DOROTHY MORRELL

Buckin' Horse Rider

Barbara A Smith

To Jack & Pat,
If one is good,
two are better.
Besides, there are
fewer typos in this edition
Barbara

1

When I began to write Dorothy's life story,
I supposed it would be a type of essay.   A long essay.

After searching out many primary source documents,
the time came to fill in the blanks between them
with a most likely scenario
and chapters were born.

One chapter led to another and then as
in any work of creative nonfiction,
the line between "what" happened and "how" it happened
became blurred.

The basic events are documented,
and though most of the characters in this story
once lived and breathed a century ago,
they didn't say everything or do things in the exact way
I wrote about them, but they were kind enough to let me
boss them around for a while!

I take full responsibility for their attitudes, quirks, and personalities.
They may have been kinder and gentler –
Maybe even rougher around the edges or
Tougher in their actions than I made them out to be.

Their strengths, I'm sure, are all their own.

Thanks to:

- *All the strong women in my life, and the men who love us*
- *Chris, who introduced me to Dorothy*
- *Nicki, for sharing photographs of BF and Sue May Robbins and cheering me on*
- *Jerry Frank, for searching out and sharing a copy of Foghorn Clancy's "Memory Trail" with me*
- *Dale Robbins, for sharing photographs of Bill and Dorothy*
- *The unspoken challenge to document that in 1914 Dorothy won her title "World's Champion Ladies' Bucking Horse Rider" at Frontier Days, Cheyenne, Wyoming, and not Pendleton – nothing against Pendleton, of course*
- *Bill Schiess, who introduced me to the love of the hunt and the chase for primary source documents*
- *The unnamed thousands who spend countless hours creating data bases for newspapers, census, marriage, death and birth records – the list goes on*
- *Lissa, who inspired me to write more than I knew I could*
- *JM Wild, my North Star*
- *Liz, who read every word*
- *Corb Lund, for writing all those rodeo songs – especially the one about a buckin' horse rider who even won ol' Cheyenne once*

- *Last and never least, my Auntie, the best big sister a big sister could ever have.*

Cover designed by Barbara A Smith

This is a work of creative nonfiction. While the story in this book is true, it may not be completely factual. In some cases events have been compressed; in others I have created events to logically fill the gaps between documentable evidence.   Some names and identifying details have been changed to protect the privacy of the people involved.

Barbara A Smith
Visit my websites at https://gramngrumpi.wixsite.com/barbaraasmith
https://www.pinterest.com/grammabobbi/dorothy-morrell-bucking-horse-rider/

Printed in the United States of America

First Printing: Nov 2017
Independantly Published

ISBN- 9781973386827

CONTENTS

I - SPRING 1913 - FROM CALGARY TO CALIFORNIA

The California sun beat down on the arena and warmed the woman to the center of her being. Sitting in the grandstands of a small town arena, she couldn't be more content. Dressed in long sleeves to protect her arms from the sun and under a wide-brimmed white hat, she thrived in the heat. She smiled – so far from Winnipeg. She treasured every mile between the wooden planks beneath her and the dusty prairies of Manitoba behind her.

She loved the rodeo. She loved everything about it. The horses, the cattle, the men. *No*, she smiled, correcting herself, *the bronks, the steers, and always the tall, lanky cowboys. Hell, even the short, round ones.*

The bronk busters, the steer riders, the steer wrestlers. The contests – the battles of muscles and will between men and beasts. The trick ropers and riders, daring and brazen, straddling and standing on the backs of horses Roman-style, galloping at breakneck speed around the arena.

Women, too, wrestling steers and riding bronks, spinning ropes, stepping in and out of their loops as if dancing with a partner. From her first rodeo a year ago in Calgary, she had been hooked.

Guy Weadick had organized a huge rodeo for Calgary in the fall of 1912 to coincide with the Calgary Exposition. Everyone in the city and countryside for miles and miles around who wasn't in jail or in the hospital attended. Indeed, Weadick gave the world a new meaning to the word *Stampede*.

This was no ordinary rodeo or frontiers day event. Not just a wild west show. This was to be the beginning and end of all rodeos. It was bigger, badder, better. That September the Calgary Stampede had been born.

Word of the events of the six-day exhibition, complete with the First Nations People, pioneers and prospectors, and always, always the cowboys – the very visage of the mighty Albertan ranching industry sadly now giving over to cash crop farming – made its way into newspapers all over Canada including the Winnipeg Tribune. She was sure it been read aloud in the evenings by her father. Cowboys from all over Canada, the United States, why even as far away as Mexico, had answered the call to come and compete, the very best against the very best.

She smiled as she imagined her father's soothing voice reading column after column to his children. Even Maria would listen in though always busy either in her kitchen or with her hands. Long winter stockings flowed from her knitting needles. Dolly and her husband, August, had finally moved out on their own leaving just Henry, Willie, Julie and baby Gus still at home to listen spellbound to Friedrich's mellow voice.

She pictured him in her mind's eye, sitting next to the front window to catch the last of the evening light; Friedrich would have read of parades, merry-go-rounds, Ferris wheels and showmen attracting people who came by railroad, horseback, in wagons. Some were even said to have come on foot. Farmers, ranchers, business men, families. From near and far.

Opening day, the Grand Parade was "the greatest pioneer pageant that had ever traversed a city's streets" Weadick declared. His procession included First Nations people from all over Alberta in their full native regalia. Pioneer missionaries marched, and Mounties rode tall in the saddle. Why, even smugglers, bootleggers and whiskey traders were tolerated in the throngs that celebrated the debut of The Calgary Stampede.

Among the spectators were the Duke and Duchess of Connaught, even the Governor General of Canada – Prince Albert, son of the Great Queen Victoria, and his wife, the Princess Louise Margaret and their youngest daughter, the Princess Patricia; yes, indeed, another Princess, watching from the royal viewing box built especially for them high above the hordes of common people.

But she had no need to listen to her father reading newspaper accounts. She had no need to wonder how it would be to have been in Calgary, at the Stampede. She had no need to imagine for she had been there.

She had gathered her belongings, the few articles of clothing, her meager stash of hideout cash she had squirreled away while working as a nurse for the doddering old doctor, George Morrell, God rest his soul, and she had quit the city of Winnipeg for good, buying a one-way train ticket to Calgary.

Calgary was so unlike Winnipeg. Long ago, the settlement at the site that would become Winnipeg had begun in 1738 as a French trading post to support fur trade with First Nations People. When the railroads crossed the village in 1881, it exploded and even now, thirty years later, it was a still a burgeoning city, growing at breakneck speed. Urbane, mechanized, productive. Surrounded by miles and miles of tiny farms growing crops in tidy fields. The cradle of a newly spawned culture would not be the host to Wild West Shows or rodeos – at least not now.

But Calgary was different. It was surrounded by ranchers who battled harsh winters and short summers, who had to raise hay to keep their cattle herds alive through the long winters. Not milking breeds in need of constant tending but stout, heavy muscled meat producers. Cattle to feed the hungry, to produce leather to shod bare feet.

After getting to Calgary, she had raided her meager stash to buy a ticket for a less expensive afternoon show at the Stampede. She could imagine her mother's wrath at the thought squandering such hard earned resources, but it didn't matter. She was no longer in her mother's home to be cowed into submission by Maria's scolding or tears.

Even now, as the California heat made sweat trickle down her back, she relished the memory of the thrill of climbing the stairs to find a seat in the grandstand built around the arena. The opening acts were stagecoach races, followed by fancy roping, relay races on horseback, Indian pony races and wild horse races.

And, God all mighty! The women! Not to be outdone, they rode at breakneck speeds in relay races. They rode bronks to a standstill. They danced, partnered with the twirling loops of their lariats. They roped and pig-tied steers. She remembered watching in awe as Tillie Baldwin rode Roman style – she "drove her twin mounts at a gait which would frighten many men . . . to death." Those were the words the newspaper reporter wrote. Words Friedrich would have read to his family.

All too soon, the afternoon show was over and the spectators made their way back to their homes, boarding houses or hotels.

Most spectators, that is. She knew she could not be borrowing from her stash again, so to extend the wonderment of the afternoon, she made her way around behind the arena to where the rodeo stock was corralled.

It was somewhat disappointing to walk past pens of steers lying with legs tucked underneath them, languidly chewing their cud as if for the world, there was nothing more important. The same placid creatures

11

which in just the last hour, had run from ropers, trying to dodge the loops of the lariats - trying and sometimes succeeding in dislodging riders, and hooking their way past pickup men.

The late afternoon sun of early September in Calgary was mild and pleasant as she picked her way past the cattle pens and stacks of hay. Busy with the tasks at hand, pitching hay or hauling water, no one seemed to mind or pay attention. Even the buzz of flies and the odor of manure did nothing to dampen the contentment she felt as she made her way to the horse corrals.

Now these were animals she could believe were fighters. She marveled at their frolic – high stepping, side stepping, half-hearted bucking. Snorting and rolling their eyes at her, they danced now nearer and then turned to move further away. Cautiously and slowly, she carefully stepped up to one of the corrals. Standing next to such energy and power, though separated by the corral poles, was exhilarating and breath-taking. She thought better than to reach through the fence, to try to stroke a velvety muzzle or satiny neck, but surely there was no harm in simply talking to the horses.

"Ah, *Schatzi,*" the German endearment slipped out unexpectedly from her mouth. She smiled. Her mother was nowhere near to hear it.

"Yes, you. You are a pretty girl." *Maybe a girl.* The gray horse stood facing her, switching its tail at flies, tossing its head and fluttering its nostrils to catch her scent.

"There, there," she continued, unaware of the woman approaching behind her. The gray mare noticed, though, and flung its head up and whirled away on nimble hooves.

"What the hell do you think you are doing?" The soft-spoken voice belied the words being used.

She refused to be intimidated or to turn around.

"These are not hobby horses," the voice continued. "You don't just walk up to them to try to make friends."

"I'm just looking at them," Carlina finally replied, knowing she sounded just like a child who had been caught with a hand in the cookie jar.

The woman held her peace and stepped up to join her.

"Hmmm, I see."

Carlina could tell the new arrival was not Canadian. Her words were slow and her vowels long. The woman offered her hand to Carlina, shaking as a man would.

"Dolly Mullins."

"Carlina Eichhorn," she replied.

They stood watching the horses milling among each other until again the gray mare began to make its way nearer to them.

Eying Dolly carefully, the mare sidestepped away from her and arched its neck toward Carlina.

"You do seem to have a way with her," Dolly began. "She's one who has never had the buck taken outta her. Some never do. They either end up at the slaughter house or here in the rodeos."

Carlina turned at last to get a close up look at the woman who had joined her. Dolly was about her own age, maybe a year or so younger or older. She couldn't tell for sure. Though dressed for rodeo competition, there was absolutely nothing masculine about her. Her blouse was full bodied to allow freedom of movement. A silk scarf was tied loosely around her neck, its knot centered on her chest. Her split-skirt was leather, fringes still swaying in the light afternoon breeze, just below her knees. Beaded leather gloves were folded together and tucked into the waistband of her skirt. The dusty leather boots on her feet were encircled with the leather straps of her silver spurs.

Dolly smiled, her dark brown eyes smiling as well.

"You ride much?"

"A little," Carlina replied. *The plodding farm horses of family friends, always on the sly. Trying to kick them to a gallop took extended effort which seldom paid off.*

She noticed that the long ringlets cascading over Dolly's shoulders were actually part of a hair piece. No wonder these women always looked like they were fresh from a hairdresser.

"You ever wanna ride a horse like this?"

Carlina drew in her breath in surprise.

"No. I mean, probably not. It really hasn't ever crossed my mind."

"Yet, here you are. Sweet-talking a bad girl." Dolly shrugged.

"I just didn't want to leave yet. This afternoon was . . ." *Was what? Thrilling? Exciting? Overwhelming?*

"I know," Dolly replied, nodding. "It makes life at home seem pretty dull.

Dull? Carlina hadn't thought of that word. Was constant work dull? Washing, ironing, cleaning, cooking, planting, harvesting, and starting all over again each morning no further ahead than the morning before. And at last, needing to work at a paying job outside the home a few hours every day for just a pittance, just to justify living in her parents' home – bringing some sort of income to the house although she carefully hoarded the portion that was her own.

Drudgery, yes. Never-ending, yes. Dull? She thought on it. Yes, definitely dull.

"Tell me about yourself," Carlina carefully asked.

"What's to tell? I work where I find it and do what I can. There's money to be made riding whether in rodeos like this or maybe Wild West Shows like the Miller Brothers 101 Ranch. You don't have to be a rodeo contestant to ride for pay. Then sometimes moving picture studios hire riders to be stunt doubles or even movie extras. That's money, too."

"What about California?" Carlina asked. "Is it hard to be a . . ." what had Dolly called it? "A. . . a movie extra?"

13

"Tss," Dolly shook her head. "The hard part is standing in the sun all day while the film makers have every one do everything over and over again. They are always looking for people to fill in the background. There is a lot more to movies than just the star actors."

Carlina had never been to a moving picture show. Money was just too dear.

"You could get work easily," Dolly promised as she looked Carlina over with a critical eye. "You're young, pretty. Your smile is nice."

She gave Carlina a nod. "Yes, you could do it. But, girl, you've got to lose that German name. No one wants anything to do with anything German these days."

"But what?" Carlina had never considered being called anything but her own name. "What would I call myself?"

"Anything! Anything would be better than Car-leen-ah!" Dolly drew out the syllables perfectly mimicking how Carlina had pronounced her name. "And Eichhorn! My god, girl! The name screams, 'Look at me! I'm fresh off the Kaiser's boat!'"

Carlina stiffened. Bad enough to argue with her mother about her nativity, but now a perfect stranger?

"Oh, sorry. I didn't mean to offend. It's just a name like Carlina Eichhorn will never do. Not for show business."

"But don't actors and riders just go by their own names?"

"Well, yes. Some do, if they have names like Bertha or Florence or Hazel. But some of 'em have made up monikers, like Prairie Rose, or Skeeter Bill or Hoot. Now there's a character."

"Don't you have a nickname?" Dolly went on. "Take me, now. My name is Dorothy, but no one ever called me that. Dolly - that's me. Carrie, perhaps? Carrie Acorn has a ring to it."

Carlina's teeth were set on edge. How many times had a school yard bully called her and her brothers The Acorn Kids? She smiled through it, though.

"Perhaps just a different name," she replied. She thought of all the girls' names she had heard and loved, other than her own, of course. Dolly stood smiling at her, white teeth shining, dark hair glistening.

"Dorothy, you say," Carlina repeated. "Dorothy . . ."

The old doctor's face came back to her. It was his wages which had brought her here, had allowed her to escape to Calgary, which would buy another train ticket this time for southern California.

"Dorothy Morrell." She thought on the name for just a split second and then nodded. "Dorothy Morrell. That is who I am."

"Fantastic!" Dolly smiled, circling Dorothy's shoulders in a friendly embrace.

"Now, girl!" Dolly had one last bit of advice for Carlina. "Never let facts get in the way of truth. It doesn't matter what was written in any dusty forgotten record, nothing gets in your way of moving forward. You write your own story.   You create your own truth.   You say it.   You believe it.   You live it. You are Dorothy Morrell."

II - FEBRUARY 1891 - HAMBURG

L ittle Carlina hugged her poppet to her chest with one arm and tried to wrap herself into her *Mutti's* long full woolen skirts with her other hand.

"Lina," her mother scolded half-heartedly, thoroughly exhausted after days of travel and weeks of preparation before that.   "Come out, *Schatzi*, dearest, just hold onto *Mutti's* skirt."

Her *Mutter*, Maria, and *Vater*, Friedrich Eichhorn, stood huddled with their three tiny children on the docks of Hamburg, sardined among scores of other impatient immigrant passengers waiting with them.

Young Friedrich, four years old, sturdy and solemn, took his job of watching over all their earthly belongings seriously as they waited to board the ship that would be the next step of their journey.

Carlina, almost three years old, wistfully clutching her rag doll baby to her, was wishing she were back in Oma's cozy, warm kitchen waiting for strudel to finish baking instead of shivering as the misty fog dampened their cloaks and drew in the cold.

Baby Julianne, only six months old, was bundled in blankets and nestled into a huge basket, whimpering and coughing. Oma had scolded and worried that Julianne was too frail and small to make the long journey. Oma, their *Grossmutter*, always had time to sing and trundle colicky, crying babies – always had *Lebkuchen* tucked away in the bread box ready for hungry little hands. Oma, who had cried silent tears as Opa bounced Friedrich one last time on his knee. Who would never be seen again by her *Kinder* nor *kleine Enkelkinder* on this earth.

Jacob and Lydia Ettel, close friends and dear neighbors from back home in Bethanien, crowded with them on the dock, their own five *Kinder* cloaked against the cold. Johannes, at eleven, seemed to tower over the combined brood of Eichhorns and Ettels.

Christoph, nine, wished he could squirm and wriggle away from the press of arms, legs and baggage and make his way down the piers to find a better spot to watch the ships and boats as they docked and were unloaded and reloaded with cargo or passengers. But his mother had charged him with keeping a hold of his brother Heinrich. Heinrich, five years old was constantly trying to wander off to explore his enticing new surroundings. Christoph thought that perhaps they could slip away together until he glanced up at his mother. The anxiety on Lydia's face told him to stay put.

Anna stood shoulder to shoulder with Carlina, her almost twin, her best friend, wanting Carlina to trade her baby doll with her. The two often traded their baby *Puppen* as they pretended to visit one another. Anna sighed. Carlina was sad again and could not be cajoled into play and would not pay attention to her at all. Baby *Bruder* Jacob lay tucked into the huge basket alongside Julianne, sleeping soundly in spite of the cold and the hustle and noise. Anna stubbornly put her thumb into her mouth, turning so that her *Mutti* would not catch her.

Together, the Eichhorns and Ettels left Russia weeks ago, traveling from the German colony of Bethanien in the Volga Valley north by rail to Moscow. From there, they traveled east to Hamburg, arriving to find the port city packed with other hopefuls waiting to continue on the next legs of their journeys to the New Promised Land.

Maria turned to her husband, Friedrich, worried, anxious and almost complaining.

"What is this I hear about ships sinking in this very harbor? Just five days ago no less?"

Friedrich sighed. Once Maria began to worry over something, it was hard for her to turn it loose.

"I heard that it was a cargo ship that had been plagued with hardship. Yes, it capsized and sank right here in the harbor."

Jacob took up where Friedrich had left off in reassuring their nervous wives.

"Just look at her," he said pointing up to the funnel and rigging of the ship they were waiting to board.   "The *Rhaetia* is a sound steamer, a sturdy workhorse of the *Hamburg-Amerikanische Packetfahrt-Actien-Gesellschaft,* the Hamburg America Line, sailing under capable command of Captain Kühlewein.   There was no need to be worried about the our safety."

Maria closed her eyes to keep Jacob from seeing her eye roll.   *Gott im Himell,* but it sounded as if he were the advertising agent for HAPAG instead of a "second deck" passenger, waiting for the first and second class passengers to board.   She quickly opened them again to once more count her children.   She listened as young Friedrich with Christoph and Heinrich, making a game of counting the tall masts on the *Rhaetia, eine, zwei, drei.* She lifted her eyes to see what had caught their attention. Thee tall masts, foremost of which was wrapped with sails; the emergency backup power to keep the ship on her way should the steam engines fail.

The February wind, though fairly calm, added enough to the chill in the air to bite and pull at them as they waited to board with the nearly one thousand other third class passengers who would travel on the so-called "Second Deck."

The same siren call, the promise of rich, virgin farmland, which had enticed their great-great grandparents to leave Germany over a 130 years earlier, again beckoned to them; the lure of land, opportunity, new life, but always land, land that would truly belong to them, not be on loan dependent upon the benevolence and whim of the Russian czars.

Catherine, the Great German Princess turned Czarina, had lain in her grave over a hundred years and the promises she had made to the world in general and to her Germanic cousins in particular had been nullified, legislated out of existence. Rescinded. Revoked.   Replaced with harsh expectations, loss of self-governance and local control over schools, taxes and the dreaded demands of military service.

The Eichhorns and the Ettels were among the many who had left the Volga steppes after the Czarina's promises had melted away. Farming was the very being of their souls.   Friedrich and Jacob hoped to start over again on the great plains of North America, whether in Canada or the United States.

At last, after all the first class passengers had loaded on board and cleared the decks, the steerage passengers began to slowly make their way up the gang planks.   Their names, ages, and places of nativity had already been carefully recorded by the immigration agents of the *HAPAG.*   They anxiously crowded into the steerage compartments below deck.   The Hamburg America Line proudly declared the steerage deck to be *'spacious, light and well ventilated, and [having] separate compartments for single men, women and families.'*

17

Friedrich and Maria, as well as Jacob and Lydia shepherded their tiny broods into the cramped space that would be their home for the next two weeks until they would disembark, not in New York City proper, but across the Hudson River in Hoboken, New Jersey, the point of contact for the Line.

"*Ach, was ist los?* What is this?" cried Maria, in dismay, as she and Lydia realized that a "separate compartment" for families did not mean a separate room for each family but was in actuality more like two long dormitory halls, one on each side of the ship with tiers of berths built over the top of each other with solid head and foot boards separating one sleeping area or compartment from the next.

"We have come so far," Lydia said, comforting her friend. "Surely we can make do for just a few more days."

"Fourteen days! That is two weeks!" Maria argued and shook her head as she surveyed the long corridor lined with beds. There was less than a meter of headroom between the bottom and top berths and about the same between the top one and the ceiling. They seemed to be about two meters in length but less than one wide. There were straw-filled mattresses covered with a thin blanket. Life-preservers served as pillows.

The Eichhorn and Ettel families were each assigned two berths, one upper and lower, across from one another. Lydia sighed. A small favor – being able to be across from their dear friends. It almost seemed cozy. The two women began to stow their families' belongings under the berths.

"*Achtgeben, Frauen!*" A steward demanded Lydia and Maria's attention as he pushed through the crowds of passengers, all working to stow their belongings. "*Nein, nein!* There can be nothing on the decks. All must be stowed on your berths." He shook his head to add further enforcement to his orders.

Exasperated, Lydia put her hands on her hips. "*Weiso nicht?* – Why not! There is plenty of room!"

The steward rolled his eyes. How many times must he repeat himself to these people? Hadn't they read all the rules and expectations posted on the walls? He took a deep breath.

"First," holding up a forefinger, "the decks are to be swept daily. Second," another finger raised, "there may be moisture, water or . . ." He paused. " . . . other filth collecting on the decks." He straightened as if remembering it was not his place to have to answer to these peasant women. "It is the rules. The only storage is on your bunks!"

He strode off to preserve his dignity as well as he might, weaving in and around the teaming hordes of passengers all intent on getting themselves and their belongings into the tiny spaces allotted them.

"*Ts, ts,*" *Tante* Lydia hissed through her teeth. She pointed her own forefinger into the air and continued, "And last but not least, *meine leib Frauen, die Ratten und Maeuse* need their spaces, too!"

Maria smiled half-heartedly and nodded as they each picked up their bundles from the floor and placed them on the bottom berth.

After the long wait on the pier, the little ones laughed and chased one another until their mothers insisted on perching them into the top bunks while they sorted out arrangements, extra clothing, especially that which they would wear the day they would finally disembark in New York was stowed against the walls.   Carefully they divided their bundles of belongings and stacked them at the heads and feet of each berth.   In bewilderment, the women tried to decide where to keep the eating utensils. Their living space seemed to shrink as Maria and Lydia worked to find places to keep things where they could be easily found or kept out of the way.

Johannes frowned at the thought of being stacked like cord wood in with the little boys and Anna until Maria insisted that Anna sleep next to Carlina in the Eichhorn's upper berth.   Carlina and Anna would sleep toe-to-toe with Friedrich and Julianne, while Johannes would share the top portion of his bunk with baby Jacob with Christoph and Heinrich at his feet.

Johannes often felt lonely since leaving Bethanien.   He loved his brothers and his little almost-cousin, Friedrich, but they were *Jungen*, too young to be companions for him and no substitute for his older cousins, Peder and Wilhelm.   Peder, daring and rebellious, taking chances and dares when the *Eltern* were out of sight.   Wilhelm, thoughtful and cautious, who made it through all of Peter's wild hair schemes with never a scrape or broken bone.

Unless his *Onkel* and *Tante* left the Volga, in a few short years Peder and Wilhelm would be conscripted into the Russian military forces to serve the required time of six years of full time service. His cousins would be far away from the fields of wheat, millet and rye, far from the farms of the Volga and lost to their families until at last by the grace of *Gott*, they may return.   But still they would not be free of the Czar's demands and his unsatiable need for human flesh at the battle front.   Nine more years of reserve would follow.   Nine more uncertain years.   His *Vater* as well as "*Onkel*" Friedrich swore their sons would never be fodder for the Moscow war machine.

He wondered what Peder and Wilhelm were doing just now?   Pitching hay to their family's cattle?   Splitting kindling should the fires go out in their stoves and cooking ovens?   Sledding in the snow down the rolling hills of the east side of the valley?   Sighing, he wondered if Peder were here now, how different life would be for the next two weeks, what would be planned to liven the long hours below deck or to celebrate a few hours of fresh air and freedom on deck.   It was pointless, he told himself.   Peder was not here.

✻ ✻ ✻

"*Stille!*"Maria was exasperated with Carlina and Friedrich, perched once again on the top berth with Annika and baby Jacob.   The long dreary days at sea were finally at an end. The other Ettel *Kinder* had been hoisted onto the top berth facing them.   All their faces had been scrubbed, their hair and hands washed, Carlina and Annika's hair plaited into tight braids.   At last they were all dressed in their *'getting-off-the-ship'* clothes.

"You remember how long we waited to get onto this floating *Miethaus*?" Maria continued, "Well, we must wait our turn to get off as well. Stop your fussing."

Carlina moved to sit closer to Annika, their baby dolls snuggled between them.

"Where is Papa?" Carlina was bored and tired of not being able to run and hide and yell and twirl.   Anna, she knew, was, too.

"Papa and Onkel Jacob are waiting for the Captain to let us know when it is our turn to see the inspectors."

The entire passenger population on the ship had been given a clean bill of health.   Thankfully, there were no serious contagious diseases among them.   Now to have their names, ages, and places of birth recorded once again.   Then to wait for all the first class passengers to make declarations and sign documentation as to the contents of their luggage.

Those huge horse hair trunks with their rounded tops and the steamer trunks had to be packed tightly with all sorts of treasures.   Carlina and Annika had seen the trunks and were sure they were big enough for little girls to play house in.   Imagine having so much that one needed such closet-box to carry it all with him.

Carlina wriggled closer to the edge of the bunk and tried to swing her legs over the railing to relieve the cramping of sitting on the hard and unforgiving mattress.   In seconds, Anna had followed suit.   Maria and Lydia scolded their little daughters and set them back away from the edge again.

Carlina pouted and wished again for Oma's soft touches and gentle words.   And her gingerbread cookies.

"Where will Oma be waiting for us?" Carlina asked suddenly.

Maria looked sharply at her tiny daughter.

"What makes you ask such a thing?" her voice surprised.

"Oma told me she would be waiting for us on the other side," Carlina explained.   "Now we are on the other side of the ocean.   You said so."

Maria frowned.   Little children!   What do they know?   How to explain?

She softened her tongue, simply saying, "*Nay, Mausi,* our Oma will not be here.   She is still in Russland, still in her kitchen.   The other side she spoke of is still far, far away."

Carlina was crestfallen, not understanding at all, and hung her head to hide the tears gathering in her eyes.   It would never do to cry over this to her mother.   "*You are a big girl now.   If you need something to cry about, I'll give it to you.*"   Carlina had no desire for a spanking this early in the day.

All sense of order seemed to have been abandoned as the eager passengers had gathered their belongings, tying some of them into bundles inside the thin blankets that had been on their bunks, cramming tightly rolled clothing and bedding into baskets, and for some rearranging small traveling trunks.   The steward had haughtily assured them that they could take the atrocious blankets with them, fresh new ones would be provided for the next passengers. Lydia had once again mocked the man behind his back.

"*Meine lieb Frauen!*" Lydia placed one hand on a hip and raised the other, jabbing the air with her index finger. "You poor unwashed pieces of humanity! No one wants your dirty, used up piece of rag of a blanket! Off! Take them all off with you!"

She and Maria laughed, happy that the long and arduous voyage was finally at an end.

The blankets had been poor protection from the cool and the damp on the poorly heated *Zwischendecke* - the second deck. Not even the heat of the scores of bodies, stacked so closely together in the bunks, could ward off the cold. After the first few nights, Lydia and Maria no longer insisted that their children change into their night clothes. They loosened the ties and buttons, put their own stockings over their children's stockinged feet, and covered them over with their coats and cloaks.

Maria carefully wrapped the one teacup and saucer her mother had given her as a keepsake into some linen handkerchiefs and stowed them carefully into a stew pot, a hand-me-down not only from her mother, but her mother's mother. Maria managed to pack all their belongings into two bundles, but with her added number of children, Lydia ended up with three. Johannes, sitting quietly in his family's bottom berth, knew he would be lugging the third bundle.

"Maria." Lydia's voice was soft with worry. "Maria, you must talk to Friedrich again. Your family must stay here in New York with us. There is work here. There are places to live among *die Volksdeutschen*. You know you can stay with us until Friedrich finds a job and you get your own place to rent."

Maria kept her feelings for Lydia's pleas hidden deep behind her no nonsense mask. What more could she say to Lydia to convince her that the Eichhorns would never be city dwellers, fenced in by buildings reaching for the skies, where there was no place for chickens, dogs, horses, cows . . . no vegetable garden, no wheat fields melting into the horizon? She loved Lydia and *die Kinder*. Her Friedrich and Lydia's Jacob had toiled together in the planting, reaping and gathering in of wheat and rye since they themselves were *Kinder*, their families living side-by-side since 'die Grosseltern' had arrived in the valley of the Volga so many years ago. Brothers could not have been closer.

"Lydia, you know how stubborn *mein Mann* is." Maria softened her tone of voice. "You know how he loves the land. We simply cannot stay here with you in the city. There is land waiting in the land called Manitoba to the north in Canada. It is you who should be coming with us."

"You have told me this over and again," Lydia's voice rose in frustration. "But how do you know? How do you know there is land waiting? Remember the stories told of *die Urgrosseltern?* Our great-grandparents were promised homes and land and barns and cattle!

21

Remember their first winter in *Russland?* Their only shelter was living with the peasants in their hovels! The horror of living at the mercy of those people! Even now, over a hundred years later, they are still bringing their chickens and sheep into their huts in the dark of winter! Maria, how do you know that there will not be the same deprivations in this Manitoba?"

Lydia shook her head in anguish, begging Maria with her eyes. But there was no change in Maria's attitude. Lydia hung her head to try to hide the tears gathering once again in her deep blue eyes. Carlina and Anna rocked their babies as if doing so could ease Lydia's grief. Their mothers' anxieties tilted their world out of kilter. Mothers were not supposed to cry or argue.

"Besides," Lydia whispered, continuing. "You know our moneys are spent. There is nothing left to take us further. We are told of a place in the city. When the ferry lands, it is a short walk to where there is housing, *die Miethausen* - apartment buildings are stacked story upon story to the sky, where many of *die Volksdeutschen* have created a little piece of *das Vaterland* here in this new place. There is work. There are schools. There are churches."

Maria smiled and hugged her friend. "And beer and bread. Yes, I know. You have told me this over and again." She stepped back and waited to see Lydia's reaction to her words being reflected back at her.

Lydia laughed, not a laugh of joy or mirth, but of one who knows the argument cannot be won and continuing would be in vain.

It was time.

Jacob and Friedrich made their way through the crowded aisle with word that at last the children should don their coats, scarves and mittens. They would need the protection from the raw March wind that was whipping the lightly falling snow into swirling blankets. Blankets now obscuring the skyline of New York City, the great city just across the river from Hoboken. Jacob and Friedrich, each shouldering some of their families' bundles, led the way from the ship docks at the foot of First Street the short ways to the Christopher Street ferry offices. Maria and Lydia shepherded the little ones, each holding a handle of the basket carrying the babies, Julianne and Jacob, nestled among the Ettels' belongings. Young Johannes threw his bundle over his shoulder just as his papa and Onkel Friedrich had done and did his best to keep up with the men.

Carlina and Anna clung to each other's hands while tucking their babies under their free arms. Carlina skipped and pulled on Anna's hand. Instantly Anna joined her and the two little girls giggled as they kept ahead of their mothers. They knew better than to get ahead of their fathers. Johannes sighed as he watched them. Little *Kinder*. What did they know?

* * *

Carlina and Anna had long since given up their skipping. Since getting off the ferry on the New York City side of the North Hudson River, it seemed they had trudged forever behind their fathers – while being cajoled, reminded and finally ordered by their mothers to keep walking. As the little procession made its way eastward down Houston Street, the children alternately stumbled over the rough cobblestones used to pave it and tripped over piles of frozen muck. Here and there on the streets and crosswalks were yet unfrozen puddles of horses' urine and worse. Maria and Lydia did their best to shepherd the children around the pools of stench and filth, finally thankful for a reason to be glad that the little girls' skirts had grown so short in the past several months.

At last, the little parade came to a halt as the families reached Bowery Street and Jacob pulled a scrap of paper from his wallet. He confirmed the address and turned to make one last invitation to the Eichhorns.

"Jacob, you are as my brother."

Friedrich interrupted him before he could even begin. "You know it pains me to leave you and Lydia and your little ones, but we cannot stay here." He turned to face the street. "Listen to the city."

Street venders shouted, horses leaned into their collars pulling dray wagons, carriages, and carts, harnesses and chains squeaking and jangling, dozens of iron shoes striking paving stones. Overhead, elevated railroad tracks promised the clatter of steel wheels on steel rails and the groaning of wooden trestles when the el-trains passed overhead. Passing street cars made it nearly impossible to hear one another as they went by.

Crestfallen, Jacob laid his bundle on to the sidewalk and he and Lydia reached to embrace Friedrich and Maria one last time. Lydia's eyes again filled with tears. She shook her head but said nothing as tears streamed down her cheeks. Young Joannes was puzzled by the sorrow in his parents' faces. The memories of his cousins back in Bethanien were more sorrowful than the impending separation from all these fussy little children. *Tante* Maria was a hard one to get along with, if anyone cared to know his opinion. *Onkel* Friedrich, quiet, soft-spoken and unassuming most of the time, was easy to overlook.

Anna and Carlina took advantage of the stop to trade their baby dolls as they often did, crooning the lullabies their *Omas* had sung to them. They paid no attention to their Papas and Mamas or the words they were speaking as they sat on a cleaner space on the freezing curb and leaned into each other's shoulders.

As Maria lifted Julianne from her nest in Lydia's basket, she tried to comfort her almost-sister, "*Ach*, Lydia. We will meet again. If not in this world, surely in the next."

At last Lydia found her voice. "That is what worries me and gives sorrow to my heart. I don't want to wait until the next world to see you again. I want you here. I want our children under my feet. I want to sing to your grandchildren."

Her words faded as a new round of tears flooded her face. Lydia embraced Maria as best she could, pressing Julianne between them. Maria returned Lydia's embrace and the two clung tightly to each other.

Friedrich cleared his throat. "Jacob, if you ever change your mind, we will be in Manitoba. Find the *Deutscher* in Winnipeg and you will find us there. We will always have an open door and supper on the back burner for you," he concluded, trying to lighten the somber mood.

Jacob nodded. "We will find you if we ever need to leave this place. Perhaps we will not be so far behind you after all."

Friedrich hesitated, not wanting to break the moment but realized the necessity of hurrying on. The next leg of their journey would be a short ride on the very tracks above their heads to Grand Central Depot.

"*Kinder*," he gently said, "we must go now. Say good-bye."

Young Friedrich mumbled to Christoph and Heinrich through his exhaustion, "*Auf Wiedersehen*," and the three shook hands as they had seen older men do.

"Come, Carlina, it is time to say good-bye to Anna. You will not be seeing her again for a long time." If ever, he thought glumly to himself. Startled, Carlina and Anna were confused, having ignored all that was going on about them.

"But, Papa, why?" Carlina was puzzled, hungry, tired, and suddenly very cross and out-of-sorts. "I don't want to say good-bye to Annika." Anna, her constant companion all the way from far off *Russland*, sleeping, eating, sharing, sometimes even quarreling but never far away.

"*Liebkind*," answered Friedrich, choosing his words carefully. "Annika and her family are staying here in this city. They have only a few more blocks to walk until they will be in their new home."

He sighed. "But we still have days to travel before we reach the land that will be our new home. Come now, *meine kleine Mädchen*."

He knelt to gather both little girls in his arms. Shyly, Carlina reached to touch Anna's face. Neither girl understood what was about to happen. They only knew that for now, this evening, Anna was going to continue to walk down the street with her family and Carlina would climb the stairs to the waiting platform to board a train car.

Anna giggled. "*Ach*, Lina. You tickle." She threw her arms around Carlina and they laughed at their old familiar game. Slowly, the girls separated and made their ways back to their mothers.

On the street level, the Ettels watched and waved as the Eichhorns made their way up the stairs, watched and waved until they could no longer see their friends through the gathering dusk, watched and waited as the train came clattering and steaming to the stop above them and then chugged into the evening.

Suddenly the noise of the city seemed distant, the din all but forgotten as Jacob now shouldered his bundle and lifted the basket handle that Maria had carried. Johannes fell in step behind his parents.

"Christoph! Heinrich! Take your sister's hands and keep up with us." Lydia spoke with unaccustomed sharpness which hurried the boys to do as they were told.

As the boys reached for her hands, Anna hugged her baby doll to her, and then began to cry as she realized Carlina still had her doll and she had Carlina's.

III - JUNE 1901 - WINNIPEG, MANITOBA

*E*ntschuldigen Sie, bitte!"   Speaking German, even at home, grated on Carlina's sense of appropriateness especially after ten years in Canada, but she desperately wanted her mother's attention. Maria's eyes narrowed briefly, she took a deep breath and turned to her daughter standing just behind her.

"No, you are not excused!   Now go and I will speak to you in the kitchen when I am finished," she ordered, speaking German of course. She then turned her attention back to the census taker sitting next to her at her dining table – though truth be told, it was just a table spread with a bobbin lace cloth in the front corner of the front room that ran across the front of their home in Winnipeg.

Carlina turned on her heel and stalked into the kitchen.   The rich smell of borscht simmering on the back burner made her mouth water and for a moment she forgot how angry she was with her mother.

Maria was proud of her grandmother's recipe and made sure Carlina could recite it from memory.

It is as simple as eine, zwei, drei - here Mutti always smiled.   *Now, Schatzi, run to the garden.   Find three great beets and pull them with care to keep their tops on.   Scrub them.   We boil them whole with 3 great spoons of vinegar and a full pot of water in Oma's soup pot. Remember?   The pot that came with us on the ship across the ocean* - Mutti's eyes looked backward through the years to the Old Country.   *- Yes, with their tops.*

How long, you ask? As long as it takes us to hang out the clothes on the line and wash the breakfast dishes.   Then set aside the beet broth.   Cool the beets just until their skins can be slipped.   Ah, that is good, Carlina. The beet juice will wear off your fingers in a day or so.   We dice the beet hearts.   Here, you set the cubes and the tops inside the ice box.

Now, daughter, we make the mother soup.   Chop one onion, mince three fingers of garlic, slice 3 ribs of celery, 3 long carrots, dice 3 potatoes, crush 3 sprigs of dill, add one head of chopped cabbage and always one soup bone.   We will simmer for the afternoon. When evening comes, and the lovely vegetables are tender, skim the fat from the soup to save for soap-making day.   Chop the beet tops fine. Stir them and the beet cubes to the warm soup.

And last of all, we will find Oma's teacup.   Yes, yes, the one with the handle broken.   Fill your Oma's teacup three times with this morning's cream and pour it into the soup.   Gently stir together while the table is being set for supper. There you have it!

When Carlina was very young, she asked her Mutti once, where the two – zwei – came from.

Salt and pepper!   Maria smiled and folded her daughter into her arms, then kissed her daughter's forehead- *and you and I, of course.*

Carlina lifted the lid on the stew pot. The liquified fat floating above the rich mix of vegetables was shimmering and ready for Carlina to use a large mixing spoon to skim it off.   She turned her hands to the soup and her ears to the front room.

Back at the dining table, Maria smiled indulgently at the agent.

"Now vhere vere ve, Meester Grieve?"   *Such a strange name for a strange man.*

Who would have thought that the Canadian government cared enough about its citizens to send out information gathering people to ask so many questions?

Mr. Grieve sighed.   He had hoped the daughter, though only in her early teens, would have been able to take over the conversation about the members of the household.   Mrs. Eichhorn – Frau Eichhorn, she insisted – was nearly impossible to understand.

"We were just going over the names of your children.   You stated that your oldest is Carline."   Such a strange name for a boy, he thought to himself.   Carl, yes, Collin, of course, but Carline?   Foreigners.   Strange people with strange ways, he decided.   Who could explain them?

"*Ja,* dis iss de name of mine eldest *Tochter,*" Maria replied, *the rude one in the kitchen who needs another lesson in manners,* she thought to herself.

Mr. Grieve scratched his head.   He wasn't sure what *Tochter* meant, but he wasn't going to try to get Missus – make that *Frau* – Eichhorn explain.

"And then you have a daughter named Dolla, a son Willie, a son Henry, and another son Fred."   He stopped and puzzled at his notes. Perhaps she had said "Ed" but Frau Eichhorn didn't correct him so he went on.

"And your youngest is a female child, Julie."

"*Ja, ja,* dis is so," Maria nodded firmly, counting off the children on her fingers as Mr. Grieve read from his notes.

Speaking slowly and carefully, he asked, "All right, Mmm, Frau Eichhorn, please tell me the birthdays of each of your children beginning with the oldest."

"De birt' day?" Maria was a little concerned.   How should she remember which day of the week her children were born on?

"Yes, ma'am, their birth dates, starting with the day of the month, then the name of the month and the year," Mr Grieve explained, patiently holding his pencil at the ready.

"*Ach, ja.* Of course, of course."   Now she understood.   She began with Fred's birthday and listed each of her other children in the order that they were born.

Mr. Grieve carefully recorded each date next to name of each child on his list of family members.

"Now, Frau Eichhorn, please tell me the name of the country where each family member was born."

"Mine husband and I vere born in *Russland* as vell as de eldest two.   De rest of de *Kinder* vere born here in Vinnipeg."

Listening from the kitchen, Carlina was overwhelmed with sorrow. Again.   Sorrow that never seemed to quite fade.   *Nein, Mutter,* but then she shook her head angrily, impatiently.   She must stop even thinking in German. *No, mother!   Your first <u>three</u> children were born in Russia.*   Oh, how she missed having a sister nearer to her own age.   A secret-sharer.   An accomplice. How she longed for her sister, Julianne, her baby sister Julie Ruth's name sake.   Julianne, the tiny bundle who didn't make it through the first winter on the Canadian prairies.   Oma had been right.

Lost in her thoughts, Carlina paid scant attention to the next part of the conversation between Mr. Grieve and her mother.   Of what importance was it when the family arrived in Canada or the church they belonged to?   The next question, though, brought her attention fully back to the conversation.

"You say your husband and your son work for someone else? How many months during 1910 were they employed?"

It pained Maria to answer. The dream of owning land and farming here in Manitoba had never been realized. Friedrich took on any work he could find, working hard, an honest day's labor every working day, to provide for his family. His diligence kept food on the table and the roof over their heads.

"Mine husband vorked 6 month and mine son has vorked 7." Maria firmly held her head high and looked Mr. Grieve square in the eye as she recounted these facts.

"And their earnings?"

Maria nodded and smiled proudly. "Mine husband brought two-hundred fifty dollars into *de Haus* and our good son brought seventy. He is sixteen, you know, but soon he vill be earning a man's vage as vell."

Mr. Grieve smiled indulgently back at Mrs. Eichhorn. "And I suppose it is safe to say that German is the language spoken in this home." A question that hardly needed to be asked based on the curt conversation of just a few moments ago.

"*Ja, ja.* Dis is so." Maria was proud of her heritage, her family and their customs. She would need to bear down on Carlina and help her to see the short-sightedness of trying to put all things *Deutsche* behind her.

"Well, now, Frau Eichhorn, it looks as though we have covered all the questions needed for our count." He hurried to his feet after closing his notebook. He was proud of his thoroughness, the information in neat and tidy columns ready to be rewritten and recorded on the official census sheets by the copyists. He gathered his coat and hat and turned for the door.

"Thank you, again, Mrs. Eichhorn." He caught his error but decided it was hardly worth correcting himself at this point.

Maria rose to her feet as well and ushered him to the door.

"Good-bye, then," she called after the man as he strode down the sidewalk, each glad to be rid of the other.

Closing the door firmly, she took a deep breath. Now to deal with her impertinent, impulsive and disrespectful daughter, counting Carlina's weaknesses as she marched into the kitchen.

"Carlina, you listen to me," she began as always speaking the German dialect unique to those families whose generations had spent over a century surrounded by their Russian neighbors. It was old fashioned, mingled with occasional Russian words and phrases, hard for other German speakers, those from the Fatherland, to understand.

"How is it that my daughter - my good German daughter - has the audacity to try to interrupt me when I am speaking with another adult? And an official man from the government at that?"

"Oh, Mother," Carlina tried to reply.

"Do not speak English to me in my own kitchen!" Maria instantly exploded.

"*Ach, Mutter!*" Carlina began again. "The man did not understand you."

"How can you say such a thing? Of course, he understood me. I speak the English just as well as you. Just because I don't go to school every day and read pretty words and write pretty letters, I can speak as well as anyone."

Carlina knew better than to argue that point, so she went back to the reasons to support the idea that Mr. Grieve and her mother had not been communicating clearly.

"Mutter, the census taker got us out of order. He wrote that Fred's name is Carline - me! What kind of a name is that for a boy? I listened, Mutter. He wrote that I am Dolly - and why did you tell him that was her name? Nathalia is her name. You say that we must be proud that we are German but then you tell the man our baby names? What is wrong with Heinrich or Wilhelm? But no, you tell him Willie and Henry. And the man wrote that Fred - Fred, not Friedrich - was born between Henry and Julie!"

"Oh, you do not know these things! How can you tell how the man wrote down our family? You were not sitting there, Miss Know-it-all!"

"I was listening, as you remind me to do so all the time. I was listening, Mutter, and he got it wrong."

Maria huffed and placed one hand on her hip. "I do not think you are right, Carlina, but even if you are, what does it matter? Those records are just for the government people counters. No one cares. No one will ever go back and read a word that is written."

She stopped to take another deep breath. Carlina had a way of twisting a conversation away from the case in point. The census man and his silly notes were not what was the most urgent and pressing items on Maria's mind. It was Carlina's constant attitude of disrespect and sassiness.

"You must remember your duty in this life," Maria started again, taking another deep breath before directing the conversation back to Carlina's shortcomings. "You are my daughter and you are to grow to be *ein gute Deutscher Frau,* one that any of the *die wundervoll Mannschaften* in this entire city - even this whole province - would be honored to marry, and you will be honored to be his wife and to bear his *Kinder,* to keep his house and cook his meals."

Carlina was horrified.

"*Mutter,*" she all but screamed. "I am *not* a German girl who can grow into a good German woman! I am not a German. You are not a German. We are nothing! Germany didn't want us. Yes, you can tell the people-counting man that we are *russisch,* but that is not true either. We don't speak Russian. We don't say Orthodox prayers. We don't eat peasant food. *Mutter,* listen to me now! I hardly remember *Russland.* I was still in short skirts when we left. We only passed through Germany on a train. I don't remember a damn thing . . ."

Maria's hand shot out and slapped Carlina hard across her face. "Not in my kitchen! Not in my house! Such filth from my daughter's mouth."

But Carlina would not be quieted.   Not this time.

"I remember nothing at all about Germany except freezing nearly to death waiting to board that ship!"

She stopped to take in a deep breath.   It was now or never.

"Mark my words, *Mutter,* I am not marrying any of your *wondervoll Deutsche Mannschaften.*   None of them.   I will not!   I will not spend my life having children nor cooking and cleaning until I die! I will not!"

Now it was Maria who was horrified at her daughter's words.   "Dear God in Heaven!   What have I done to fail you as a mother?"

She reached out gently to take Carlina's cheeks into her hands while tears began to course down her own.

"*Liebste,*" her voice softened.   "Is my life so horrid that you hate it?   Is your father such a disappointment?   Is your brother an embarrassment?   What is it that you cannot abide?"

Carlina leaned into her mother's embrace, allowing her mother to smooth her hair and kiss her forehead, all the while knowing that smoothing over their feelings today would not change her hopes and dreams of tomorrow.   Her mother would never understand.   Carlina decided to save her words and use them to mark her own path.   She *would* leave this god-forsaken place, Winnipeg, the mushrooming, pompous, self-centered city surrounded by miles and miles of lonely, wind-swept prairies.   She would never grow old and die in Canada.

One day she would follow her nose, and find a better path.

IV - OCTOBER 1913 — ROSIE

*L*ieber Gott im Himmel, why did I ever agree to get on that damn donkey? *Not just once, but twice.*

Lying on the boards of a front row bleacher seat, Dorothy cursed the day that donkey had been born.   The damp bandana over her forehead was warm now as she reached to turn it over.

She'd been under the weather for a couple of days now, and as always, Frank Griffin, Mr. Rodeo Boss, had been complaining and fussing at her, about not keeping up her end of her "daily appearance contract."   After all she a moving picture star – now that she actually had a few "extra" appearances behind her – and Boss Griffin expected some might come just to see her riding at full tilt during the opening ceremonies.

'Hell, there isn't anything to it,' Griffin had growled at the doctor.   *'All she's gotta do is smile, wave her hat and ride around the arena.'*

Well, there *was* a little more to it than that. The "daily appearances" she'd been hired to make were to ride at a lope in a figure eight and then once around at a high gallop to the center of the arena. Her mount had been trained to rear up on its hind legs, punching the sky like an equine boxer with its forelegs. This was when the hat-waving came into play. It kept her busy during the summer months when the studios making moving picture shows were on hiatus. But the doc hadn't given his go-ahead to any riding in the arena for several days now, so grousing was about as far as Griffin would go.

Today, finally, Doc had actually given his okay, so she and also Eloise had agreed to ride that Trick Burro, Rosie, a sort of spoof that would surely go off without a hitch. Surely that would fulfill the "daily appearance" clause.

The first time she climbed onto the donkey's back, she was unseated in no time, but her landing had been almost graceful and practically a non-event. Then Eloise had taken a turn and came back down to earth just as gracefully, but with a bigger grin. She always came up grinning. Grinning, ear to ear and all teeth showing. Nothing could slow her down or get her down. For Dorothy, though, the second time being thrown from the burro, was anything but graceful, landing on her left cheek and forehead and being knocked unconscious.

Boy, that brought all the cowboys running. Off the fences, gates and grandstands, they gathered, a half dozen carefully lifting her from the ground, carrying her over to the rough sawn planks of the front row of bleacher seats. Their efforts had been poorly rewarded as Eloise rushed in to shoo them away.

"Goddamn! Give the lady some breathin' room!" Eloise barked. "And somebody make theirselves useful and git me a damp kerchief or something."

A tall, lanky cowboy had been first to present Eloise with his bandana, dipped in a watering trough, no doubt, but wrung out.

"Thank you kindly, man." Eloise glanced up at the cowboy. Up and up. *This here galoot is treetop tall. Could be he's that Mr. Robbins. What's the rest of his name?*

She shook her head. It would come to her. She laid the bandana across Dorothy's forehead.

A newspaper reporter, seeming out of place in his bowler hat and checkered vest, stood on the fringe of the crowd around Dorothy and Eloise, furiously making his pencil fly across the page of his pocket notebook. He smiled and licked the tip of his pencil once more as he surveyed the crowd, writing, stopping now and again to catch just the right word or expression. His camera man stood in some near-by shade, bored and smoking a cigarette, his box camera still attached to its tripod, at the ready should any photographic opportunity present itself again.

"Shoo! Now shoo! All you, now git!" There was no mistaking the firmness in Eloise's command. One by one, each of the men gathered around the two women finally turned on his heel and walked away to resume watching the stunt riding between the main events.

"Hey, mister! You, too!" Eloise stood up to emphasize her orders. "You're just underfoot. You can trust the doc, here, can take over the care of our Miss Morrell."

Dorothy caught the last of Eloise's words as her eyelids fluttered and she tried to focus in on the faces still forming a ring overhead. As he turned to leave, the last cowboy - recipient of Eloise's tongue lashing - seemed to be a giant, albeit a slender one, his height accentuated by his boots and tall hat.

She closed her eyes again and shuddered. Boss Griffin was sure to fuss and fume over this one.

Eloise left Dorothy under the care of the Boss's company doctor, although he was more interested in watching the riders in the arena than worrying about her now that she had come back to consciousness. Eloise hurried away to try to find some vender who would let her dampen her own clean handkerchief with the icy water collected in the bottom of his ice box.

The only thing good about being unseated from Rosy, the Bucking Donkey, Dorothy thought to herself, was that the she hadn't been the only one to be thrown.

Chagrined, she listened to that pompous newspaper reporter as he muttered, reading back the notes he had written to himself: *Miss Dorothy Morrell attempted to ride "Rosie," the bucking burro, and was thrown heavily. Miss Eloise Fox suffered a similar fate when she bestrode the diminutive animal.* He nodded, smiled and flipped the notebook closed and tucked it into the inside pocket of his vest. With a cheery salute, he melted into the crowd.

Heavily? *o Gott!* Heavily! She groaned and sat up, swinging her feet, heavy in her knee high riding boots, to the ground.

Dear Eloise! She was a pistol - she never let anyone or anything stand in her way of getting where she wanted or needed to be. Had Eloise heard the reporter's mumblings, she would have taken him to task and corrected him, of that Dorothy was sure. - *Hey, mister! Don't you go callin' me Eloise! You better write that* Fox Hastings *took a tumble from that damn burro, or don't write nothin' at all!*

She didn't mince any words telling the story of her life in the Wild West shows, either.

"My pa was a horse trainer an' all I ever wanted to do was work them horses just like him. Hell, not 'like him,' but 'with him.' He never had no sons, just me and my little sister. I figgered I'd be good help for him but him and my mama wanted a proper little girl, ladylike, pristine, you know the type."

Eloise wrinkled her nose, shrugged and grinned.

"Especially my mama. How many times did she tell me what a disappointment I would be to my *grossmutter*, rest her soul. Gawd, them German grandmas'll be the death of you. So, to try to fix me up right, they sent me off to a convent school when I was twelve to be finished. Hmm! Finished! Like I had parts missing or stitches loose.

"By gum, all the good it did 'em. Money down a rat hole. From day one, all I done was figure one way and then another to get outta there."

Here the details of her story always jumped ahead. So "one way or another," she'd run away from that boarding school and married Mike Hastings, Wyoming cowboy and bulldogger. Why, the ink was hardly even dry yet on the marriage license when they took to their first show.

"Been married to Mike a while now. He been showin' me the ropes of bronk ridin' and I been watchin' and practicin' them fancy ridin' tricks those trick-ridin' gals do."

Dorothy wondered about marrying a cowboy. How could one split her heart between horses and a man? And riding for a rodeo boss like Mr Griffin was demanding. How would one divide her days? Her nights? The show must always go on. Like today, Boss Griffin's reaction to Eloise being thrown was, "Hope your landing won't delay the rest of your rides this afternoon."

Of course, nothing ever stopped Eloise from a ride. Not bruises, nor scrapes, nor sprained wrists, surely not that burro, Rosy.

Oh, but the pain in Dorothy's head was pounding and her wrist throbbed. Feeling peaked and under the weather – more like a thunderstorm, was one thing, but this sprained wrist might slow down her getting in the saddle. She could hardly move it. Maybe she could get Eloise to help her wrap it.

Eloise came running back with the sopping bandana.

"You won't believe this!" she crowed. "Old Jack down the way put a couple chucks of ice inside this here kerchief. Hold still now. What're you doing settin' up? Lie back down."

Dorothy winced as Eloise carefully washed her face again with the warm damp bandana before applying the cool fresh one over her forehead. Hard to believe this was Eloise's first year on the circuit, as they called following the fairs, Wild West shows and rodeos. *Just like me, only that's nobody's business but my own.*

In the year since Calgary, she'd made great inroads into creating Miss Dorothy Morrell, the - *famous Canadian rider, cowgirl and motion picture horsewoman* - as she had been called in the write ups about her in numerous newspapers throughout southern and central California. She'd found a few bit parts in several movies, in some she was even astride a horse or two, so that part about "motion picture horsewoman" was surely true enough. Cowgirl, well, here she was, all duded up in a split skirt just as Dolly Mullins had been, neckerchief knotted around her neck and shoulders, fancy beaded soft leather gauntlets – so necessary to protect her fingers and hands when handling the reins. She certainly looked every bit the part of a cowgirl. And she was absolutely sure that somewhere in Canada, someone would think she was famous, even if it were only baby sister Julie Ruth - if only she knew about her older sister. She had herself a signed contract with Mr. Griffin to "appear daily" in his shows, and so, by gum, she was well on her way. Now to get healed up and back into the real saddle every day and keep the dollars rolling in, even if ever so slowly.

"Hey, Dot," Eloise began, smiling wide and nearly dancing with delight. "You feelin' better yet? Wanna take a walk with me? Come on. You gotta come see my new saddle. Well, you know, it's new to me. Mike just got it today. With Boss calling us for that burro ride, I forgot to show you."

"Dot?" Dorothy laughed and carefully got to her feet. "I suppose now you want me to be calling you Fox!"

"Hell, yeah," Eloise replied. "You know, Fox's my maiden name, and I ain't no maiden no more!" The blush on her cheeks was more than the heat, but quick in passing. "Fox Hastings! That's who I am now. Eloise is too sweet a name for the likes of me."

"Okay, Fox," Dorothy said, trying the name on for size, "you lead the way."

Fox puffed up like a big bullfrog, swagger to match, and strode past the racetrack, Emeryville's makeshift rodeo area, toward the tents on its far side, on behind the temporary holding pens and corrals housing the rodeo stock.

Dorothy followed, though still feeling light headed and sporting a screaming headache.

"Ain't she a beauty?"

A touch of reverence mingled with the pride in Fox's voice as she led Dorothy to a sawhorse supporting the saddle.

"Lookie them straps here in front of the pommel. These'll be what I'm standing in next time I take a turn doin' the hippodrome around the arena."

She fingered the tough leather straps lovingly, as she should, Dorothy supposed. To Dorothy, though, at first glance, the saddle seemed quite ordinary although the horn was a bit taller and the cantle hardly raised itself at the rear of the seat. It did have a breast strap which some riders insisted on using as a must for keeping the saddle on the horse with all the pull and the shifting of weight that went with trick riding. But Fox was quick to point out the strap for the back bend and a belt for the stroud layout, and how to hook a stirrup over the horn to lean off the horse in a side-saddle layout.

"There's other stuff we could add . . ."

Fox went on but Dorothy had stopped listening as she nodded in awe at the joy Fox had in her husband's gift of the saddle. All Dorothy ever wanted to do after swinging up onto a horse, was to stay on, though riding in the parades opening the rodeo shows was hardly a challenge. The challenge was sometimes keeping a tight grip with her ankles as her horse was rearing and pawing the sky. For now, she would gladly leave the trick riding to girls like Fox.

"Too bad we cain't just wear britches like them cowboys do!" Fox stood with her hands on her hips, still smiling at her saddle.

Dorothy was a little taken back. True, some girls bloused the bottoms of their split skirts when riding. Some even made the blousing permanent, gathering the hems of their fabric split skirts and sewing a band around the bottom. Liked to call them bloomers, but there was no doubt that the bloomers were ladies' wear. To put on a pair of cowboy's jeans was beyond Dorothy's imagination, definitely not for her. She would be sticking with her leather skirts forever.

"Well, we gotta get back. Boss'll be hollerin' his head off if I'm late for the last rides of the day."

Fox took out at a pace that made Dorothy take double steps to keep up. Fox did more than "appear daily," she took to riding bucking bronks, too. She made it look easy most days. *How would it be?* Dorothy wondered.

Back in the grandstands surrounding the racetrack, Dorothy took a seat near the end, away from the hustle of those who wanted the better view of the afternoon show. She concentrated on watching Fox, Nettie Hawn and Babe Dukes as they rode bucking bronks as a lead-in to the cowboys' rides. She shook her head. Any old cowboy was welcome to risk his hide, even his life, and sign up to ride to ride the meanest, wildest, buckingest bronks, but women had to pay their dues, before being allowed to take chances, *"show the stuff they were made of."* How do girls show the stuff they are made of if they weren't allowed to compete? Dorothy watched as each rider either rode her horse to a standstill, or as she had with Rosie, lost her seat.

Dorothy marveled at how quickly the pickup men moved in for both those who finished their rides or needed to be helped out of harm's way once on the ground and in danger of being trampled.

Ahh! Dorothy was glad for the mid-October weather which had cooled and was pleasant. If her head would just quit pounding, life would be damn near perfect.

"Excuse me, miss," a young voice broke into her musings.

"Yes?" Dorothy turned to see a boy about 13 or 14, dressed in short pants that ended just below his knees and a white shirt and tie, suspenders over his shoulders.

"Are you Miss Dorothy Morrell?" he asked, trying to muster an authoritative tone.

Dorothy smiled. "Why, yes, I am."

"Then I have a letter for you, miss. Told to deliver it to nobody but you." He handed her an envelope, waiting a moment, hoping for a tip, but Dorothy's pockets were empty and would likely stay that way if she didn't get back in that saddle again.

"Why, thank you!" She smiled her most winning smile at the boy and took the envelope, scrutinizing the painfully perfect block printing across the front. *Miss Dorothy Morrell* was all it said.

"Will there be a reply?" the boy asked, still waiting.   Even before opening the envelope, Dorothy shook her head.   Even if she had wanted to write a reply, she had nothing to write one with.

The boy shrugged, gave a quick wave, and then threw his leg over the back of his bike and took his seat.   He leaned forward, and the bike began to roll even before he found his pedals and started on his way.   *An iron pony, fueled by the muscle and blood of its rider, pedals for stirrups, handle bars for reins,* Dorothy thought as she watched him pedal away.   *Could a boy ever love his bike the way a cowboy loved his horse?* she wondered.   Hard to tell, kids these days.

Turning the envelope over in her hand, she saw that the flap had simply been tucked in and not sealed.   Not too worried about privacy.   Pulling the flap open, she was surprised to see the contents had been written on lined paper.   The sight took her back to her school days in Winnipeg.

As she unfolded the paper, she could see the same precise printing, smaller though, as on the front of the envelope.   It wasn't a letter, per se. There was no date, no greeting, no signature, just three stanzas of poetry:

> *Top notch rider - and purty as well,*
> *Is our Wild West Gal, Miss Dorothy Morrell.*
> *She came with Boss Griffin to ride for the Show*
> *But that's not what today's tale is to tell.*
>
> *When to center arena, "Rosie" did go,*
> *A nasty old brute, famed bucking burro.*
> *Up on its back Miss Dorothy did step*
> *Only to come back down hard, nothing to show.*
>
> *Do we need to teach Rosie some manners, I ask?*
> *She needs to treat cowgirls with much more class.*
> *Too bad she's pig-headed*
> *For no matter the schoolin', she'll still be just a dumb _____*   **

Dorothy threw her head back and laughed her first real laugh of the day. Hell, maybe the whole week.   Her spirits lifted as the clouds of disappointment in her ride, the humiliation of being thrown by the burro, and the frustrations with Boss Griffin melted away.   She glanced back down at the sheet of paper.   There was a post script: *I also seen you in some of those moving picture shows.   I love how well you seat a horse.*

"What? What is it?" The nosy reporter had just walked up again with his camera man.   Dorothy was dumb-founded.   Who in heaven's name did he think he was?   Moreover, who in the world did he think *she* was that a letter to her was so important?   There were bigger names than hers riding today right here for Boss Griffin, most obviously, the 1913 Cowgirl Champion of the World, the lady bronk rider, Nettie Hawn.   They said she'd made a beautiful ride on a wicked horse called Snake, earlier this fall in Pendleton at the Round Up. But then again, Nettie was pretty busy now, riding, most likely, not available to talk to some nosy reporter.

Never let the facts get in the way of the truth, Dolly's words echoed again. She put on her best meet-the-press face and smiled coyly.

"And who might you be, sir?" she began. It would never do to discuss personal business with a nameless person.

"Oh, sorry!" The man stuck out his hand. As she offered hers in return, Dorothy couldn't get over the Americans always wanting to shake a woman's hand. "Name is Harvey Doolittle, though I do my best to live down my name, from the Oakland Tribune. I just thought maybe we could get a new angle on . . . uhm . . . horsewomen and the rodeo."

Indeed, a different angle than, being "thrown heavily."

"Well, now, this is just one of many letters I have received from well-wishers," Dorothy began, glancing down through the verses as if reminding herself of the content. "Although a lady never divulges what a man has written to her."

"A sweetheart?" Mr. Doolittle's voice was hopeful as he whipped out his notebook and turned to a fresh page.

"Oh, no! Not this writer. Mind you though, he did speak of love," Dorothy danced around the edges of truth, delighting in the man's haste to write every word from her mouth.

"So, you have met this man," Mr. Doolittle plied for details.

"Well, he writes that he has seen all my moving picture shows and has fallen deeply in love with me." *Oh, Dolly!* She laughed to herself. *Creating her own truth.*

"He claims to have even watched me ride in some of Boss Griffin's rodeos. Sort of admiring me from afar, I suppose. His only introduction was that he was among the crowd who rushed to my aid today when I was thrown from that diminutive beast, Rosie." She paused for effect, but Doolittle kept on writing, apparently not catching her veiled sarcasm.

"But, goodness, there were . . ." she continued counting on her fingers. "Well, there were more than I can tell. Of course, I have replied that I will not be setting on Rosie again any time soon." Or she would have written had she actually replied. She shrugged and folded the sheet of paper to put it back into the envelope.

"No, no, Miss Morrell! Leave it out. Please, we need a photograph of you with your letter!" Doolittle interrupted her in the middle of trying to tuck the folded paper back into its envelope. "Trout, get over here!" he called to his cameraman.

Mr. Trout languidly unfolded himself from the nearby bleacher where he sat smoking. Again. Without any hurry at all, he took a last drag and then ground out the butt with the toe of one of his well-worn leather shoes.

"Is this how you hurry?" Doolittle was exasperated.

"Hold your horses, Doo. This ain't no action shot. The lady ain't goin' nowhere."

Doolittle scowled but held his peace.

"Now, Miss Morrell, how shall we set up this shot?" Trout said while unfolding his tripod. When he had finished, he turned his attention back to Dorothy, and stepped back and looked her over, head to toe. "Push up your sleeves, miss, it ain't winter yet. Here, now, hold yer envelope and gloves in yer left hand."

Dorothy pulled her gauntlets from her waistband. Trout lifted both of her hands a little higher.

"That's it. Now hold yer mystery man's letter out in front of you with both hands. No, a little higher. Let's tip that hat up some." He lifted the brim of her gray triple-x beaver hat ever so slightly. "All righty! Smile purty."

Dorothy felt like she was back on a movie picture show set, being ordered around by the director. Only then she was getting paid. She refreshed her smile and tilted her head slightly.

"Nice! Yes, nice! Now turn yerself just a hair so yer quartered to the camera." He paused and smiled sardonically at Doolittle. "I think we got us a keeper. Whatcha think, Doo?"

"You're the one with the eye for the perfect picture. Let's get on with it."

Mr. Trout adjusted his lens and then took a couple of exposures while Dorothy stood rock steady still. "That should do 'er," he nodded to Doolittle.

"Great! Now we won't have to use the picture from earlier today – the one with the burro."

Dorothy was horrified to think that evidence of her graceless landing might have been captured on film, but she maintained her smile and tried to look excited to be talking to Mr Damn Nosy Newsman Harvey Doolittle.

"Now, Miss Morrell. I'm afraid I didn't get all the details from your ride earlier. The ride on . . . erh . . . Rosie. Would you be so kind as to fill me in on the details of how and why you and Eloise . . ."

"Fox," Dorothy interrupted. "Fox Hastings."

"Never heard her called that." Doolittle frowned. "Never mind. Back to the question, how and why you two ladies got set up to ride that burro."

"But, of course." Dorothy shrugged and smiled wider. "Be glad to."

Glad to add her two bits – her own twist on reality – plus she knew Boss Griffin would be just as thrilled with this kind of "daily appearance," photograph and all, even if it didn't make the front page. Anything to catch the eyes of the readers and peak their curiosity. A ticket sale was, as always, another dollar in the bank.

Mr. Doolittle found a fresh page in his note book, pencil at the ready and smiled back at her, Miss Dorothy Morrell, famous Canadian horsewoman and motion picture star.

V – APRIL 1914 – ON A DARE!

The spring rodeo season was just beginning and Dorothy was thinking back to last fall. All the Main Streets, all the arenas, all the faces blurred together - Salinas, Emeryville, Oakland - she couldn't keep them or all the others straight. The only one she was sure of was Emeryville. She shook her head. No need to dwell on the negative - rather she should remember how thrilled Boss Griffin was with two, not just one articles in the paper thanks to Rosie!

She was pretty sure this was Fresno, but then again, it could be Bakersfield. It didn't seem to matter where they were, the shows were the same.

The morning chill of late spring had burned off fast, the day promising to be fair and warm.   She had done her riding through the arena on a tall roan during the opening ceremonies for the first show of the day, and now sat idly watching the ladies' bucking contests.   The horses being drawn were anything but up to snuff.   After being seated in their saddles, the ladies were being disappointed with half-hearted bucking, a little crow hopping, and general low scoring rides.   It was going to be a long day.

Dorothy took advantage of the slowness to take inventory of where she was just now on her life's new road here in California.   The newness and thrill had definitely worn off of the parades, the pageantry, the endless smiling, the waving.

There had to be more than this.   Maybe she could talk Boss Griffin into letting her ride a trick or two to add to the dash around the arena.   That would wake up the crowd!   She wondered where Fox was just about now. Dorothy hadn't seen her since the tiny cowgirl had left the crowd in awe earlier with her repertoire of carefully practiced stands, swoops, and drags.

"I'll bet that if I should saddle a certain cayuse for yuh, yuh could ride rings around any a them girls."   Dorothy was startled out of her reverie by the soft western twang of the cowboy towering next to her.

As she glanced up, Emeryville came back to mind.   She was sure he was the tall stranger who had been last to leave the circle of rescuers.   No, there had to be a better 'memory' than that.

Perhaps I knew him in . . . Montana!   Montana wasn't all that far from Manitoba.   Closer than California, that was for sure.   Let's see, I had been . . . delivering mail . . . on the Blackfoot Indian Reservation . . . where I had polished my horse riding skills . . . riding for the Pony Express.   Yes, the Pony Express riders delivered mail, hadn't they?   But they hadn't ridden bucking horses.   What a pity!

"But I've never been on a bucking horse in my life," the words spilled out before Dorothy could catch herself.

"Don't make no difference.   I bet yuh kin outride any of them gals here. I dare yuh to try!"   The cowboy smiled down at her and raised an eyebrow. "What do yuh say?   Shall we make a go of it?"

Oh, so it was now a dare!   He had dared her to ride.   Fred, her brother had dared her many a time to break – or at least bend –   one of Mutti's many rules.   She had never backed down then and she wasn't about to back down now.   But, criminy!   A bucking horse?

"Well, go ahead!   Bring 'er on!"   Dorothy stood up, dusted off her leather skirt and started climbing down from the bleachers to the ground level.

"By the way, I'm called Skeeter Bill."

"I thought I recognized you," Dorothy replied, smiling her best, though she wasn't about to remind him of Emeryville, as she offered her hand. "Dorothy Morrell."

"I know," Bill replied, "I know."

Her heart was – what would Fox say? – about to jump out of her throat? She was on high alert now. Was it the horse or the man? Didn't matter. She'd work that out later.

"Go ahead. Bring on your horse."

"Come along, then." Bill offered Dorothy his elbow before heading for the back side of the arena. As they walked, he had some words of advice for Dorothy. "Listen now. Yuh say yuh ain't never been in the hurricane deck on a bucking horse before, but I seen yuh burn the breeze in a few arenas. Yuh seat a horse well."

Dorothy's pulse rose at hearing the phrase. The mysterious poet of Emeryville was no doubt at her fingertips even now.

"I know yuh kin do this," he went on. "Yuh got a natchral rhythm and feel to yer riding. Yuh'll do good."

Good to know, she thought, hoping this would not be a repeat of Rosie's Ride.

"But of course!" was all she replied.

"Here's a little advice for yer first time up. Every time that cayuse hits the ground, yuh raise yer hat as high as yuh can, and when he comes up again, hit him right between the horns . . . ears! Hit him between the ears."

"Got it. Head down, hat up. Head up, hat down."

Dorothy followed Skeeter Bill Robbins into the arena as he waved over to a group of cowboys leaning against corral poles watching as skittish horses nipped and chased each other.

"Hey, Jess," he called, "how's about we saddle up that horse we's talkin' 'bout earlier?"

The man called Jess nodded, as Skeeter Bill shook out his lariat and stepped into the corral. The nervous mustangs milled away from him as effortlessly and gracefully his loop floated out and settled over the head of a long legged dun, black mane and tail and stripe down its back. It snorted and reared, then pulled back against the rope showing the whites of its eyes as it fought to escape.

Leaning backward himself, Bill walked his hands up the rope, slowly approaching the bronk and crooning softly to the horse as it pulled and sidestepped away from him. Jess pulled a saddle off the top rail of the corral and quickly ran to Bill's side.

Both men were trying to sweet talk the horse into standing still – just still enough – to throw the saddle across its back. By this time a couple other cowboys were now crowding the horse's front quarters. Hands out to steady its head. Hands running over the quivering shoulder muscles. Hands to help in any way they could. Jess stepped in and threw the saddle across the horse's back only to have the horse side step out from underneath it before he could reach under the dancing legs to grab the cinch. Hands retrieved the saddle and threw it back across the horse's back, and then tossed the cinch under its belly. Jess caught the cinch and threaded the latigo strap through the cinch ring and back up to the saddle's d-ring pulling it tight as he went.   By now the horse was fairly quiet, though still dancing on its front toes now and again.   Jess tied off the latigo and turned to Skeeter.

"Reckon we're ready."

All of the men were breathing heavily.

"So you cleared this ride with the rodeo boss?" Jess asked.

Bill simply smiled and nodded.

Surprised, Dorothy glanced from one man to the other.   They were grinning ear to ear at each other.   It appeared to her that there had been a plan in place and she had stepped into something a little bigger than a dare.   She could feel her hackles rising on the back of her neck.   *By damn!* she'd show them.   She didn't know who she should be mad at, or if she should be angry at all, but Boss Griffin's constant training was paying off as she returned their grins for a brilliant smile of her own.

The horse was "led around" to the center of the arena, where Dorothy reached for her gauntlets but discovered she'd left them with her saddle and bridle after her morning ride.   No matter, now was time to climb into the saddle.

"No, I don't need any help, mind you," she was firm in that regard as she stepped into the stirrup.   As she settled into the seat, she experienced one of the strangest sensations she'd ever felt in her life.   The horse was quivering beneath her as she adjusted her weight in the saddle, tightened her knees and took the hackamore rope firmly in her left hand.

Gott im Himmel, keep me safe in your hands, she prayed.   She also prayed she'd keep her seat for at least a few good jumps, as she scanned the arena for any soft place to land.

No time for anything but the here and now!   The cowboys all let loose of the horse at the same moment.   Somebody gave a whoop and the dun bowed its neck and went at it, "boiled over," as they say.   With every jump, there was a terrible jolt that made her feel like her bones would let loose of their joints.

O, Gott! Head down, hat up!   Head up, hat down!

With her right hand, she grabbed her hat from her head.   At times she could look straight down over the saddle horn and see the dusty, dirty surface of the ground.   Other times, she was sure the ground was raising up to meet her, only to be twisted and turned away from it once again.

Fanning the horse's head, Dorothy managed to keep well forward and stay with the bronc while its front end was in the air, and to keep her seat when it jarred its forelegs into the ground, kicking and bucking with its hind legs.   Hope began rising as the seconds passed and she determined to herself that she would stay with this horse even if it bucked every tooth out of her head.

At last, the dun slowed, finally finishing its bucking, but it took to racing across the arena.   Dorothy felt exhilarated as the pickup men who had been flanking her ride, closed in.   One leaned into her and held out his arm to her.   She grabbed it and threw herself on the rump of his horse behind the seat of his saddle.

Now, how in heaven's name had Bill managed that? she thought to herself. He must have had his own horse saddled and at the ready after all, it was his dare that had put her here, possibly in harm's way.   Maybe this was his way of trying to be sure that no harm would come to her.

No matter!   Dorothy was ecstatic as she clung to Bill's waist.   The thrill of adrenaline coursed through her body and it seemed that nothing else mattered except the horse behind her, the horse beneath her, and the man in front of her.

The crowd was a blur, then cowboys seemed far away, all she could think of was she had really done it!   She, Dorothy Morrell, had ridden a bronk.   Not just ridden it, but ridden it to the end.   To what?   To a score? Had she scored?   It was more than she could hope for.

She and Bill rode to the rear of the arena where another saddled bronk was waiting to be lead out for the next lady rider.   She slid to the ground as Bill threw his leg over the saddle horn and jumped lightly to land next to her.

"Well, now, gal!   Whatja think a that?"

His grin told her everything she needed to know about how pleased he was with her ride as he threw an arm around her shoulders.

"Oh, God!   I can't wait to do it again! Oh, my heavens!   That was the most – the most – I . . ."   Words failed her.

She smiled up at Mr. Skeeter Bill Robbins and one thing she knew and knew well.   She was not just the opening act for Boss Griffin anymore. She was Dorothy Morrell, bucking horse rider!

VI - MAY 1914 - CAPTAIN OF
THE COWBOY COMPANY

I believe I read something about your cowhand feller in one of the papers the other day. Something about wanting to go to Mexico with a bunch of cowboy soldiers," Boss said to Dorothy as he counted out her final wages of the season. As usual, his 'office' was an empty holding pen, now shoveled out and raked clean of manure and debris.

"Oh, and just who is 'my' cowhand fellow?" Dorothy asked, smiling up at Boss as she folded the bills into her pocket book.

"That Mo-Skeeter cowboy," Boss replied, grinning down at Dorothy. She was surprised to find that Boss Griffin could be relaxed and even jovial when the cares and worries of the day were far away.

"Oh," Dorothy blushed. "Haven't seen him since . . ." She thought back. "Since last month, I think."

"Well, girl, your luck is about to change. Better or worse, couldn't say, but it's gonna to changing all the same," Boss replied, nodding through the dusk of the evening in the direction of the holding pens. Most were still full of bronks and steers waiting to be shipped out in the coming days. She followed Boss's gaze and discovered Skeeter Bill Robbins making his way through the rodeo grounds. He certainly seemed in no hurry, stopping to talk and laugh with nearly everyone he passed. Was Boss actually onto something, though? Had Bill really shown up to see her?

Changing the subject, he said, "You're sure you're not coming back next season." Though a question, his tone of voice made it a statement.

"Yes, but thank you," Dorothy replied, smiling and nodding. *Always leave them smiling!* Boss's number one rule of thumb.

He turned to the next cowgirl in line and Dorothy stepped out into the cool of the evening out behind the chutes.

This had been the last show on her contract with the Boss and she was glad to be moving on. Hopefully, to the bigger and the better.

Watching Bill from the corner of her eye, keeping him in sight, Dorothy hummed a nameless tune while she packed her gear. She didn't have much to gather. Leather gloves, a rope, an extra blouse or two. For now, the daily bronk rides had been on Griffin's saddles, though she had been faithfully squirreling away dimes and dollars since that first ride. First thing she learned was that saddle bronk competitors used their own saddles and gear. She smiled. She liked the sound of that - *Saddle bronk competitor.*

So much about her had changed in the weeks since Boss Griffin had sputtered and fumed after learning of her first ride on a bucking horse. She shook her head remembering.

"Beginner's luck!" he thundered at her after calling her into his "office" - a horse stall behind the chutes. The chutes on the far side of the arena. "What were you and that dim-witted cowhand thinking? You could have been killed or worse!"

Dorothy wasn't sure but what most of Boss's anger came from the fact that she had ridden a wild horse outside her contract with him. Ridden and taken the chance of being injured. An injury that would keep her from fulfilling her daily appearances. Always, always, those daily appearances.

She also wondered what could possibly be worse than being killed but thought it likely better not to ask. Wouldn't be in her best interest to show much curiosity about that right at that moment.

"Doesn't matter what we were thinking," Dorothy answered, keeping her voice even despite her annoyance. "Fact is, I placed second in the money. Hard cash.   I want to be rough riding on a bronk in your afternoon shows every day that we perform from here on out."

"From here on out?" Griffin's voice went from booming thunder to icy cold with disbelief.   "You can't.   I mean, all the afternoon shows have already been planned and the programs have been pre-printed.   You know that.   All ready to stamp the name of the arena on them."

Dorothy waited for the man to further cool down.   Her silence made him nervous.

"You're kidding me, right?" he finally blustered.   "Just another part of these schemes you and old Skeeter What's-His-Name cooked up!" He slammed a fist into the palm of his hand.

"No, no, and no," he continued to storm.

Dorothy hated to play her ace of trump, but Boss left her no choice, although a small compromise might be in order.

"I'll tell you what," Dorothy began.   "I'll finish the season riding in the opening show and you'll let me ride one mustang a day."

"No."   Boss was adamant.

"Well, then it's been good working for you."

"What?   You can't quit.   You're on contract."

Dorothy stood and smiled up at him, refusing to say another word.

Boss fumed. He was not used to being out negotiated by anyone, let alone a girl who couldn't even stay on a burro.

"Tell you what," he finally said, "you can stay and rope or ride, whatever, in the afternoons but you are one of my drawing cards and you are still opening all the shows.   But the first scrape, bruise, or bloody nose you get coming off a horse and Doc will make sure that hurricane seat disappears so fast, you won't even remember ever being in it."

The thankfulness Dorothy felt was far overshadowed by the extreme bitterness in his voice and pompousness in assuming that unlike any of the other riders, Dorothy had to be immune to the slightest of injuries.   It didn't matter, he would never know unless she wanted him to.

"And I'll want my daily wage increased." Dorothy hammered the deal home.

Boss said not a word but pulled a tattered notebook and the stub of a pencil from a pocket.   He licked the tip of the pencil and began scrawling across the page.

"By the way," Dorothy continued as she watched him writing, "there is going to be a follow up article in the Oakland Tribune about my mystery letter writer.   Remember the one last fall?   Mr. Doolittle is writing it.   It's sure to entice more than a few folks into coming to your afternoon shows," Dorothy added.

And of course, as far as Mr. Doolittle knew, the Mystery Man was still a mystery, Dorothy thought to herself.   A girl was under no obligation to discuss every detail of her life with anyone, especially nosy tell-all reporters like Mr. Doolittle or cranky bosses.

"Humph," Boss snorted as if he didn't give a fig about free publicity. He finished the contract by signing and dating it and handed the notebook over to Dorothy.

Frank Griffin Wild West Show and Rodeo will pay a wage of one dollar and fifty cents per day to Miss Dorothy Morrell for the following daily appearances in all scheduled shows for the rest of its spring 1914 rodeo season: riding in all parades mounted on a horse, fancy/trick riding and/or roping during each show's opening act, and the opportunity to draw and ride in one ladies' bucking horse contest per day. Payment will be drawn weekly. Griffin Wild West Show and Rodeo will no longer provide room or board for Miss Morrell. Any injuries which will exclude her from fulfilling this contract will render it null and void.

Dorothy breathed a sigh of relief even though the loss of room and board would cut into the raise in daily wage that Boss had given her. No matter. She was now a bucking horse rider, and she knew she was going to like them a little tougher than most. The better the fight in the bronk, she had observed, the better the score at the end of the ride. Life was like that sometimes.

The changes had been rougher than she had imaged. The hard landings brought on sore muscles. Bruises. An occasional scrape or two. All of which she carefully doctored herself. But still, more often than not, she had made it to the end of her rides and had come out on top, the victor in the daily battles of will – her will to stay on the horse and the horse's will to be free from the pesky little rider on its back.

And the dirt. Dirt in her hair. In her eyes. Her nose. Dirt in her clothes. Most of the cowboys didn't bother to change after their rides – change out of shirts grimy with dust and sweat, sometimes caked with fresh manure but not her. An extra blouse was always a part of her daily gear. She snapped her carpet bag shut.

The tall figure finally stepped up to her out of the shadows of the dusk.

"Howdy there, girl," called his familiar voice. Dorothy's heart skipped a beat.

"Hi, Bill," Dorothy answered, looking up into Bill's friendly face.

"Walk yuh home?" Bill asked.

"Sure, it's not far. Just a boarding house down the road a piece." Dorothy replied. Bill picked up her bag and offered her his elbow as she smiled up at him once again, glad to be going and gone. She slipped her hand into the crook of his elbow and they started making their way carefully to the street.

"Got any plans fer the next little while?" Bill asked, tentatively.

Dorothy pondered on the question. What was he really asking?

"You mean like shows or rodeos? There's the rodeo in Salinas next month," she hesitantly replied.

"Yeah, Salinas," Bill nodded. "You wanna do some ropin' stuff with me? A good partner is hard to come by."

Dorothy thought of the fancy roping tricks she seen other couples perform.

49

"Anything as long as there is not a figure eight involved," she laughed.

"Well, now, I bet yer thinkin' a ridin' them figger eights 'round the area, but there's figger eights in ropin', too," Bill reminded her.

"You're right." Dorothy nodded. "But no more opening the show."

"Ahhh, I see - was it really all that bad?" Bill asked, though his voice was full of both kindness and concern.

Dorothy thought on the question for a while before she answered.

"No, not really. It was more the fact that Boss acted as he believed that was all I was good for." *Dorothy Morrell, Moving Picture Star,* smiling pretty, waving at the crowds.

"I felt like I was supposed to be a one-trick pony and all I was good for was looking good."

"I wuz wonderin'. Might a figgered that," was all Bill said.

How wrong Griffin had been when he had called him *'That dim-witted cowhand!'* Dorothy thought, remembering the Boss's unkind judgement of Bill. Not only unkind, but untrue as well. Pretty sharp, this cowhand.

"I'm thinking of finding a place in Oakland to rent for a while," Dorothy said.

"It's a good spot," Bill agreed, nodding. "Kinda in the middle a anyplace yuh might need to go. Trains go outta there all day long an' half the night."

"What's going to be keeping you busy the next little while?" Dorothy asked, hoping he wouldn't be far.

"Me? I'll be scourin' the countryside, checkin' out ranches, lookin' fer some good buckin' stock. Keep them rodeo bosses happy with fresh talent." He paused.

"Plus I got me some strings a relay horses. Most rodeos got relay races for both the cowboys and cowgirls."

They walked on, listening to the night sounds of crickets, the whisper of light breezes in the leaves above them, the fading echoes of automobile traffic as the darkness deepened.

"Yuh hungry?" Bill asked as they passed a diner. "Maybe a piece a pie?"

"Sure," Dorothy answered, glad for a reason to spend just a little more time this evening with the cowboy who she hoped would become a familiar fixture in her life. *No, not a fixture. Fixtures were ordinary accessories, overused and overlooked, forgotten and never thought about unless the need was immediate. Bill was not a fixture.* What exactly though, she thought to herself, remained to be seen.

Bill opened the door for Dorothy and they walked in and seated themselves at the counter.

"What'll it be, folks?" asked the waiter, friendly enough, though one eye was on his customers and one eye on the clock. Closing time was still a half hour off, but they had the place to themselves. Maybe he had been thinking of closing early.

"Apple pie with ice cream and coffee for me," Dorothy answered.

"And I'll be havin' what the lady is havin'," Bill said. Coffee was poured into thick, sturdy mugs before the waiter disappeared into the back to serve up the pie.

"Boss said he'd read about you in the paper lately," Dorothy began.

"Oh? Hope it was good. Course, if it was all good, it might a not been all true," Bill grinned at her.

"Something about going to Mexico?" Dorothy wished she'd been paying more attention to Griffin and had asked for more details.

"Well, as yuh know, I spent this past winter cowpunchin' up in Oregon – cowboys gotta eat between rodeo seasons. So it was just before I started back down here to California when them sailors was arrested and harassed in Tampico. Humm, 'bout the first part a April."

Dorothy nodded – she figured Tampico must be in Mexico somewhere, and more than likely on the coast if sailors were involved, but just where, she didn't know and truth be told, didn't care.

"Go on," she said listening carefully.

She loved watching his face when he was explaining things or storytelling, how the lines around his eyes crinkled, then smoothed as he talked. Smile lines, not quite dimples, lent emphasis to his words. His eyes sometimes took on a faraway look as if he had to see exactly what it was he was telling her about. His was the face of an earnest, hardworking but fun loving man. A face she felt she might trust. Some day.

"Here you go, folks." The plates of pie were set in front of them, and Dorothy followed Bill's lead in wasting no time in cutting into the pie with her fork and less time getting it into her mouth.

"Hmmmmm," Dorothy said, ignoring Mutti's oft repeated warning not to sing to her food.

"So bein' arrested wasn't the worst insult," he continued. "It was that them sailors was booed and hissed and whatnot whilst bein' herded like cattle down the streets a Tampico t' jail.

"They wasn't even in jail all that long, but the Admiral, the navy boss down there, he demanded apology from them Mexicans," Bill said, reaching for his coffee cup.

"I thought he got it," Dorothy said quietly.

"Well, a verbal 'we're sorry' is all he got, but the Admiral – Mayo, I think his name is – insisted on a 21-gun salute for Ol' Glory, which he was refused."

"I see," Dorothy said, although she didn't. An apology was an apology in her mind.

"So in the Oregon National Guard up there, they's a bunch a Spanish American War veterans amongst 'em, an' they wanted to organize a bunch a volunteers just in case President Wilson ever got approval from Congress to send in troops. You know, to let them folks down south know we ain't happy bein' messed with.

51

"That's when me and the boys thought we could be of service to the President and the country. Them fellers elected me as Captain of the Cowboy Company, unofficial company, mind yuh, an' I sent a telegram to Wilson lettin' him know of our willin'ness to serve."

"So, any word back from the President or his office?" Dorothy asked, hoping this wasn't a touchy subject, glancing sideways at Bill as he forked another bite of pie. The answer was self-evident, of course. He was sitting next to her at this very moment.

"Not a thing," Bill snorted. "I kinda think that nobody takes a bunch a cowboys serious."

"Maybe it isn't that," Dorothy replied. "Maybe it's that the whole affair down in Mexico was - what do they say? - a tempest in a teapot?"

Bill nodded somberly. "Perhaps, but it don't seem like it to me. Yuh let somebody push yuh around a little, they end up pushin' yuh around a whole lot."

Bill laughed then and shook his head. "I s'pose we are a little rough around the edges. Anyway, nothin's come of it and by now, nothin' will. Not for the Cowboy Company, anyway."

"I, for one, am glad," Dorothy said, smiling up at Bill. "If you and those cowboys had run off to Mexico, we wouldn't be sharing pie right now, and I'd need a big stick, walking home after dark all by myself."

"Oh, there'd probably be someone to walk with you," Bill countered.

"Like who?" Dorothy was incredulous. "Boss? You think he'd care?

She smiled up at the would-be-Captain of the Cowboy Company. "No, Mr. Robbins, I'm glad for your willingness to be of service to the country, but I'm more glad you're here with me tonight."

"You don't say!" Bill grinned back at her.

VII - 18 JUNE 1914 - BEGIN WITH BREAKFAST

Her own kitchen. Her own table. Her own place. True, it was little more than a hole in the wall, as Bill had observed. A tiny bedroom behind an all-purpose room - kitchen, dinette, and front room rolled into one. But it was hers, the first place ever she had ever had to call her own. Being alone in her own tiny home during downtime was delicious.

And for the first time since leaving Winnipeg, she had some place to actually call home. Sure, it was only tiny, but it had been newly built in just the past few years. The earthquake eight years ago had melted San Francisco's flimsy multi-story tenements into the ground but had affected Oakland as well though in a far different way. Within just a day or two after the earthquake, Oakland's population had doubled as survivors fled the fires and rubble and with that sudden explosion came the need for more housing.

Her flat had running water from the tap over the galvanized double sink and a tiny cook stove that had come standard with the place. And a flushing water closet just down the hall! In fact, every floor had one of these indoor conveniences. Gone were the days of lugging chamber pots down the stairs every morning to the outhouses in the back or worse yet, just tossing the contents out the window of the front room. "Front room" – a snobby thing to call the kitchen–dining–living area that opened up into a bedroom hardly big enough for a bed.

Dorothy hummed as she turned the potatoes - spuds, Bill liked to call them- and the slices of thick German bratwursts - sausages - frying in the heavy cast iron skillet. Coffee was percolating. Biscuits were baking. Eggs were lined on the tiny strip of counter top, ready to be scrambled as soon as her breakfast company arrived. Her breakfast company. Bill. Her heart sang.

A quick survey of the table assured her that she really was ready for Bill anytime he arrived. She smoothed the long apron she wore over her every day dress before she poured herself a cup of coffee and tried to decide who should sit on the one chair at the table. She felt that as the hostess, she should sit on the upended wooden fruit crate and let her company sit on the chair. She laughed to herself though. *That would be the day! Skeeter Bill Robbins would never sit in a chair while a woman sat on a box!*

She set her cup on the table and took the biscuits out of the oven, turning them into a basket and setting it on the tiny table. She turned the potatoes and sausages again and decided it was time to crack the eggs and beat them with a little cream.

Tum-ti-ti-tum-tum came the knock on the door. Smiling with anticipation, Dorothy set the bowl of egg mixture down and ran her fingers through her hair before opening the door.

Bill was grinning, eyes sparkling. He was bursting with excitement.

"Good mornin', ma'am," he said, as if he were announcing an undisputable fact, rather than as a greeting.

"And good morning to you!" she replied, caught up in anticipation. "Come in and have a seat."

She wondered if she would ever get over the impulse that she should be standing on tiptoe to kiss him on the cheek by way of a greeting. It had been her mother's practice which she had passed on to her daughter. Then again, Maria Eichhorn was not of a custom to ever greeting gentlemen in such a way – maybe her sons, occasionally her husband – no, just her women friends, so that didn't really explain Dorothy's thoughts, either.

Ah, well, she smiled up at Bill before pouring the beaten eggs over the potatoes and reaching for the coffee pot.

Bill set himself right down on the wooden box exactly as Dorothy had guessed he would.

"Good to be back in town," he announced, still grinning. Dorothy was beginning to wonder what he had up his sleeve.

"Good to have you back!"

"Whatcha got goin' this weekend?" Bill asked, no longer able to wait but still not quite getting to the point.

"About the same," Dorothy smiled over her shoulder, hoping for anything but the same.

"How's about goin' with me across the Bay to San Francisco for a couple a days?" he asked.

She was taken by surprise and it showed, delighting Bill all the more.

"What's in San Francisco that isn't here?" Hesitantly replying with a question of her own.

"That's exactly the point! We're gonna be seein' things there that ain't here," came his cheerful reply.

She laughed. "But of course."

Bill had quite the knack for drawing out a story for optimal effect. Well, he would just have to wait a minute. Eggs, potatoes and sausages were ready to be dished onto plates.

Setting their plates onto the table, she finally sat down across from Bill, and said with a grin of her own, "Now tell me all about San Francisco."

"Well, there's beaches with sand," he began, a bite of potatoes already in his mouth.

"Hmmm." Dorothy did not believe this would be the reason for his excitement, though it sounded great to her. How would it be to walk along a seashore, looking out across the waves knowing there were thousands of miles of ocean before her? "Sounds very inviting but I think there is a beach closer to home."

"True, but it ain't on the mighty Pacific Ocean. An' then there's Golden Gate Park," Bill added.

"There are lots of parks here in Oakland," she pointed out, still puzzled.

"But ain't none here like Golden Gate. I hear it's bigger'n Central Park in New York City. Three miles long an' a half mile wide, so they say. 'Course, I ain't walked it, but I'll take their word for it."

"And . . ." Dorothy let the word hang midair, waiting for the reason to clinch the deal.

"An' the site for the Panama–Pacific World's Fair!" Bill exclaimed with a satisfied look on his face.

"But the Exposition doesn't start until next year," Dorothy said, wondering how this could possibly be what was so exciting for Bill.

"Yup, I know," he said. "But just this week, I been talkin' with Tom Mildrick. He's a rodeo promoter and livestock provider I been acquainted with for quite some time now. He helped get the rodeo put together down in Bakersfield a couple months ago."

"I remember," Dorothy replied. *And so much more. Her first bucking horse ride. The ride that changed her life.* "At least I think I remember who he is."

"Well, he been recruitin' for Joe Miller, of the Miller Brothers 101 Ranch Rodeo."

"Aren't they out of Texas or Oklahoma?" Dorothy could not figure a tie between the 101 Ranch to San Francisco.

"Oklahoma," Bill replied, "but the 101 Ranch is bringin' part of their show and rodeo out here next year for the Exposition and Tom says they're wantin' all the performers they can get their hands on."

"Ahh, I see!" Dorothy nodded, finally picking up on a possible reason for Bill's excitement. She grinned and raised both eyebrows. "Quite possibly could one of those performers, as you say, be you?"

"Yup, I signed on. Can yuh believe it?" he laughed. "Me, signin' a contract for 'daily appearances.' So, it ain't competition so much's it's entertainment. No prize money, but then again, ain't no entrance fees. Just ridin' for the brand, as they say, and gettin' paid to do it. Though, I bet it makes one Miss Dorothy Morrell wonder what the world is comin' to!"

She nodded, although she could see the logic in Bill's decision. "Sounds like steady work! Can't ever beat that."

Then she frowned, still puzzled at the invitation to go to San Francisco now and not next year.

"But what does this have to do with going over there this weekend?" Dorothy asked and Bill laughed at her quizzical expression.

"Well, I hear they been openin' up the exposition grounds on Sundees for sightseers for a couple a months now. Lotsa folks like to take a stroll and look around to see how the buildin's an' grounds's comin' along. They say there's lots to see already though the exhibition halls and concessions ain't close to bein' open yet."

Dorothy nodded, clearly seeing that Bill was still wound up and had more to say.

"I figgered one a the things we could do is go check out 'The Zone' – as the Avenue of Fun is gonna be called – see how the arena is comin' along. Yuh know, seein's how that's where I'll be every day startin' 'bout the middle a next February."

Dorothy's eyes lit up with at the thoughts of all the possible things they could see and do.

"An' I got a friend who's got a couple a rooms he and the Missus rent now and again. We can stay there and not have to come back over here to Oakland at night. Won't cost us much. The Missus' food'll be topnotch, I can promise yuh that much right now."

Dorothy nodded. "I suppose that by the time you figure the cost of going back and forth by the ferry, staying there wouldn't be too bad."

But she was mentally counting the bills and coins in the socks hidden in the toes of her boots. Under her bed. Pushed back into the corner as far as she could reach.

Bill grinned wider. "Speakin' a ferries, you hear a the Airy Ferry?"

Dorothy snorted in a way that would have made her mother cringe.

"You mean that aeroplane service that crashed into the Bay last month?" Dorothy asked, narrowing her eyes across the table at Bill.

"Well, now, the pilot called it a 'forced landing.' I guess the engine quit on him but he got it landed just fine. 'Plane had to be towed back to its dock but it's been good ever since." Bill defended the pilot and then hesitated, watching Dorothy's expression. He was pretty sure he would have to do some pretty smooth talking or she wasn't going to be persuaded to go on any such adventure.

"He only charges a dime per passenger. His 'plane can take four at a time. I hear it's only 6 minutes to cross from Oakland to San Francisco," Bill said, paused before adding, "an' I thought anybody who can ride them wild horses for fun wouldn't hesitate a tall at a chance to fly across the Bay."

"Well, I think maybe you thought wrong. I do ride wild horses but I don't know about being that far in the air," Dorothy said, though she really was sure that Bill would be able to convince her otherwise. "We'll be a lot higher than 6 or 8 feet off the ground."

"Yuh been thrown higher than 6 or 8 feet a time or two," Bill teased. "I sure know I been!"

"Maybe so," Dorothy agreed, "but this is different. A lot different."

"Think on it! I bet traveling by way of 'planes is gonna take off and be the next big thing," Bill grinned. "But, either way you wanna get there, I was thinkin' we might go over Saturday and maybe come back Monday or Tuesday."

"I'd love to go," Dorothy said. "I haven't ever been over to San Francisco. It's a little out of way. Not a place Boss ever took his Wild West Show."

"Nope, but sure as shootin', there's a Real Ranch Rodeo comin'," Bill said.

"Maybe we can check out Mr. Christofferson's aeroplane service," Dorothy conceded. "Maybe if we watched it cross over and back . . ." She let her own words do the convincing of her heart that things would be okay.

"Oh, there's another thing I wanna talk to yuh about." Bill's voice became a little more serious, though only slightly.

"Soon as we're done at the Salinas rodeo next month, I'm headin' for Cheyenne. So 'round the first week a August."

Dorothy nodded.

"Rodeos 'round here's good for gettin' yer feet wet, gettin' in some experience, but if yuh really wanna move up in the ranks, yuh need to go to the big ones. Cheyenne. Pendleton. Calgary. Hell, it don' matter if yuh place in the money or not -   though it'd be nice to get some a yer entrance money back now and again, but just bein' there is like goin' to school. Yuh watch an' learn."

"I'll miss you till you're back here again," Dorothy said a little wistfully.

"No, I mean, I'm thinkin' *you* oughta come with me," Bill explained. "This year promises to be bigger and better."

"Bill, I don't see how I can do it," Dorothy began hesitantly. "Couple of reasons. Have I really ridden enough to qualify to enter the saddle bronc competition? I've only got one actual rodeo payday under my belt so far," she explained, then added, "You know that any cowboy fresh off the range can put his money on the table, and buy into the game."

"For women, though, it's different." She was starting to sound annoyed. "We have to 'prove our mettle' before rodeos will even consider letting us put our money on the table. We've got to show our stuff. Be above injury. It's quite exasperating – women need experience to be allowed into the competitions, but how do they get the experience if they aren't allowed to complete."

"But, yuh been ridin' for Griffin," Bill argued. "So yuh ain't a stranger to the saddle. That's gotta count for somethin' even if ridin' for Boss wasn't for prize money. I bet yuh'll be able to ride with the best of 'em and hold yer own."

"Maybe."

The kitchen was quiet as each mulled over their own thoughts and worries.

At last, Dorothy said softly, "Bill, it's not just lack of experience that's holding me up." She hesitated even longer. It wasn't her way to discuss money – or the lack thereof – with anyone, not even Bill.

"Hey, if yuh need someone to walk yuh through the ropes," he grinned his crooked grin and winked, "or better yet, walk with yuh through a lasso, yuh always got me. I been chasin' rodeos a lotta of years now. Ain't nothin' to it."

Dorothy smiled across at Bill. "It seems to me that you, Mr. Skeeter Bill Robbins, believe that anyone can do or accomplish anything that comes their way. Isn't there anything that ever worries you?"

He nodded and thought for several moments before answering her. " 'Course there's things that bother me, but when they come along, I first think t'myself: Can I fix this? If the answer's 'yes,' I git right on it. If there ain't nothin' I can do 'bout it, I just leave it behind me and I git on with life."

He lifted his cup of coffee before realizing it was empty.

"See what I mean here? M'cup ain't got a thing in it. So, I can pour me some more, I can ask someone to pour for me, or I can do without. Simple."

"I see," Dorothy said, as he reached for the coffee pot.

He cleared his throat before continuing on. "But back to what yuh was askin'. I always got this little naggin' thought me in the back of my mind, especially every time I start to thinkin' a headin' back to Wyoming. Lotsa folks back there remember me as 'just one a them Robbins boys,' always hangin' 'round horses, never quite breakin' into the big time. Hell, next month when I git to Cheyenne, I'm gonna be ridin' in the 'amateur buckin' contest.' I know it already, but it ain't gonna trip me up, I'm gonna be there, doin' my best and maybe 'nother year, I'll be movin' up."

"Go on," Dorothy said taking one of his hands in hers across the table.

"But I ain't gonna let that naggin' voice, nor my worryin' 'bout what the neighbors's thinkin', or my rankin' amongst the 'boys keep me away from doin' what I love.   Ridin' horses, ridin' steers, twirlin' a rope. Gonna git it done."

He suddenly stopped, looked Dorothy full into her eyes as he held both of her hands in his.   "Yuh said it ain't just lack of experience holdin' yuh up.   What else could there be?"

Dorothy shrugged a little and then shook her head, deciding her worry about the means to get to Cheyenne was definitely not something she was going to discuss with Bill just yet, so she simply said, "It's not important. I'll just think on your advice and decide what I'm going to do in August."

Then she brightened, squeezing his hands and laughed a little.

"But I know for sure what we're doing the weekend.   Come hell or high water, we're going to San Francisco!"

VIII - JULY 1914 - SAN FRANCISCO ACROSS THE BAY

At her her table on her own chair – the only chair in the flat – Dorothy was making a packing list. She'd never had to make a list before. She'd just collected everything she owned; packing it tightly into the carpet bag she'd "borrowed" from her parents and boarded the train.

This time would be different.

As she stewed over her list, she thought back to – she counted the weeks – it was July now, so back four weeks ago, to that June morning when Bill had burst into her kitchen bringing sunshine. That's what she needed right about now. Some sunshine.

Sunshine. There had been lots of sun on the Saturday she and Bill went to San Francisco, though it was cloudy the day before and it had worried Bill. So unlike him.

"If this rain keeps up, that fly boy ain't gonna be flyin' the Airy Ferry t'morrow," he complained, searching the overcast skies for any sign of a break in the weather.

"It's only light showers now and again. It'll probably clear up well before tomorrow," Dorothy assured him, though at that point, it really would have been all right with her if the weather hadn't cleared.

Bundled up in light coats, they were standing on the Oakland Pier looking across the Bay to the far off skyline of San Francisco. Only three or four miles to opposite shore, but only a limited number of ways to get there.

"So, six minutes by aeroplane," Dorothy said, both her hands tucked into the crook of Bill's elbow. She should have brought a pair of gloves with her. "Thirty minutes by ferry. Either way, it's far faster than taking a train all the way down to San Jose and back up the peninsula."

Bill laughed. "Sometimes train trips ain't all they're cracked up to be. 'Specially if yer in a box car with the steers 'r horses."

He looked down at her fondly. "Speakin' a train trips, you thought much about goin' to Cheyenne?"

"Surely not if we are going by boxcar!" Dorothy retorted. "Just how often do you travel like that?"

"Hardly ever," Bill answered. "I was just joshin'. So what do yuh think?"

"One day at a time, mister," she laughed back, "one day at a time."

By midmorning when Dorothy and Bill arrived back at the pier on Saturday, the low lying fog had burned off and the day promised to remain bright and clear. Unlike yesterday, when Christofferson and the Airy Ferry were nowhere to be seen, a short queue of eager passengers was waiting to take their turns flying across the bay.

"Yer sure yer alright with this?" Bill asked one last time as they stepped up to the line. "We can always go on the regular ferry."

"As long as the pilot hasn't had any 'forced landings' by the time it's our turn, I'm sure I'll be fine."

All too soon, she and Bill were the next passengers in line. Up close, Dorothy felt a little more reassured. The belly of the seaplane looked a lot like a small skiff that had sprouted not one pair but two pair of wings. It had twin propellers mounted from the rear of the top pair of wings which were powered by a single engine. Dorothy watched as the pilot, Silas Christofferson, tossed a rope to a man waiting on the dock who secured the aeroplane to the pier. Christofferson quickly stepped out of the aircraft and helped the incoming passengers carefully step out of the aeroplane, gently rocking in the water, to the more solid footing of the pier.

Faces flushed with excitement, one of the men turned to Christofferson and said, "By golly, it would be worth the fare just to fly back over there again. And back."

"Glad you enjoyed your flight, sir. Be happy to fly with you again anytime," the pilot graciously answered. As soon as the incoming passengers had untied their life jackets, they took them off and handed them to Christofferson.

"How you doing, folks?" Christofferson turned his attention to Bill and Dorothy, as well as the couple standing behind them. "You ready for the quickest trip possible between here and there?" He nodded in the direction of San Francisco.

"Only ten cents per person," he said, indicating it was time to pay up. "And please tie yourself into your life jacket before getting into the flying boat!"

Dorothy found her way into the life vest, fumbling to tie the straps in front of her as Bill slipped into his. Dorothy noticed the pilot was not bothering with a vest. An encouraging sign, she thought.

Two narrow leather upholstered bench seats, one in front of the other, were behind the pilot's seat. All the seats were open to the air. Bill held both of their carpet bags in one hand as he and Christofferson helped Dorothy to step across the short gap of open water and into the belly of the flying boat.

Bill followed and folded himself down into the seat next to her, placing both bags into the limited space on the floor. The second pair of passengers was soon seated as well. Christofferson untied the rope that had secured the aeroplane to the pier and then a couple of men using the wings as leverage maneuvered the flying boat around to face out across the bay.

"Folks, have a great flight," Christofferson shouted as the engine was started. As it roared into life, Dorothy was sure she had never been so close to anything so loud in her life. It was as if a train engine were behind her and bearing down fast.

Dorothy reached for Bill's hand for reassurance as the propellers began pushing the craft out across the waves of the bay. Their vibrations thrummed through her whole being. The flying boat – which suddenly seemed more and more flimsy to her – bounced and swayed slightly as it began to pick up speed. Spray from the underbelly skimming across the water settled over them.

Just as Dorothy felt that she couldn't stand one more second of the bouncing and jarring over the waves, she felt the flying boat being lifted from the surface of the bay. Even with the deafening roar of the engine and propellers, an instant feeling of freedom and peace flowed through her as the little ship broke free from the drag of the waters and the pull of earth's gravity and they climbed higher and higher into the air.

For just an instant, an urge to close her eyes for the rest of the flight came over her, but as they continued to climb into the sky and the incredible visa unfolded before her, the urge was just as quickly forgotten.

Looking back over her shoulder, the pier looked like a narrow stick of wood floating on the waters and the passenger sheds of the ferry terminals seemed to be blocks of wood that children might play with. The people on the pier become tiny black dots that soon disappeared behind them.

Dorothy looked up into Bill's face. He was grinning like - what? - Christmas morning? He tried to say something to her, but his words were completely drowned out by the cacophony created by the engine, the propellers and now the rush of wind past their faces. She just smiled and shook her head as the wind whipped through her hair. Thank goodness for hat pins.

Bill shrugged, taking his hand from hers, pushed his own hat more securely onto his head and then slipped his arm around her shoulders and pulled her close to him. She felt herself relaxing into his embrace, tension and anxiety melting just as the fog had earlier. She reached for his other hand and was surprised at how warm it was. She was quite chilled from the dampness of the sea spray and the wind in her face.

As she surveyed the earth below, she was amazed at the number of islands, some larger, others quite small, dotting San Francisco Bay. Rugged mountains she had never been aware of ringed the oblong body of water. More quickly than she could have ever imagined, the city of San Francisco came into focus below them. As Christofferson flew around the northern end of the peninsula, the wide expanse of the Pacific Ocean came into view, the horizon line lost between the blue of the sea and the blue of the sky.

So high above the earth, Dorothy felt smaller and more insignificant than she ever had. At five and a half feet, she was a good half a head taller than many of the other women in the rodeo business - no, she had never felt small. As for insignificant, that feeling had been forgotten for years now.

Christofferson piloted the seaplane to the ferry terminal on the sea side of the exposition grounds. Dorothy saw that it was far less crowded than the dozens of main piers on the northeastern coast. A huge clock tower predicting and boasting "1915" stood tall and proud facing the sea as it seemed to be inviting the entire world to the upcoming Panama-Pacific International Exposition. A thrill ran through her as she looked over the many gleaming buildings beneath her. Dozens of walkways spider webbed their way off of the main pedestrian thoroughfare. A tiny world unto itself unfolded before her eyes.

Bill let go of her hand to point to something below them. She just smiled. He could have been pointing at just about anything and she knew he would explain it just as soon as their ability to hear one another after the insane noise of the flying boat had quieted.

The pilot set the seaplane down onto the water, once again raising spray. He cut the engine and the aircraft coasted toward the pier, the sudden silence only broken by the hiss of the spray and the sound of the belly of the flying boat gliding over the water. Men were ready to catch the rope Christofferson threw to them.

A little unsteadily, Dorothy stood, her ears still ringing. Christofferson and one of the men on the pier helped her to step out of the aeroplane and onto the pier. Before she even untied the ties on her life jacket, she turned to Bill.

"Bill! It was the best!" She beamed but couldn't think of anything more expressive to say.

He grinned down at her. "Better than that horse in Bakersfield?"

"Much!"

"Yuh gonna quit the rodeo and take to flyin'?" he teased.

"Not likely, but who knows?" she joked back.

Handing their life jackets to the next set of passengers, Dorothy and Bill linked arms and made their way passed the fairgrounds and into the city.

"I'm purty sure I could pick out where the 101 Ranch is buildin' their arena," Bill told her as they walked along.

"Ah, so that was what you were pointing out to me?" Dorothy asked.

"Yup, though I figgered from the look on yer face, yuh didn't really know what I's pointin' out." Bill grinned. "It's gonna be great comin' back here t'morrow and seein' everything up close."

"But I will say, it was incredible seeing everything from the air," Dorothy said. "It's a lot different being that high off the ground when you're not worrying about keeping your saddle underneath you!"

"Hadn't thought of it quite that way," Bill agreed.

They caught a street car and rode it to the part of town where they would be staying. As they walked down the street, Dorothy was suddenly surprised to see an empty lot overgrown with tall grass. Not that an empty lot was surprising but the gated wrought iron fence around what was once a yard, a cement walk and steps leading to nothingness brought a sharp reminder that this was a city still in recovery from the earthquake and deadly fires only eight years ago.

Dorothy began to feel a little uneasy as Bill announced they finally arrived at their destination and he opened the gate of a white picket fence. A cozy bungalow sat at the end of the front walk, flowering bushes brightening the front of a covered porch that ran the entire width of the front of the house.

"Bill," she whispered. "Are you sure this is the right place?"

"Yup," he replied as the front door of the house burst open and a pair of young boys appeared on the porch.

"Uncle Bill," they called, excited to see their company.

Dorothy turned a nervous eye to Bill. "You didn't tell me we were staying with relatives."

He chuckled. "We ain't. Them kids just call me that. Been a friend a the family fer years."

Dorothy wasn't quite sure why she was relieved but she was.

"Ma, they're here," the older of the two hollered into the house and then joined his younger brother in running down the steps to greet their guests. Dorothy was a little taken aback at the little boys' delight in meeting them.

"Hey, Uncle, who's this . . ." the younger one began.

"Hush, now, you," called a pleasant looking woman from the porch. "Give Bill a chance to introduce everyone."

"Here, take our bags. We thought we'd drop 'em off before we headed out to see the sights," Bill said, handing one to each of the boys.

"Boys, just bring them up here and set them by the front door," their mother said.

"Dorothy," Bill began, "this is Mavis Thompson and her boys, Critter One and Critter Two."

"No, we ain't critters," exclaimed the younger of the two sternly, getting an equally stern look from his mother.

"Ah, pardon me, miss," he corrected himself. "I'm Lester and this is my brother, Delbert."

"Pleased to meet you," Dorothy replied, smiling as the two somberly stepped forward to formally shake her hand.

"But nobody calls us by our whole names," said Delbert. "They call me Del –"

"And I'm Les," his brother finished proudly.

"And pleased to meet you, too," Dorothy said as she stepped forward to greet their hostess.

"Oh, Mavis, this is Dorothy Morrell," Bill finished. "Yuh might a read a her in the papers."

Dorothy laughed, self-conscious of the awe in the boys eyes as they looked up at her.

"Are you as famous as Uncle Bill?" asked Les.

"Now, boys, let our company have a moment's peace. Come in, come in," Mavis offered. "Bill, you are sleeping on the back porch."

Dorothy's eyes widened.

"Not to worry, Miss Morrell," Mavis began.

"Please, Dorothy is fine."

"The back porch is enclosed and Bill has slept there many a night when he comes to town. Del, will you please get Miss Dorothy's bag and show her up to the room upstairs?" Mavis asked.

"I wouldn't have known there was an upstairs," Dorothy said to Del as she followed him.

"Lotsa people are surprised when they find out," Del explained, leading her up a narrow staircase. "It used to be just the attic, but Pa put in a window and it's a pretty nice bedroom now."

The room, though small, was larger than her bedroom back in Oakland. A colorful and intricately pieced patchwork quilt covered the bed. A wash bowl and pitcher of water were setting on a small corner table. The dormer window faced the backyard of the house.   Cozy.   Del placed her bag on a chair and hurried back down the stairs.

Dorothy took off her jacket and started to hang it on the hook near the door, but remembered she and Bill would be going out and about.   Taking one last look around the comfortable little room, she turned to follow Del, though he was long gone.

Dorothy joined Bill and Mavis in the front room.

"Supper still at six?" Bill asked.

"Sit down is at six.   Food's on the back burner until seven.   After that it's bread and milk," Mavis laughed, "as I am sure you well remember!"

Bill chuckled, but seemed to be a little embarrassed.

"No need to bring that up," he said, grinning as he and Dorothy stepped out the front door.   "Daylight's burnin'.   We better get on our way."

IX - JUNE & JULY 1914 - THE LIST

Come on!   Take off your boots and stockings," Dorothy urged, looking up at Bill, as she herself was standing barefooted in warm, dry sand.   She and Bill were still a ways from where the Pacific Ocean was pushing waves, long and foaming, washing them to where they were breaking on the smooth sandy beach, row on row.

"Standing here in just one spot feels like, well, like I'm slowly sinking - I can't really tell you exactly how it feels.   You need to get your boots off and see for yourself."

"Ah, naw, I ain't been barefoot for too long to remember," Bill protested.

"But look around!   There are quite a few people out wading," Dorothy said encouragingly.

"When I's a kid and I'd go to my mother with that argument, she'd always say somethin' sassy, like, if all yer friends was jumping off a cliff, wouldja do it, too?" Bill replied stubbornly. "Besides there's scads a people just like me who ain't got their shoes off."

Dorothy smiled over at Bill. "Suit yourself, but I'm going in."

"What? Yer in yer dress!"

"I'm only going to wade in the shallows and get my toes wet," Dorothy explained, making her way first through the dry sand that tugged at her feet, slowing her steps.

"Oh!" she cried, hesitating momentarily.

"The sand gets cooler here where it's wet," Dorothy called to Bill as she continued on out to meet the waves.

When she got no reply, she turned to find out what he was doing. She was delighted to see he was sitting in the sand, pulling his boots off and stowing his socks inside of them.

"Yuh think our shoes and socks will be okay waitin' here for us?" Bill asked. Dorothy studied the other beach goers. No one seemed interested in a large sized pair of cowboys boots nor a pair of lady's shoes.

"I think so," she answered.

"Are you going to roll your pant legs up?" she asked, but he already was.

Bill joined Dorothy and hand in hand, they stepped into a tiny riffle of water as it rolled its way up the sand and covered their feet.

"Oh, my," Bill's eyebrows shot up in a look of wonder. "Ain't never had the earth melt away beneath me b'fore!"

"It does feel pretty strange," Dorothy agreed, "but in a delightful way."

They watched the sea water receding back into the larger waves. Another wave started its way up the sands and covered the tops of their feet. Dorothy swung her toes through the water, and then quickly tightened her hold on Bill's hand as she nearly lost her balance when the sand shifted again beneath their feet.

"Oh, here comes another one!" Before the words were completely out of her mouth, Dorothy realized this wave was deeper than the others had been. She reached down to snatch her skirt up and save it from being drenched but she was too late. Both the bottom of her skirt and Bill's pant legs were instantly soaked.

Bill laughed at the startled look on Dorothy's face.

"What are we going to do now?" she said, holding her soaked skirts out wide.

"Well, we come this far, might as well let 'er rip!" Bill hollered and bent to scoop up water with his hands.

"Oh, no!" Dorothy yelled back, laughing, stepping away but reaching for her own water to throw and the fight was on and soon they were soaked to the skin. Dorothy grinned sheepishly up at Bill. "Guess my dress got wet after all."

"Yup, I'm all done in," Bill said as they trudged together back to higher ground. "But my mother used to say if yer feet's dirty, yer hair's a mess and yuh got sparkles in yer eyes, it's been a damn fine day."

"What else might your mother say about now?" Dorothy teased, breathlessly lengthening her stride to keep up with Bill.

"She'd prob'ly still be pitchin' water, knowin' her." He grinned. "She don't back down from nothin' - might pick 'er battles on occasion, but she don't back down.

"An' what'd yer mother be sayin'?" Bill returned the question.

Dorothy shook her head and sighed. It was if clouds had suddenly covered the sun. "It doesn't matter. She's not here to say it."

"That bad, huh?"

"Yes," was all Dorothy would say.

Bill put his arm around her shoulders to comfort whatever sorrows he couldn't see.

"Yuh wanna walk a ways down the beach?" he asked.

She nodded, and slipped her arm around his waist as they walked back to where they had left their footwear.

"Sorry for being a spoil sport," she said as they continued to walk barefoot through warm dry sand. Bill squeezed her shoulders but said nothing for a while as they continued down the beach.

"The wind's from the west," Bill said, at last, taking in a deep breath of tangy ocean air. "Wonder how long ago it was this air was in Jay-pan 'r China?"

The soft knock at her kitchen door brought her back to the present with a start. She smiled happily. It would be Bill, no doubt, here to share a cup of coffee just like he'd done so many times he was anywhere near Oakland.

"Come on in," Dorothy opened her door and greeted Bill. "Got time for a cuppa joe?"

Technically it wasn't the instant brew that the Belgian percolator "Geo" Washington was peddling these days - and making a good go of it, too. No, instant coffee was not for her.

Dorothy prided herself in her carefully brewed coffee, only grinding the amount of roasted beans needed to fill the basket of her percolator for the next fresh pot. Her coffee was never as dark and strong as Mutti's had been, but then Mutti wasn't here and wasn't likely to ever be, either.

"How's my girl this morning?" Skeeter Bill Robbins smiled down at her, as he took off his hat and sat on an upended wooden crate, the seat he claimed at the tiny kitchen table as his own. Dorothy wasn't sure she like being called anyone's girl, even from a great guy like Bill.

"I was thinking back to San Francisco," was how she answered though, as she filled his cup. "So glad we went."

"Cain't wait to go back and see how the fairgrounds will look when they're finished."

As he reached for his cup of coffee, Bill noticed Dorothy's carefully written list.

"So, whatcha got here?"

"Making a packing list for Cheyenne," she answered.

Bill slapped his thigh and grinned.

"So you're gonna go! Yuh won't be sorry! I bet yer gonna kick up some dust and do just fine at Frontier Days! Tell yuh, it makes them little shows 'round here look like grade school, little kids reading outta McGuffey Readers. Yer goin' to the big school now!"

"Bill! I told you, I'm not sure I've passed the rigors these 'little shows' around here as you call them," she reminded him. "I'm still not so sure this is a good idea."

Bill took a deep breath. Dorothy knew there was going to be a lengthy explanation and sat back with her own cup of coffee to enjoy it.

"Hey, even though in the past few years, they's been a few 'ladies' exhibitions' – as them Frontier Days boys like to call 'em - rough ridin' and steer ropin' - there ain't never been a real competition. Couple a years ago, some pretty big names in ladies' bronk ridin' started makin' some purty good rides in Cheyenne but all they got was braggin' rights.

"Yuh heard of Bertha Blancett - now she was the first lady to . . . ah. . . fork a bronk in Cheyenne." His hesitation made her smile. Dear Bill. Dear Lord!

"So up till now there ain't never actually been any right official competition for the cowgirls - yuh know, prize money, saddles, fancy bridles an' silver spurs - but that's all changin' up this year." He lifted his coffee cup in a mock toast.

"It ain't like Pendleton. Up there, the ladies been competin' for maybe a half dozen years 'r so. Now, even though they's been ladies who's ridden bronks in Cheyenne, they ain't been ridin' as competitors. Not many of 'em're even makin' a show of goin' to Cheyenne this year. Not a enough of time between Cheyenne and Pendleton, I guess, if yuh get busted up."

Dorothy noticed their cups were nearly empty and thought now would be a good time to bring the coffee pot back to the table. Bill's enthusiasm was contagious.

"Yup! You, Miss Dorothy Morrell, are gonna be gettin' in on the ground level in Cheyenne and there ain't no way to go but up."

It was easy to get caught up in Bill's optimism, his grey eyes twinkling and his hands drawing pictures in the air.

"So what's on your list so far?" Bill was curious what Dorothy thought was so important she had to write it down. Clothing, maybe. The second hand bronk riding saddle she'd finally saved up enough to buy. But what else could there possibly be?

"Well, I don't need to write down every piece of rodeo outfitting I own. All of that goes as a given. But I was trying to come up with a list of provisions to take with us.

70

"Bread, I think two or three loaves; cheese, two pounds; boiled eggs, maybe two dozen; three or four canteens for water, tea or coffee . . ." Dorothy looked up from her list expecting Bill to add an item or two of his favorites. "A few blankets, maybe?"

"Why're you planning to bring all this stuff?" Though puzzled, Dorothy's list had done nothing to dampen Bill's enthusiasm.

"Aren't we going by train to Cheyenne?"

"Yes."

"Isn't it going to take two or three days to get there?"

"Yes."

"Well, I've been on long train trips in my life. Trips that took days. I think I know what I need to bring."

The look on Dorothy's face told Bill that she thought her reasoning was self-evident. He picked up his cup of coffee, blew across the top of it and took a sip. Hmmmmm, good. He followed with another sip. He shook his head slowly.

"Nope, I'm sorry. I don't follow. Why are you planning to bring this stuff?"

Dorothy's eyes narrowed. Was Bill deliberately trying to aggravate her?

"So we'll have something to eat while we're on the train and have something to keep off the chill while we sleep on the benches?" Her statement was really a question.

"Ahhhh, I see." Bill's grin grew wide again. "I guess I didn't tell yuh we's ridin' the Southern Pacific to Cheyenne. Even in second-class, we'll be sleepin' in berths and eatin' in the dinin' car. It's like a hotel on wheels."

The surprise on Dorothy's face told him he probably should have told her earlier.

"I don't have that kind of money, Bill. I am sure we can manage with a less elaborate way to travel."

Panic began to rise in Dorothy's voice. She lived frugally but there was no way she could afford to travel that way, even second-class was far beyond her savings. And she wasn't about to let Bill start making decisions about her life and worse yet, paying for them.

"Relax, cowgirl," Bill teased. "Yer gonna clean up in Cheyenne. Yuh can buy the tickets home. Yuh won't be beholdin' to me for long a tall."

Dorothy busied herself by pouring herself a fresh cup of coffee as she pondered her new understanding of how they were going to be traveling to Cheyenne.

She couldn't imagine staying in a hotel, especially not "on wheels." Her life since leaving Winnipeg had been spent in boarding houses, sharing rented rooms with the other show girls, sometimes sleeping on cots in company tents. Even the winter months while she was working for the moving picture studios were spent in Spartan living conditions.

This tiny apartment seemed spacious yet cozy compared to most of her living quarters for the last few years. Her ability to cook meals for herself, sit at her own window and watch the world go by, sleep in her own bed without having to listen to anyone else's deep breathing or worse snoring was a pleasure.

"I don't know about this," Dorothy started. "I'd really like to go to Cheyenne but it just doesn't seem quite right you buying a ticket for me. I'm not your wife. I'm not a business partner. You don't owe me anything."

She could tell by the change in Bill's expression that she had offended him.

"Please, Bill. Know that I am very grateful for the changes you've brought to my life. Riding that bronk in Fresno."

"Bakersfield."

"All right, Bakersfield. Anyway, giving me the opportunity to stand up to Boss Griffin and now," her laughter now sparkled across the room, "changing the course from being a pretty face to pretty good rider."

"Dorothy." Bill spoke slowly and carefully after gathering his thoughts but mincing no words. "My mother would shoot me if I disrespected yuh in any way and believe me; I am *not* spending thirty-six to forty-eight hours in third class coach listenin' to all those cryin' kids, scoldin' mothers and impatient fathers tellin' the whole kit and kaboodle to hush it up. To my way of thinkin', expectin' *you* - no, *allowin'* yuh to travel back there with all noise and confusion while I'm up front enjoyin' peace and quiet, well, that would be far more disrespectful than sharin' a berth - separate beds, mind yuh," he was quick to add, "- they's not like yer thinkin'. It's not like there's individual rooms in them sleepin' cars."

"They got - here lemme draw yuh a picture."

He stopped his explanation and pulled a short stub of a pencil out of his pocket as well as a folded envelope. He smoothed the rumpled piece of paper across her table and began to draw.

Dorothy watched as he carefully sketched out the floor plan of a typical sleeping car complete with vestibules at each end, a smoking room, a drawing room, the open seating and the seats available at a "slightly extra cost" - Bill refused to say how much - which could be folded down and made into beds by the attending porters and as well as the upper bunks that folded down from the upper walls near ceiling. The sleeping "compartments" were made only somewhat private by pulling curtains closed during the nights.

"Yuh see," he smiled, "it's not like we'll be sharin' a room. 'Less yuh count it as sharin' a room with all the rest a them passengers in the sleepin' car we're gonna be in."

Dorothy took in a deep breath and held it before slowly letting it out, considering the pencil sketch on the table before her. She looked up into Bill's face and nodded, finally smiling.

"It'll do." She shrugged and started to crumple her list. "I guess I don't need this list at all," she said with a turning up the corners of her mouth in relief.

Bill smiled back.

"So, now back to what yuh was sayin' a while ago.   Yuh know . . ." his voice trailed off.   He leaned forward, elbows on his knees but looking earnestly up into her eyes.   "About yuh not bein' my wife or a business partner.

"Yes," Dorothy answered hesitantly.

"Wouldja ever consider marryin' a rough-stock ridin', rope-spinnin' cowboy?   Say one that is tall and skinny, and maybe even from the hills of Wyoming?"

Dorothy's brown eyes shone, sparkling and hiding the sudden wave of confusion bordering on panic rushing over her.

"Well, now, mister," she replied coyly, stalling for a few extra seconds of consideration, tapping her chin with a forefinger for show.   "That would surely depend on whom that steer wrestling, trick roping, poetry writing cowboy from the wilds of Wyoming was.   If the right one came along, I'd be sure to consider it."

She gave one sure nod of her head to reinforce to herself what she had just said to Bill and then repeated, "Yes, I'm sure if the right one came along, I'd lasso, tie and brand him in record time. . . if."

She let her last word hang in the air between them, but smiling all the while and Bill smiled back at her.

X – 6 AUGUST 1914 – TRAIN TO CHEYENNE

Just one last thing before we board," Bill said, pulling the hand trolley stacked with his trunk, and overnight bag as well as Dorothy's old carpet bag *and* new suit-case plus several hat boxes toward the Western Union counter. "Quick telegram to Mike, at the Cheyenne paper, lettin' him know we started on our way.

"Cain't never get too much press," he added with a grin. *Well, usually,* he corrected himself.

"No, not according to Boss Griffin," Dorothy agreed. She listened as Bill dictated his message to the State Leader.

"Leaving San Francisco by afternoon train. Stop. Accompanied by Miss Dorothy Morrell. Stop. Cleaned up at Salinas. Stop."

Dorothy found Bill's way of saying things refreshing, if not sometimes confusing. When Mutti 'cleaned up,' it was with lye soap and a scrub

74

brush. Papa 'cleaned up' with a razor and shaving soap. Bill cleaned up by placing somewhere among the top three contestants in his competition.

And in actuality, they were leaving Oakland, but no one outside of the Valley seemed to know where Oakland was.

"So, *I* am accompanying *you*? What about *you* accompanying *me*?" Dorothy joked, as they left the telegraph counter.

"Then yuh woulda needed to send the telegram," Bill said, grinning and reaching for the trolley handle. "Ready?"

The excitement he was feeling was both electrifying and contagious.

"I've never seen you like this before a rodeo," Dorothy observed, slipping her hand into the crook of his elbow as they walked toward the platform.

"Yuh never seen me on my way to the Daddy of 'em All, now have you?"

"The Daddy of Them All?" Dorothy asked. *These Americans!*

"No, the Daddy of 'em All!" Bill corrected. "Been around now almost twenty years. Pendleton cain't even say that. Cheyenne's just been a little slow givin' the ladies their proper due, is all!"

A porter took over their luggage as he checked their tickets and directed them down the line of passenger cars to the one that would be their home for the next few days.

"I'll just stow the rest of your luggage in the baggage car," the porter informed them as Bill reached for Dorothy's carpet bag and his war bag, "and you can pick it up on the platform when you all get to Cheyenne."

Bill nodded, tipped the man, and took Dorothy's elbow as she stepped onto the boarding box before stepping up the permanently attached steps at the front of the car. Just as in Bill's sketch, the first area they entered seemed to be more like a living room than a train car. Though there were no sofas or overstuffed chairs, but on either side of the aisle were cushioned seats wide enough for two or three people to face each and share a window. Two smartly dressed women sat facing each other, smiling coquettishly toward Bill until they realized he was with Dorothy. Their smiles turned to smirks. Dorothy ignored them, although she was quick to notice that Bill hadn't even paid a bit of attention to them. Could it be that he towered so far over them that he hadn't noticed them?

Dorothy and Bill stepped through the doorway between the drawing room and the main part of the car, sectioned off into the seating compartments that could easily be converted into sleeping areas. Partial walls, ceiling to floor, divided one seating area from the next. The ends of the walls nearer to the aisle were hidden behind curtains that were gathered and fastened for the day.

Another porter stepped out of the smoking room at the rear of the car, his cheery smile and wave letting them know he was available to help them find where their seating was. After showing their tickets, they found their section and Bill stowed the bags under one of the seats, making a grand flourish with both arms.

"Welcome to your new abode, Miss Morrell."

75

He was still in high spirits.   She sat and made herself comfortable on the seat facing toward the front of the train, knowing from past experience that sitting backwards to the direction of travel would soon have her feeling ill.

Bill sat down across from her and crossed one leg over his knee. Almost as an afterthought, he reached up and took his tall Stetson hat off his head.   He frowned a moment and then carefully set it next to him between himself and the window, hat brim up, crown down.

"Wouldn't it ride better the other way?" Dorothy asked.

The shock on Bill's face made her giggle as he explained in a droll voice, "Yuh never wanna put yer hat on its brim.   All yer luck'll run out, so make sure it's upside down."

Dorothy raised an eyebrow.   "Really?"

Bill shrugged and grinned.   "Really! . . . or so they say!"

It wasn't long before the last boarding calls were shouted down the line, the whistles blown, and the train began chugging its way out of Oakland, starting up into the Sacramento Valley through first farm fields and orchards.   Grapes, apples, plums, raspberries and even lemon groves were standing at the ready to harvest.   Now and again they passed the huge tracts of land of cattle ranching operations.

"So, Bill, where are you from in Wyoming?" Dorothy asked, hoping to get Bill talking about himself.   She could be an interested listener for as long as it took to get to Cheyenne.

He nodded.   "Well, my mum sez that if yuh put yer finger right in the middle of a map a Wyoming and then move it just a little to the right, yuh'll be right over our neck of the woods.   'A little to the right of the middle of nowhere,' as she says.

"So, sure as shootin', I's born in a homestead cabin, just as she says, a little to the right of the middle of nowhere."   He stretched his legs out in front of him and crossed his ankles.

"My dad moved from place to place all his life till he got to Wyoming.   I b'lieve he was born in Kentucky.   Dad told how when he was about ten years old or so, his dad, my granddad had a falling out with his dad – my great-grand, I s'pose, so granddad, pulled up roots from Kentucky, loaded his family into two or three covered wagons and took to moving further and further west every few years.   They never stayed very long in any one place ever again.   Maybe a year or so.

"My dad's name was Benjamin Franklin Robbins."   Bill waited for some comment or reaction from Dorothy about such a name, but none came.

"Yes?" she finally said, wondering just what the significance was.

"Benjamin Franklin?" Bill hinted.

Dorothy nodded but really had no idea who he was talking about.

"Ahh, I see.   You Canadians, being Brits, right, don't seem to care too much about American history."

He waved it off and continued, "Well, Benjamin Franklin was what a lot of folks down here like to call one of our Foundin' Fathers. A leader before an' after the Revolutionary War."

Getting little reaction from Dorothy, Bill decided to go on with his own story as she didn't seem to be too interested in a history lesson.

"All right. Well, my dad went by BF or sometimes just Frank cuz his dad's name was Benjamin Franklin Robbins, as well."

Dorothy smiled, nodding, now only vaguely aware of the country side they were passing through.

"I never met my grandparents Robbins. Once the family got to the gold fields of Colorado, him and most every one of his brothers went their own way. Most of my uncles went to work in the mines.

"But my dad was always partial to horses and being on the go, I guess bein' raised on the move like he was. Now that he was on his own, he begun to haul freight by teams an' wagons. No railroads yet. He had several freight wagons, and he'd connect up two or three of them, and hitch maybe five or more teams together for the original freight trains. For a few years after he and my mum were married, he hauled freight 'tween Denver and Cheyenne."

Dorothy nodded, intently watching the smile lines around Bill's eyes. They seemed to be punctuating his story.

"And Cheyenne, this is where we are heading, right?"

"Yup," he replied and then continued. "They homesteaded up on Boxelder Creek in Wyoming a few years before I was born. Even after they settled in Boxelder, he continued to haul freight, 'specially for the US Army.

"They say he wuz also a horse tradin' fool. Buyin', sellin', deliverin' herds. The army out here in the West was movin' on the backs a horses, and they was always in need a new mounts. He might've arranged for a few horse races on the side with a little money to be made – bettin' on which horses would come in first, second or third. Or at least them's the stories I heard now and again."

How different from her own father, Dorothy mused. Friedrich might have loved horses once in the previous life when he had been a farmer, coaxing grain from the sandy, once marshy steppes of the Volga Valley but once they got to Canada, farming had been a thing of the past. The Eichhorns had settled into Winnipeg and were relieved to be among fellow countrymen, to be a part of a cultural community familiar and comfortable, Friedrich glad to find work where he could.

"So tell me about Manitoba," Bill asked. "Was your dad a rancher? A farmer? When didja start riding horses?"

Dorothy laughed, hoping she was covering her nervousness. Reporting The Truth was easy among strangers or casual acquaintances, and Bill was long since neither.

Perhaps she could tell of the summers that the Eichhorns had visited their old friends the Ettels on their farm. It would be easy to transform Papa into the land owner.

"My Papa was a . . . ," Dorothy looked across into Bill's friendly gray eyes filled with interest but tempered with patience.   Dorothy took a deep breath and began again.

"My Papa was a hardworking man.   One summer, we all went to our *Onkel*, Uncle Jacob's ranch."   Dorothy corrected herself quickly, hoping Bill hadn't picked up on the German word.

"I was about 14, I think.   Uncle Jacob needed more help on his ranch, well, it was more like a farm.   There was more to do that summer than just he and his boys could handle."

Bill nodded thinking back to his own early years.

"That spring, we all took the train from Winnipeg to Boulton."   Dorothy laughed.   "One of those 'pack your own food and blanket trips.'"

"It was great fun.   So different than our lives back in Winnipeg.   Miles of open prairie.   They had a daughter about my age, Anna . . ."

"Your cousin?" Bill asked.

"Well, yes, my cousin," Dorothy agreed.   *Cousin?   She couldn't place a family relationship between the Ettels, Jacob and Maria to her parents; just the memory of always having called them Onkel and Tante.*

"Anna and I loved to ride the prairies with the wind in our faces, sailing over the billowing grassland."

Dorothy smiled a little at the memories of their homecomings. *Tante Lydia's sternly worded scoldings: Anna Ettel, you know better!   These horses of ours, they are not racing horses.   Good Gott, they are not even saddle horses. You and Carlina have no business trying to race them down the lane.*

Anna had gravely agreed with her mother but the next time the two girls had permission to ride sturdy Cross Drafts again, they docilely walked their patient mounts down the lane and over the rolling swales until they were out of Tante Lydia's sight. Then heels to flanks and off they went, Anna and Carlina pushing their horses to speeds farm horses seldom saw.

"At the end of summer, I was a little sad, getting back on the train, thinking how Anna could be riding her horse to school, my brothers and I walking."   *It could have happened, Dorothy reasoned.   Anna could have ridden a plow horse to school at least once in her life!*

"Other than that, there's nothing really interesting about how I grew up.   We lived in Winnipeg just a few blocks from the Red River.   Life was pretty ordinary, I think.   My mother was determined to raise me up to be a woman who could cook and clean and keep house.   Back in Winnipeg, I would have to sneak off if I ever wanted to even think about riding."

That much was certainly true – though as for *sneaking off*, she'd only done that once, when she had finally made the break from her old life to her new one.

Bill nodded, puzzling through the idea of having to sneak off to ride. He had no memory at all of when he first was on a horse.   Horses had been a part of himself all his life.   Learning to ride had come early, just as learning to gentle and break horses for riding and ranch work had been much of what he'd known in those early years.

"Incredible." Bill shook his head now. "Just incredible. Ever'thing I do in a rodeo arena, whether ropin', ridin' rough stock, steer wrestlin', ev'ry one a them things wuz work I had to learn to just work ever' day on the ranch. They wasn't for show nor competition, just what we done day in, day out."

A comfortable quiet settled over them as outside the windows the fields, orchards, and pastures were replaced by rocky outcropping and pine forests.

"I think I'll go down to the smokin' room for a spell," Bill interrupted their reverie.

"If you don't mind, I'll go, too," Dorothy replied.

"Now, Miss Dot, what's a nice girl like you gonna to be doin' in a smokin' room with a bunch of smokers?"

Though teasing, Dorothy could tell Bill hadn't caught onto the fact that she, too, was a smoker now and then. It was her turn to be the coquette.

"I'll be bumming smokes off you, I guess," she replied, smiling coyly.

For a half a second, Bill seemed speechless, but then he chuckled and said, "Well, ma'am, seein's how you put it that way, I just might be able to oblige."

Dorothy had wondered if perhaps, Bill's surprise had anything to do with the fact that very few women she knew who smoked would ever do so in public, but as they were the only ones in the smoking section of their car, it didn't seem to matter one way or the other.

"How stout do yuh like 'em?" Bill asked in regard to how much tobacco to roll into her cigarette.

"Not too." She wondered if that was really an answer, but he seemed to understand as he rolled a thin cigarette for her and a more generous one for himself.

The instant feeling of relaxation as she pulled her first drag was exactly what she needed after being on her toes all afternoon long during her conversations with Bill. Sure, they'd spent a lot of time together in the last three or four months, but never so many hours in such close proximity with little to do except talk.

Today's conversations were going far past pleasantries, past the business of planning and arranging. Deeper into protected places, pastd the carefully orchestrated Truths of Miss Dorothy Morrell.

In the falling dusk of evening, as the train began to climb ponderously up the foothills of the Sierra Nevada, Bill stood and offered his hand to Dorothy, inviting her to her feet.

"Mind yuh, Miss Dot, meals is included on these here tickets. Let's go see what they might be offerin' us for supper."

Companionably, they began making their way through the vestibule and the connecting by-ways from car to car until they arrived in the dining car. Only a few diners were still seated at the tables lining the outside walls of the car.

"Here you go," Bill offered as he pulled a chair out for Dorothy.

"Thank you."

Dorothy had never had anyone seat her at a dining table before. She could get used to this she thought to herself.

The waiter arrived with a coffee cart. "May I offer you dessert?" he asked.

They must have missed the dinner hour. It suited Dorothy fine. It seemed a little late to be eating a full blown meal.

"Apple pie, please," she informed him. "And coffee."

"I'll take the same," Bill added.

The waiter poured their coffee and dished up small plates of apple pie, as Dorothy smiled across the table at Bill, stirring cream and sugar into her coffee. She watched as he turned his attention to his pie. He smiled as he ate the first bites, nodding his approval of the pastry.

Dorothy took a bite of hers and had to remind herself not to compare the crust to her mother's. Mutti's pie crusts were legendary, lard, flour and icy cold water precisely measured. Not that there anything wrong with this pie, she reminded herself but the water should have been just a little colder before it was added to the lard and flour mixture.

As talkative as Bill had been earlier, he was quiet now and concentrated on his light supper. Eating must be serious business in the life of a cowboy, a working cowboy, out on the range all day. She smiled to herself. *Range all day.* She wondered what that would have been like.

She'd been an extra and even a stunt double a time or two in a few moving picture shows that featured ranch life but she doubted a movie set was hardly any equal to where Bill had been raised – rather a minuscule, shallow imitation of his wide open world.

As they finished their pie and coffee, the electric lights in the car came on as dusk turned to darkness. The porters were ready to fold down the upper berths and make down the facing seats into beds so Dorothy and Bill made one last trip down to the smoking room as their beds were made up.

"How'd yuh like this kinda travelin' so far?" Bill asked as he rolled another cigarette for himself as Dorothy had declined one for herself.

She pondered a moment before answering. "It's all been so new and different."

She tried to look out through the window, but could only see the reflection of herself and Bill.

"I guess I hadn't taken time to stop and think about whether I liked it or not." She turned to smile at Bill. "But make no doubt about it. I like it!"

Bill smiled back and nodded. He liked it as well. Far too often in the past, he and other cowboys had "bunked" in the boxcars with the horses as they made their way from rodeo or show to another, but that was no way to travel while being accompanied by Miss Dorothy Morrell.

He contemplated his cigarette, and decided to slow down his smoking.

"I'll be along shortly," he said to Dorothy. "Yuh just go get settled in for the night. I'll try not to step on yuh too hard when I climb up into that top bunk. It's the bunk I always preferred, so good thing it's mine."

He seemed serious in his joking.

Dorothy was thankful for his thoughtfulness in providing her the privacy she craved to prepare for the night. She made her way passed the open seating area of their car to where her and Bill's compartment was. When she stepped passed the curtains, now drawn for the night, she noticed that the porter had not only made down the beds but had already pulled the window shades down as well.

Looking up into Bill's bunk, a trickle of memories made their way from the very back of her mind. Memories of her childhood rose like wisps of fog that slowly took form. Oh, yes, she remembered clearly now the bunks on that ship. The ocean crossing ship. The bunk she had shared with – Anna? She nodded to herself. Of course! The Ettels.

The similarity between the sleeping sections of the steerage passageways of the Rhaetia and this railcar was striking.

"Ahhh, Anna," she whispered. How long had it been since she'd thought of the ocean crossing? Many, many years. Not even the summer visits with Anna had jostled the long forgotten memories to remembrance. Memories of bunkbeds, games of hide-and-seek, of tag. Maria's constant exasperation.

She breathed another deep sigh and began unbuttoning the front of her dress. From the way she looked today, no one could guess she was the Miss Dorothy Morrell, "celebrated lady rider who had tackled some of the toughest horses ever saddled."

Sometimes she thought that the Mr. Doolittles of the world worked overtime to outdo each other, adding one superlative after another to their reporting. It was all right with her, though. It made getting The Truth out there all the easier.

As she slid between the sheets until her back was against the outer wall, she noticed Bill's hat was hung on a hook they hadn't paid attention to before. It was safer there.

She wondered why it was that in her nightgown, buttoned to her chin and under the covers of her bed, she felt more vulnerable than anytime during the day with arms, neck and legs uncovered and easily seen. She curled into a ball and wondered how long it would be until Bill got back. The rocking of the rails eventually lulled her into a light sleep.

When Bill stepped back through the curtains, he'd already taken off his boots. He stowed them next to Dorothy's bed and stepped up into the bunk overhead. Lying on his back, he loosened his belt, wriggled out of his cream colored pants, before unbuttoning his shirt and taking it off. He'd slept less comfortably dressed many times. This was going to be easy.

Dorothy stirred as Bill rolled over in the bunk above her. For a few minutes, she listened to the night noises of the sleeping car. The curtains muffled most of the sounds of snoring and low conversation. Bill's breathing told her he was still awake.

"Bill," she said in a low voice, not wishing to be heard by anyone outside their curtains.

"Yeah?"

She wondered about the wisdom in what she had decided to tell him.

"These beds, the way they look now, they reminded me of when I was a tiny girl."

"Oh, yuh slep' on bunk beds back then, too?"

"No, not usually."

"Oh." Bill was a patient man. He could wait until she decided to finish her thoughts.

"Bill."

"Yeah?"

"I wasn't born in Winnipeg."

"Oooooh?" His reply drawn out in a question. More silence.

"My great-grandparents, maybe even my great-great-grandparents immigrated from Germany to the Volga Valley to farm for Catherine the Empress of Russia."

"Hummmm." He was still listening. And waiting.

"I was born in Russia." She waited for any expression of disbelief or disdain. None came.

"Long ways off," was all Bill said.

"Yes, well, when I was three or four, I can't remember very well, my father and mother decided to leave the Russia and come to Canada. Another family traveled with us. *Onkel Jacob* and *Tante Lydia*."

"Uncle Jacob? The farmer – rancher up north a Winnipeg?" Bill asked.

"One and the same," Dorothy replied.

"So they made it to Canada, too?" Bill asked though the answer was obvious.

"I don't know how long it took them to get to Manitoba; our families didn't travel together after we left the ship. The evening that my family got on the train heading for Manitoba, their family stayed behind in New York.

"Another thing I remember now. Anna and I had traded our doll babies that night. We did that once in a while – watched each other's baby.

"Our *omas* - our grandmothers - had made those dolls for us. They were just little dolls with cloth heads and bodies and buttons for their eyes but we loved them almost as much as we loved each other."

She couldn't believe how hard it was to tell this part of her memories to Bill. The hard stories weren't the lighthearted tales of two hard-headed, hard-riding girls thundering across the prairie duff. Horses' hooves pitching prairie divots behind them.

No. The hard story to tell was her parents' story. Sadness she had not felt in years slowly crept back through her heart and she wondered if she should go on. Sadness reflected from Friedrich's eyes, sorrow in her mother's at the loss of their hopes and dreams. Owning their own land, their own farm.

Dorothy frowned in the darkness, trying to remember any of the faces of her past but none came. Not *Opa.* Not even *Oma.*

"And the dolls?" Bill couldn't see how the dolls related to Dorothy's story at all.

"That night in New York, we had traded our babies, and when it came time for my family to get on the train, we forgot to trade back." She sighed. "It was so long ago."

Bill thought of another little girl. His own sister, Pearl. She'd had a doll much like the ones Dorothy described. Maybe one day he would tell Dorothy of the dearest memory of his own childhood.

"Bill?"

"Yeah?" He was beginning to enjoy the routine.

"My name's not Dorothy."

There, now, she'd gone and done it.

"Well, now, Dorothy, my name's not Bill."

She suppressed a laugh.

"Of course not. I bet it's William – not a chance it's Wilhelm, like one of my younger brothers. We call him Willie."

"Nope. It ain't William, neither! Hell, I got me *two* brothers named William."

And one son-of-a-bitchin' step-father, he added just to himself.

"No! *Two* brothers? Why in the world?"

Then she thought of baby Julianne and her sister Julie Ruth. It wouldn't really be out of the question.

"My mum was born in South Africa."

Now it was Bill's turn to make a long answer for a short question.

"Oh, I see," Dorothy replied though she didn't really.

"Her dad spent his life in the service of Her Majesty, The Queen of England, Queen Victoria. Think mum said he was an engineer. As I understand a planner, a builder supervisor of some sort."

Dorothy's eyes widened in the dark.

"Served all over the world, an' him doin' what he done, he was able to take his wife an' kids with him wherever he went. Those kids's born all over the world. Like I said, my mum was born in South Africa, couple of her sisters in France. I don't know about all the rest."

"That's long ways off," Dorothy said, and enjoyed throwing the phrase back at him.

"Yep. After he retired, living his life 'at leisure' as he called it, he come to Colorado. The lure a gold, called to him, too, I guess. He still had a son an' three daughters at home when him an' his family came to the States an' my mum was one of 'em.

"I don't know how her and my dad ever got together. They's from different worlds, poles apart, so to speak, but made no diff'rence to 'em. Pretty soon, they's married, movin' around Colorado, my dad always chasin' work. Like I told ya, he wuz a teamster, hauled freight from the end of the railroad lines to wherever it needed to go. And a mustanger. After a few years, they ended up in the hills south a Glenrock, Wyoming, like I told yuh, ranchin' along Boxelder Creek wheres I was born." He repeated parts of his story from earlier in the afternoon.

And your brothers named William? But like Bill, she could wait out a story to its finish.

"My second oldest brother, they named William Jason. We just call him Jay. He's a few years older'n me.

"I see," said Dorothy, though she didn't - yet.

"After my dad quit haulin' freight between Denver and Cheyenne, he was still horse tradin' - buyin' and sellin' an' movin' horses from here to there." His voice grew quiet as the memories of his father overwhelmed him with lonesomeness, if just for a moment.

"I's about six, maybe seven years old an' it was in the fall of the year, when he was out workin' some green bronks. Him and a few a them horses was out in a pole corral. One a them cayuse took a mind to high tail it over the top rail of the fence. Bucked and kicked right into it. Broke that top pole all apart. Couple of them pole pieces come flyin' at him. One broke a few ribs. 'Nother one knocked him in the stomach purty bad. One hit him long side the head. He wasn't long for this world after that."

"I'm so sorry."

Dorothy was overwhelmed by the sorrow not only in Bill's voice as well as the thought of losing his father at such a young age.

"So, Mum, she was expectin' at the time my dad passed away. Few months later, the last a the Robbins brothers was born. She named him Frank B Robbins, after our dad.

"Them first couple a years was damn tough on Mum. Even with the half-growed sons that my older brothers was, it was next to impossible keep the ranch goin' on her own. I s'pose she thought it was a good idea to marry Mr. W. C. Kimball when he come a-callin'. I'm pretty damn sure it was the more the ranch he had in mind to marry over the woman. He sure as hell was no father to me or any of my older brothers. He sorta tolerated Frank, but soon as Frank was old 'nough to light out on his own, he did."

Dorothy had nothing to say at this. It was as if Bill had lost both his parents, one to death and one to marriage rough as it was. Her own father had been such a quiet refuge. Friedrich took the edge off of Maria's tongue, the bite from her bark.

"This ol' W. C. Kimball, he come from back east - Maine, if I'm rememberin' right. You should hear him talk. All ay-uh and no-ah. Made my ears bleed sometimes."

Dorothy smiled to herself in the dark. Bill had such a way of talking.

"Near's I could tell, not that I ever cared much, he come out west with his mother after she split the sheets from his dad. Seemed he was devoted to her, Mz Salome, more'n he was to Mum, appeared to me." The railroad car swayed gently to the rhythm of the rails.   Both Dorothy and Bill were each lost in their own thoughts for a time.

"Oh, shoot," Bill laughed. "I was supposed to be tellin' you why I got me two brothers by name a William.   With Mr. Kimball around, she had a few more kids, two boys, two girls. Their youngest is named William.   Call him Billy."

"Ahh, I see.   Two brothers named William but with different last names."

"You got it!" he chuckled.

Dorothy gathered her courage.

"Bill," she said at last.

"Yeah?"

"My name is Carlina."

"Car-leen-ah," Bill repeated her name as she had pronounced it just to be clear.

"Carlina?" This time he spoke her name as a question.

"Yes?" Dorothy replied.

"My name is Roy.   Roy Raymond Robbins."

"Glad to make your acquaintance, Roy," she whispered.

Bill laughed right out loud.   "Good to make yours, as well, Miss Carlina."

Dorothy pondered on all they had told each other.   She wondered if it had been hard for Bill to make peace with the idea of her being Russian-born.   The stillness of the night grew around them when at last she heard Bill whisper to her again.

"Dot?"

"Yes?" She blinked to clear her thoughts and push sleep away.

"Miss Dottie," he hesitated, as now he was the one who had to gather courage.   "I might've written to my mother a while back askin' what she thought about the idea of one her sons being married on horseback.   You know, in an arena at a rodeo.   Maybe like the rodeo in Cheyenne."

"So?"

"And she might've taken the time to talk to a newspaperman in the town just down the road apiece about her famous son, the one making good with a reputation as a roper and rider on the Pacific Coast."

"And?"

Bill's answer was a while in coming.   "And there might've been a front page article the hometown paper about that son getting married in Cheyenne next week."

Dorothy sat straight up in her bed almost hitting her head on the bottom of Bill's bunk.

"What in the world?" she gasped.

Bill was glad to hear surprise and not anger in her voice.

"Now, now," he tried to sooth her.   "You know how them reporters like to spin their stories better'n I like spinnin' rope.   I'm just sayin', more'n likely, there'll be some folks who'll be callin' you Missus Robbins at times in the next few days, and I thought you just might need to know why."

Dorothy pushed herself up to sit back against the headboard, taking in this newest Truth of her life.

Oh, bother! *Better get everything straight here and now! Well, most everything.*

"Bill, now you listen." She bit her lower lip and was thankful for the darkness separating them.

"I'm listening," he quietly replied, hoping he was man enough to weather any storm she was going to throw at him.

"Bill," she started, still hesitating, before going on at last. "Bill, I was married once."

Bill relished the relief flowing through him. There were no storm clouds over Dorothy's head. He smiled into the darkness.

"Could he ride a bronk?" he asked.

"No, of course not."

"Did he ever rope a steer?"

"Never!"

"Was he as tall as me?"

Dorothy laughed softly. "No. Not even!"

"Did he ever write yuh poems?" He made it sound like 'pomes.'

"I don't think he even knew what rhyming words were."

"Don't sound to me like he was worth a tinker's damn. Good thing yuh loosed yer rope and let that critter go."

Tears began to gather in Dorothy's eyes as relief and thankfulness replaced the anxiety that had been building all evening.

"Bill," she whispered, softly, not sure he could even hear her.

"Yes, Dot," he whispered back – how sweet the words.

"I'm pretty sure I found a keeper in you, Mr. Roy Raymond also known as Skeeter Bill Robbins."

"Yeah, an' I am pretty damn sure I love you, Miss Dorothy almost Robbins Morrell."

There didn't seem much more to say, the gentle rocking of the railcar and the rhythm of the iron wheels over the rails soon sang them both to sleep.

XI – 7 AUGUST 1914 – ALMOST MRS. ROBBINS

Bright, pleasant sunlight streamed its way passed the blinds to awaken Dorothy. She yawned and stretched, listening to the rails beneath her. Then she listened to hear if she could tell if Bill were awake yet. She realized that there was nothing but silence above her. No sounds of breathing, or turning over on the bunk. She reached up and knocked on the bottom of the bed overhead. Nothing.

As she swung her legs over the side of the bed, last night's conversation with Bill came crashing back.

Ach, Gott in Himmel! her mother's familiar complaint came all to easily to mind. What in Heaven's name had she done last night? It had all seemed so right, so timely last evening, but now in the light of day, she groaned.

"No man wants used goods," her mother had fumed when her daughter had finally called it quits on her marriage. "It is useless even to hope that anyone will want to marry you now!"

Dorothy remembered the argument that had followed all too well.

"I never want to be married again anyway, Mutter." Even her mother recognized her daughter's anger in being called by the formal word rather than the endearing term that all her children had continued to use well out of childhood. "I am sorry I disappoint you. I am sorry I cannot be like Nathalia! I cannot be what you want me to be."

"You just haven't tried hard enough," was all her mother would answer before going into a three day silent treatment.

Dorothy shook her head and sighed. Time would tell how things would play out between Bill and her.

She reached for the clothing which she'd hung on a hook the night before and quickly dressed. She flipped up the window shade and wondered where they were. Miles and miles of empty desert were broken up with little vegetation stretched to rocky, sparsely forested mountain chains. There was fierceness, stubborn and proud, to the landscape. She'd keep those feelings in mind.

Dorothy stepped out of their sleeping alcove and made her way to the restrooms at the front of the car. These seemed to be reserved to be used by women and children, while the ones near the smoking room were used more by the men. As she washed her hands and face, she squinted into the tiny mirror, was reminded she needed to brush her hair when she got back to her berth.

When she stepped back into the seating/sleeping room of the train car, she was surprised to see that the porters had already remade her bed into cushioned benches and that Bill's bunk was folded back up into the wall. *Good thing I am up for the day,* she thought wistfully though it wouldn't do to be sleeping at this time of the day.

Dorothy pulled the curtain closed behind her and wondered what time it actually was. Most times when she had asked Mutti for the time of day, her mother had tsked her tongue and replied, "Daytime, of course, little one!" She hummed a little as she thought on the more tender side of Maria Eichhorn.

She took her hairbrush from her carpet bag and went to work on her hair. After brushing it out, she gathered it at the nape of her neck and tied a narrow ribbon around it. She wondered how long it would be before she got up the nerve to cut it short. Something else her mother had clucked over the few times they'd ever seen young women with such haircuts.

"Doth not even nature itself teach you, that, if a man has long hair, it is a shame unto him? But if a woman has long hair, it is a glory to her!" Mutti would sniff in disdain and then as the faithful Lutheran woman she was, she always added, "Moreover, what the Bible asserts, God asserts. What the Bible commands, God commands. The authority of the Scriptures is complete, certain and final."

Knowing her mother as she did, Dorothy had been careful not to express any opinion to the contrary, because additionally whatever Maria asserted was absolutely complete, certain, and final.

A soft knock on the partial wall of the berth brought her back to the present. Dorothy pulled back the curtains to find Bill holding two mugs of coffee. Dorothy studied his face carefully for any signs of remorse or regret in greeting her this morning. All she found was happiness, joy in the new day and a cheerful greeting.

"Ah, good mornin', Miss Dot!" Bill stepped in while Dorothy fastened the curtains back for the day. "Didja sleep good?"

"Well enough, yes," she decided that sounded like she was hedging bad news, so she added. "Yes, as you say, I slept good."

"Good, good." Bill nodded. "Thought yuh might need a little somethin' to getcha up and goin' till we get to breakfast," he said as he handed her one of the mugs of coffee as they sat down. She could see that cream had been added, and when she sipped, the sugar he had added was right. The rich creamy brew spread warmth through her body and soul.

"Figgered tryin' to get from there to here with those little cups and saucers might be harder than stayin' on a bronk."

As they sat facing each other, Dorothy decided to try to enjoy the day. Enjoy her companion. Enjoy the journey, even the miles of empty desert continued to offer a certain charm. Enjoy being so far from Winnipeg.

"They's servin' breakfast, if you want somethin'," Bill told her.

"Hmmm, yes!" Something to do with their time. Her time. Something to keep her busy instead of worrying.

Together they stood, Dorothy slipped her hand into the crook of Bill's elbow and they started toward the dining car.

"I think I'm finally hungry after all the hustle and bustle of getting on our way yesterday." She had never been able to eat much when she was under stress or pressure, so eaten little yesterday.

When their plates arrived, Dorothy looked over the scrambled eggs with approval. They'd been made with just a touch of cream to lighten their texture. The sausages were crisp and browned perfectly. Buttered toast and cottage fried potatoes were arranged along one side of the plate. She smiled across the table at Bill as he used his toast to push his eggs onto his fork. She put her napkin in her lap, and decided if Bill could 'dig in' she should be able to 'shovel' a little as well.

After Bill had polished his plate with one of Dorothy's pieces of toast, he sat back a little in his chair and waved to the waiter to refill his coffee cup.

"Well, Mrs. Almost Robbins . . ."

Reassured. Refreshed. Restored. Dorothy's relief buoyed her in a better way than coffee or breakfast ever could have.

"Now, Bill, let's not get ahead of the game," Dorothy warned, though her dark eyes were shining.

"Oh, all right. Then if yer willin', let's review the last go round," Bill began. "If I may be so bold," the expression more reserved and stuffy than the Bill she'd known so far, "and if yuh don't mind tellin' me, just what kind of guy was this feller yuh let loose?"

Dorothy smiled across the table at Bill, still searching his face for any warning signs of distrust or disappointment.

"Bill, you always make me smile, feel better, feel capable – even strong," Dorothy said, remembering her thoughts about the passing landscape. The fierceness, stubbornness. The pride.

"He never made me feel any of that."

She picked up her teaspoon and used its handle to check off an imaginary list on the table cloth.

"My cooking wasn't as good as his mother's. My garden wasn't as productive as his grandmother's. I wasn't as pretty as his sister. My house was not as tidy as his auntie's. You name it, I came up short. After trying to please him for almost two years, I packed my bag one day and went home.

"My mother was not pleased. My sister was horrified and my brothers, especially my older brother wouldn't talk to me at all."

"And yer father?"

"He was sad, I could tell, but he never spoke to me of my choices. I sometimes wonder if he had decided with so many others scolding and correcting me, he would keep his peace even if he did agree with them all.

"That man never even tried to see me or talk to me again. That hurt," she frowned as she said it. "But it hurt in such a damn fine way. Good riddance."

Bill sipped his coffee studying the rugged terrain they were rolling through.

"Seems to me, there should be good wild horse country."

Ach, was ist los? Sometimes her mother's voice was exactly the one she needed. *What in the world?* She raised her eyebrows and looked out the window herself, searching for any signs of life and finding few.

Bill winked across the table.

"I come from wild horse country, myself. Mustangs's a like people – every single one a them diff'ernt from another. Some a them cayuse'll never quit the buck an' that's good for bronk riders like me – and you, I'd say. For other horses, it might take time, maybe a lotta time, but finally one day, yuh realize there ain't been no fight in 'em fer a long time, only loyalty, willin'ness to work hard, and the best companion a horseman would ever need or want." *Horseman, not cowboy.*

Grinning, he continued. "Now, we used to use my mum's biscuits for target practice. My grandmum served tea at four o'clock in the afternoon – never had much of a garden, and I ain't never met any of my aunts an' I got no sister. That makes you, Miss Dot, incomparable! And that's all right with me."

"Your grandmother served tea? Every afternoon? On a homestead?"

"Didn't matter to her she's livin' on a homestead. Her husband passed away 'bout the same time my dad did, so she come up from Colorado to live

90

with us.   Actually lived in the little homestead cabin my dad threw together while the big house was built.   Stayed on even after Mum married Mr. Kimball.

"Goldarn!"   Bill's mild cursing made Dorothy smile.   "Grandmum irritated the hell outta old W. C.   Gave me joy.   She'd been all round the world, faced down tigers, rode elephants, spoke to native Africans usin' their own tongue-clickin' language.   Wasn't no high plains sheepherder gonna make her change her ways.

"Mr. Kimball used to give us boys endless chores, send us on wild goose chases, anything to keep us way out and away from the house in the afternoons.   'Wastin' time,' he called it.   But we boys knew how to get around him most of the time.   We always got done what he told us to get done.   Got good starts, maybe even finished up by four in the afternoon. Who can keep hungry, growin' boys away from cakes or cookies or biscuits or shortbread . . ." He was nodding at the memories.   "Grandmum was a right good at bakin' most anything.   Don't know why our mum never caught on."

The waiter came by with a fresh pot of coffee and refilled both their cups.   Bill gently reached across the table and entwined his fingers with Dorothy's.

"Was it complicated?   Gettin' a divorce, I mean?"   His gray eyes soft with sympathy.

Dread once again weighed down Dorothy's heart.   She looked down and shook her head.

"I don't really know.   Left that up to him.   He was the one with means to file."   Dorothy's eyes were on her nearly empty plate as her stomach lurched and she was wishing she'd skipped breakfast all together.   She tried to pull her hand from Bill's but he gently held it firm.   "We'd been separated a year or so before I left Canada and I've been here a year."

Her throat tightened, eyes smarted, but she swallowed down the tears and finished.   "Truth be told, Bill, I never expected to - no, I never thought I'd ever want to marry again.   Divorcing wasn't important to me, getting away to find my own way, follow my own dreams, that was all that meant anything to me."

Bill's fingers were warm and comforting around hers.

"I don't think I'm in any position to be getting 'hitched up,' as you say."

He put down his coffee cup and took her hand in both of his.

"I'm sorry," she added with a whisper, still avoiding looking up at Bill.

"Dottie."   He cleared his throat before starting again.   "Carlina Eichhorn, I been waitin' for you all my life.   Watched my older brothers marry theirselves good women.   I been wonderin' for years where my Mrs. Robbins was gonna come from.   What she'd look like.   How the sound of her voice'd drive me crazy.

"So, if you'll willin' to have a footloose drifter as your partner, an' you don't mind joinin' me in followin' the shows, I'm happy to wait to make our marriage official as long as it takes to get this other thing straightened out."

Dorothy placed her other hand over their fingers and raised her eyes to look Bill full on, wanting only to ease the worry in his eyes.

"Roy Raymond Robbins," she whispered across the table. "I am willing. More than willing. I'm honored to 'have you,' as you say. It seems to me, we're two of a kind, as far as being footloose and following the shows, the rodeos, whatever comes along. I'm more than ready to hitch my wagon to your star. I'll be proud to be your Mrs. Robbins."

Bill surely wanted to lean across the table and kiss her full on her lips right in front of the whole dining car; if he'd had his hat on, he'd have thrown it in the air and yelled; he wanted to feel her arms around him as he had the day he'd been her pickup man after her first bronk ride, but his mother had raised him better than that, so he settled for quick kiss on the backs of both of her hands before helping her to her feet and tucking both her hands into his elbow.

Oh, Lord, but this day was gonna be a good one.

XII – 4 OCTOBER 1914 –A LITTLE TO THE RIGHT OF THE MIDDLE OF NOWHERE

O h!" Dorothy gritted her teeth as she was pitched forward and then sideways.

"My!" She clung to the edges of her seat as she was thrown skyward.

"Hell!" Dorothy complained. "Riding over this road in this damn – what you call it? – tin lizzie is harder than it was staying on that bucker, Lillian Russell."

She glared over at Bill, one hand on the steering wheel of the borrowed car and his left arm resting on the door. He smiled back and shrugged as they bounced along.

"Too bad there ain't no prize money nor saddle waitin' at the end of this ride." He didn't seem to mind the rough drive over the wagon road at all. "Good thing yuh pulled yer hat down tight before we started up the grade."

And that there is a hat pin going through it to hold it to my head!

"I think it would be easier if I got out and walked," she grimaced as the open-topped car bounced its way over yet another rock only to land in a pothole.

"Them's the 'xact words we used to tell our mum when we's comin' back from Glenrock in the back a the farm wagon. Once we's complainin' so hard, she just stopped the wagon and said, 'Have at 'er, boys. See yuh at home.' It was the longest walk a my life and I decided I's never gonna complain again about this road."

The first seven or eight miles south on the Mormon Canyon Road out of Glenrock were relatively smooth as they drove passed farmsteads now and again. Even the open range had been pretty easy riding before they started climbing, but now as they chugged along through the sparse timber, it seemed each mile was worse than the last.

"Don't worry. We'll top out here in a minute and start down into the Upper Boxelder. It'll be easier goin'." He grinned over at her again. "Or my name ain't Skeeter Bill Robbins."

"Humph," Dorothy grumbled. "Only thing is, is your name is *not* Skeeter Bill."

"Oh, come on, now for Pete's sake! It ain't all that bad. Try to relax a little."

Was that a hint of impatience in his voice? Dorothy decided she could keep the rest of her complaints to herself as she tried to do as he'd suggested and relax.

They rounded a turn and finally came out of the timber.

"Oh, my stars!" Dorothy exclaimed. They were overlooking a broad, high mountain valley that stretched away from them for miles. The aspen were autumn gold in the light of mid-afternoon.

"Welcome to a Little Right a the Middle of Nowhere! Ain't like no place else on earth!"

There was pride in his voice, but something else, Dorothy thought. Wistfulness? Wishfulness?

Bill stopped the car, letting it idle, as he got out to check the tires and roll a smoke.

"We're better'n half way to home and best part is the worst part is behind us now."

Dorothy gladly stepped out of the Model T Ford and stretched.

"I have never seen anything like this."

She breathed deeply of the high mountain air, sweetened now with solid ground under her feet.

"Half way? I think I'd better go check out some of those trees over there."

94

Bill nodded absently, smoking and wrapped up in his own thoughts. Six years. Six years since he'd traveled this same road but traveling north into Glenrock headed for a train. Any train. Eastbound or west, it hadn't mattered as long as it took him away from the constant complaints, reprimands, his inability to please the man his mother had married. He hadn't planned to be away so long, but one rodeo lead to another, the summer seasons faded into looking for winter work to tide him over until spring again. Bill had but one regret, the price of being shed of his step-father included being far from his mother. Thank God for the US mail.

The years had blurred by – Pendleton, Cheyenne, Salinas, Reno, Los Angeles – until he'd come across Dot in Emeryville. He let his eyes wander down the road to where she was making her way back to him. Wrapped and buttoned into a coat that fell well below her knees, with that little hat pinned to her head, she looked nothing like the Ladies' World Champion Bronk Rider crowned a few months ago at the 1914 Cheyenne Frontier Days Rodeo. What a pistol!

"I think I'm much better now," Dorothy called to him as soon as she was in earshot.

"Wait there. I'll save yuh a few steps," he called back, sliding back in behind the steering wheel.

With the worst of the road behind them, Dorothy sat back into her seat and enjoyed every passing mile.

"Tell me about your sisters and brothers still at home," Dorothy asked.

"Hard to say. Last I saw them girls, they's 9 or 10, only a year between 'em. They looked a lot like Mum." He sighed, "I don't even know if I'll recognize 'em.

"Billy back then was just a little kid. I don't know, maybe two – three. He's walkin' and talkin' but I could hardly understand a word he said at that age. The oldest of them Kimball kids is my half-brother, Bird. He was 'leven or so. By now he must be 'bout, I don't know, 16? 17? An' a course, there's my brother, Frank, but I'll bet he's not around much if he can help it," he snorted.

Bill looked down the road watching for rocks or tree roots but saw instead the shadows of a young girl. He allowed the memories of that girl to wash over him. The girl who had once been inseparable from Roy, her little brother. He glanced over at Dorothy. She was watching him watching her. No time like the present.

"I had me another sister once. Her name was – still is, I guess – Pearl. Frances Pearl after our dad, but just Pearl to us. She was just a couple a years older 'n me. Mum said the two of us was thick as thieves. I guess we was, 'specially on days Grammum was bakin'.

"I liked to dog her around, doin' whatever mum had her doin.' Gatherin' eggs, weedin' garden . . ."

"Now, wait a minute, here, cowboy! You said there was no garden," Dorothy interrupted.

"I said my grammum never had much of a garden, never said nothin' about my mum, though her garden was up right next to Grammum's cabin." His eyes laughed at her before sobering again as he went on.

"Yeah, followin' Pearl wherever she went, doin' whatever it was she thought up for us to get into. Mum says that what one didn't think of, the other did." He steered around a pothole, taking the low side of the road.

"Summer days'd find us up in the garden. It was somethin' we got away with a lot – pickin' stuff outta Mum's garden. She grew all sorts of veg'tables, spuds, beets, turnips but peas we liked the best. We'd open up them pods and eat 'em right out there in middle a the patch. It was gettin' a little late in the summer, September, I think. The peas was gettin' a little passed their prime. That was good though. Mum would let 'em dry on vine and save 'em for winter soups."

Bill grew quiet. Dorothy scouted down the road. It looked fairly smooth, hardly a challenge requiring any extra thought. She turned to study Bill's face and could see he was not seeing the road at all, rather a skinny little girl. One who shepherded him around and kept him under her wings. His jaw was tight and both hands were on the steering wheel. He shook his head.

"We's happy when once in a while, we'd find some greener pods. Those peas's still somewhat sweet even if they's a little crunchy.

"Then Pearl called to me to come on over 'cause she'd found some real soft green peas."

He shook his head again, as if he could erase whatever it was he was about to tell Dorothy. He stepped on the clutch and brake pedals and coasted to a stop.

Bill turned in his seat to face Dorothy.

"What were they?" Dorothy dreaded the answer, the one so hard for Bill to tell.

"They's nightshade berries," he spoke slowly and deliberately. "They wasn't red an' ripe yet, still just little green balls a poison."

He shook his head and it was clear to Dorothy that it didn't matter how long ago Pearl had passed away, the missing her was still overwhelming.

"When I got over to where she was eatin' them berries, she already figgered out they wasn't peas. Pretty soon she went on about how her tummy was hurtin'. We went to Grammum and she made her some peppermint tea and then sent me to get Mum. By the time we got back, Pearlie was talkin' all sorts of crazy things, claimin' they's jackrabbits in Grammum's cupboards, askin' Grammum why it was she let rattlesnakes in t'house."

Dorothy reached over and took Bill's hand in hers. Gently she caressed the back of it, wishing for all the world that she could take on some of the sorrow she could hear in his voice.

As she traced her fingers over his knuckles, he finally went on, "My dad went out to where we'd been pickin' them peas. Soon as he saw what Pearlie'd been eatin', he broke down in tears. Said he'd seen cattle killed from eatin' it. All the while, us kids was scared to death. We never seen our dad cry before nor since."

Bill swallowed hard and shook his head again before going on.

"Pretty soon Pearlie was cryin' about how her eyes hurt. Grammum put cold cloths over her face an' eyes. Mum held her in the lap, and rocked her in Grammum's rocker. Sang to her like she done with all her babies when they's fussin' and won't sleep.

"All too soon she's quietin' down her cryin' but then she goes to shiverin' like it's the middle of winter. She's still shiverin' when she finally fell asleep. Asleep but she never woke up."

"Oh, my God, Bill. I am so, so sorry. I don't know what to say . . ."

"Shhhhh! Don't." Bill shook his head, turning to look Dorothy full in her eyes. "Mostly we just don't speak about her much. It's easier that way."

He gently squeezed her hands before pulling his hand free, let out the clutch and was once again driving down the road.

Dorothy folded her hands in her lap and studied them. She hardly remembered when Julianne had died. Pneumonia Mutti said. Yes, she wondered what life would have been like if she'd had a sister more her age, but the sorrow that still clear in Bill's face totally overshadowed anything she remembered feeling.

The miles crept by until at last they topped a rise and there below them on the far side of the valley was a homestead cabin neatly surrounded with a pole and wire fence. Outbuildings and corrals skirted the yard. Still making their way down the road, Bill pointed to a small fenced in enclosure beyond the cabin, part way up the slope behind it.

"Pearlie an' my dad're buried right out there behind the home place."

Dorothy nodded. "Would it be all right - not tonight but sometime - to walk up and visit?"

Bill nodded, not adding any spoken words to their agreement but reached back over and took Dorothy's hand in his and squeezed, gently at first, and then more firmly.

Bill nodded across the valley and Dorothy looked to see what had caught his attention. She saw that their arrival had been noticed as several people began to make their way through the yard.

Letting go of her hand, Bill whooped and waved to his family.

"Miss Dot! Time to pull yer hat down tight! We got us a wild ride ahead!"

XIII – 4 OCTOBER 1914 – SUPPER

Dorothy was totally unprepared for the welcoming reception that was assembled and coming to meet them at the end of the short lane leading up to Bill's boyhood home.   Several dogs were barking and dancing, as a woman who could only be Bill's mother broke away from the rest of the group and came running to greet them.

"Roy!" she called still running.   "Roy, welcome home!"

Bill braked and shut off the car before swinging the door open and scooping up his mother into a bear hug, lifting her from the ground and rocking side by side.

"Oh, my Lord, baby!" she gasped when he set her back on her feet, tears now running down her face. She stepped back a little, still grasping his forearms in her hands. "Let me look at you, now!"

She looked him up and down and then stretched up on tip-toes to kiss his cheek. Bill smiled down at his mother.

"Good to see you, too, Mum!"

"Oh, you!" his mother sputtered, all the while smiling through her tears. "How are you, son? I've missed you so much! How long are you staying? And . . ." She looked past her son, "is this Miss Morrell?"

Bill laughed and shook his head. "No, Mum. This's just Dorothy. She's family – or will be soon enough. I'm kinda partial to callin' her Dot, myself. She might even let you call her Dot, too."

Bill's face softened as he turned to Dorothy.

"Dot, this is my mother, Sue May Robbins, now Kimball."

Dorothy stepped forward to embrace the woman who had finally let loose of Bill and now reached to give Dorothy a friendly hug.

"So pleased to meet you, Mrs. Kimball," Dorothy leaned in to kiss Bill's mother lightly on her cheek just as her mother would have done.

"Oh, my! How long has it been since I've been so honored?" Sue said as she returned a kiss to Dorothy's cheek.

"Oh, don't look so surprised," she said to her gathered children. "Just because people here in Wyoming do not do such thing, it is a very polite way of greeting people when you are introduced."

Then she gave a start as what Dorothy had called her sank in.

"Now, Dorothy, you may call me Sue or you may call me Sue May, but you need never call me Mrs. Kimball again. Mrs. Kimball is reserved for bankers or lawyers or such."

"Yes, ma'am," Dorothy answered.

"Sue." Came the correction. Dorothy loved listening to Sue's quick easy way of speaking, the lilt that spoke of far off lands, not quite British, but worlds away from the high plains of Wyoming.

Sue turned her attention to her other children now standing in a semi-circle around Bill, Dorothy and the car.

"This is William, my youngest." A round faced boy of about ten nodded in her direction with a friendly grin. "Now, Billy, you start carrying their bags up to where they belong."

"Now, Mum, I can drive in a little closer," Bill offered. "No need for him to carry it so far."

"Billy," was all Sue said and her youngest son knew her word was the one to be followed as he lifted the carpet bags from the back seat of the car.

"Roy," Sue explained, "a few extra steps never hurt anyone.

"Now these are my daughters, Julia and Josephine – Josie," Sue said as she put her arms around the two teenaged girls standing next to her. The two girls smiled over at Dorothy unsure of just how to greet her. Dorothy stepped over, gently took first one girl and then the other by the shoulders and gave each a light kiss on the cheek which seemed to fluster both of them.

"Pleased to make your acquaintance," Dorothy said to each.

"Now, girls, you two go get supper on the table, then ring the dinner bell to call your father and brother in. I expect they're close enough to hear it."

Sue linked one arm through one of Bill's and her other through one of Dorothy's and lead them up the lane and through the front gate of the fenced in yard, chatting all the way, asking question after question, but never quite waiting for an answer.

"Oh, we'll just have to catch up after supper," she finally said.

"What do you think of it?" Sue May stopped the procession to let Dorothy get a good look at the front of the home. Sturdy squared off logs chinked with mortar had been used to build the two story house. A screen door protecting the wooden front door was set between two windows facing the front yard. A brick chimney ran up the west side of the house. The simplicity of the home held its own grandeur. This was no homesteader's cabin, thrown up in a hurry with the bare minimum to satisfy the requirements of the law, but a building of substance, of permanence, steady against the elements.

"Frank built this front part of the house just after we first came up here in '86. One great room on the ground floor, at the time it was kitchen, dining and front room all in one and there are two bedrooms upstairs. We faced it to the south to catch the heat of the sun all day. Weather tends to be cool at this altitude no matter the time of year." As they walked around to the east side of the house, she pointed out the upper story window. "That was our bedroom, Frank's and mine. The children had the other one. Cut a hole in the floor to help bring warm air up to their room."

"Even at that, it's pretty cold upstairs in the winters," Bill added.

Dorothy admired the wild rose bushes planted under the first floor windows. Their petals were long gone, but vivid rose hips brightened the side yard.

The ringing of the dinner bell surprised Dorothy even though she had known it would be coming. This was no iron triangle or school marm bell, but more the size expected to be in the belfry of a school or church. Family would be able to hear the call to meals at least a mile away if not more – a comforting thought this time of day.

"Let's move along," Sue said, still linking arms with Dorothy and Bill. By now they had walked around to the north side of the home and Dorothy could see the one story addition that made a T with the front part of the house.

"All those boys," Sue May said, shaking her head, "and they simply would not stop growing. And growing." She laughed up at Bill and nodded. "We needed more room and so Frank and I added this back wing about '91.

"As you are able to see, Frank and I thought it best to offset the chimney so we might still have a window in the children's bedroom. Helps one to get up with the sun if one can see the sun.

"Ah, and here come Mr. Kimball and Bird now," Sue nodded toward the west pasture, two men, one younger, the other older were walking toward them.

Dorothy put on her opening-the-show smile and waiting for introductions.

As Mr. Kimball approached, though, she could see he was scowling.

"So have yeh finally given up playin' cowboy?" he growled at Bill. "Are yeh back home t' finally start helpin' out around here?"

Dorothy waited for Mr. Kimball's guffaw, sure to signal a joke, a slap on the back, a scuff of the toe of his boot through the fine dry dust of the lane. Bill simply looked past his step-father, gently took Dorothy's elbow and quietly shepherded her back to the front door while the older man snorted and shook his head.

"Shoulda known!" was all he said pursing his lips in dissatisfaction. Icy silence followed them all into the house.

The smells of supper were amazing, though, and raised Dorothy's spirits as she and Bill stepped through the front door. The girls had indeed "put supper on the table." A huge bowl of potatoes, riced and mixed with canned milk sat steaming in the center of the table. Boats of gravy, platters of fried meat, late season green beans and mountains of biscuits ladened the table.

Dorothy turned to Bill, the question in her eyes clear to him. He whispered, "Josie made the biscuits. You'll be all right."

"Roy! You've been telling stories on me again, I see."

Sue's laughter brightened the room as she ignored the thundercloud hovering over her husband.

"Now, Mum, I only been speakin' the truth."

Bill laughed and put an arm around Sue's shoulders as she slipped her arm around his waist.

"You may wash up in the kitchen. It will be fine just this once," Sue May defended herself to the looks of surprise from not only her daughters, but especially her sons.

She turned to Dorothy. "Most of the time, we are in the practice of washing up for meals on the back steps until it gets so cold the water freezes out there. Water barrel and basin, soap and towels all ready for taking the dirt of the day from one's hands and face - but not tonight. Let's hurry along."

The family soon gathered around the long, handmade table that stretched through one side of the front room. After being seated, Dorothy was surprised to watch as the family bowed their heads.

Bless us, O Lord, and these thy gifts, which we are about to receive from Thy bounty. Through Christ our Lord. Amen.

How long had it been since she had given thanks for a meal? Out loud? She could almost hear Mutti's and Papa's voices reciting in perfect unison, *Come, Lord Jesus, be our Guest, and let Thy gifts to us be blessed. Amen.*

Amen. Amen to the supplication at the table and the one in her heart.

"Dig in and help yourselves!"

Sue was clearly delighted to have guests at her table. The bowls and platters made their way around the table in a clockwise rotation and soon all were eating with gusto Dorothy noticed as she began to sample her fare. The biscuits were light and flaky. The gravy thick and rich on the potatoes. The cutlets had been pounded, breaded and fried making them tender enough to cut with a fork.

"Do you raise your own beef?" Dorothy asked.

Looks of surprise came from every direction as the children looked first at their mother and then at one another.

"Mr. Kimball chooses to run sheep on this place," Sue said stiffly, putting further questions at rest. "What we have before us tonight is the best venison that ever came in front of a rifle sight. Bird . . ." she nodded down the table to the quiet teenaged boy ". . . keeps us in red meat year round. Crack shot, our boy!"

Bird's ears brightened at his mother's praise. Dorothy noticed Mr. Kimball was more interested in his plate than the shooting abilities of his son.

"Mum, when you gonna start lettin' me bring in the meat?" Billy asked with a pout.

"Soon enough, soon enough, Bud," Mr. Kimball quickly answered in lieu of his wife, actually showing a hint of a smile he nodded down the table at his youngest son.

"So, who's yer friend?" Mr. Kimball grunted, though clearly he knew the answer. To Dorothy's surprise, Bill quickly put a bite of potatoes and gravy into his mouth and then shrugged apologetically toward his mother.

"Father," Sue began, patiently turning to face her husband, "as you have probably heard, this is Miss Dorothy Morrell of Winnipeg, Canada."

Dorothy tried to hear if there were the slightest trace of sarcasm in Sue's voice, but she found none.

"Dorothy, this is my husband, W.C. Kimball. Folks around here sometimes call him Dub. It's short for double-you." Sue explained as the older man gave a slight nod in Dorothy's direction. She had never been treated so coldly in her life.

"Pleased to make your acquaintance, Dub," Dorothy nodded back.

"Mis-teh Kimball, if you please," was the reply she got back complete with scowl.

"Begging your pardon."

Dorothy was now of the opinion that Bill's solution to avoiding conversation with *Mr.* Kimball was a good one, and picked up her fork.

But Sue was unflappable. "Dorothy, tell us about your rides in Cheyenne. We'd love to hear all about them."

102

Mr. Kimball instantly interrupted. "Oh, hell! What is there t' tell? One gets on a horse an' either keeps his seat or he doesn't. Evidently, in this case, this – this *woman* here managed to keep her seat."

He spat the words as if he were speaking of a fiasco that could hardly be explained.

Dorothy smiled wanly down the table at Mr. Kimball and then returned her attention to her plate as did everyone else at the table.

Quickly, Mr. Kimball finished his meal, slowing down only to sop every bit of gravy from his plate with a biscuit and then turned to Bird.

"Come along, boy, there are still plenty o' chores to be finished around the place. Never endin', they are. We don't have time to sit around gossipin' and fritterin' away the day."

With a thankful heart, Dorothy watched as the two got to their feet and walked out of the house through the front door. She could clearly feel the relief that settled over the room as they could hear the closed front door, the screen door banging on its spring.

"Dorothy, my husband is of the opinion that only noble work that can be done by anyone on the face of the entire earth is right here on this homestead. I hope you will not be put off by his beliefs."

"No, ma'am – Sue – I'm quite aware there are differing opinions about our line of work, some very unkindly."

One of Bill's sisters, she thought it was Julia, repeated her mother's question to Dorothy. "So, how were your rides in Cheyenne?"

Dorothy nodded, thinking how to answer. The joy seemed to have escaped her even though Mr. Kimball was long gone, but she smiled brightly across the table anyway.

"Mr. Kimball had it right on the money, though he left out a few of the details. I did get on a few horses and I stayed on them and didn't pull leather. I guess the judges liked the way I rode because in the end I earned the top points and a beautiful hand carved prize saddle from the Union Pacific came my way," she grinned across the table at the young girl, "and according to the folks in Cheyenne, I'm the World's Champion Lady Bronk Rider."

Dorothy kind of liked the sound of that title, *World's Champion Lady Bronk Rider - 1914.* It was what she always would be.

"And don't forget. One hundred fifty dollars in gold!" Bill chimed in. He was proud of Dorothy and it showed.

She rolled her eyes and shook her head. "Shhh! Now, Bill!" Her mother's warning came to mind. *Money is never discussed in mixed company or among strangers.*

"Made my second place showin' in the amateur buckin' event look quite . . ." Bill said, his eyes twinkling ". . . second rate."

His sisters hooted and even Billy grinned. Sue shook her head. Dorothy looked around the table, admiring Bill's family. They smiled back, especially his sisters who seemed to be warming up to her, as well.

"We read about you in the papers," Jo began shyly. "Are you really 19?"

"Oh, good Lord, no!" Dorothy laughed out loud, much louder than would have been proper at her mother's supper table.

"Josephine!" her mother scolded. "You never ask a woman her age."

"But, mum, I didn't't ask her how old she was, only if she is really 19."

Dorothy was quick to come to Jo's defense. "First thing you learn in show business is never to correct good press, and to think twice before correcting bad – I need all the good press I can come by."

"Just remember, Jo. It's not polite." Her mother had the final word. "Now, girls, let's gather the supper plates from the table and bring out the cobbler."

She nodded at Bill. "Yes, Roy. We made it with strawberry and rhubarb preserves. I'm sorry we have no cream but we've got lots of canned milk."

She turned to Dorothy. "We shall just have to wait for Mama Cow's calf to be born in the spring – lots of fresh milk, then. Cream and butter then. Oh, and she's the only cow Dub allows on the place."

"What is rhubarb?" Dorothy asked, cautiously.

"It's sometimes called pie plant," Sue explained. "Its stalks are quite sour, but compliment strawberries quite nicely in preserves and pies."

"And lots and lots of sugar," Bill finished for her. "Mum does have a way with makin' sour things sweet."

Dorothy smiled across the table, wondering at Bill's description of his mother. Was he talking about more things in life than just rhubarb? Raising children perhaps? Burying child? A husband gone too early? Long harsh winters, and short hot summers?

XIV − 4 OCTOBER 1914 − EVENING

H urry with dishes, girls," Sue called to Josie and Julia who were already in the kitchen busy cleaning up the supper dishes. "Come out as soon as you're finished and sit a while. Roy's got a lot to tell us, I'm sure."

It was a little hard at times for Dorothy to remember that Bill, her *Skeeter Bill*, was Sue May's *Roy*, though she could see that there were quite enough *Bills* around the Kimball place already.

After they filled their mugs with fresh hot coffee, Dorothy and Bill followed Sue into the westward facing side yard. The sunset was still glowing with oranges, reds, and violets framing the surrounding hills and mountains as the sun was still making its final descent below the horizon.

Dorothy could see handmade yard furniture, comfortable and inviting. She sat down next to Bill on a sturdy settee while Sue's chair was at an angle facing them. Small talk filled the time so that the girls wouldn't miss any of Bill's stories.

Sue patted the arm of the chair in which she was seated.

"Dorothy," she began, "just what do you think these are made of?"

Dorothy squinted at the chair through the dim of dusk. She was puzzled at the slender rounded wooden materials; bent and lashed together to make several chairs as well as the settee that she and Bill were sitting on.

She shook her head. "I really couldn't say."

With her fingertips, she stroked the smooth cane-like pieces lined up side by side creating the arm of the settee.

"Go on and tell her, Roy," Sue said with a grin.

Bill blew across the top of his coffee, and sipped for a moment before answering.

"Well, Dot, these here chairs an' such, are the best seats ever made from the willows growing down along the crick over there!" Bill nodded toward a now darkened line of scrubby bushes and grinned, delighting in Dorothy's look of disbelief. "Me and my brothers spent many an evenin' flexin' them willow boughs so's they'd dry in just the right shape. Sometimes we had to lash 'em together with rawhide, an' other times we had nails to do the job."

Dorothy admired the furniture with new appreciation wondering at the hours the brothers had put into each creation.

As Josie and Julia joined them, the conversation took on new energy.

"So, Roy, tell us what's been keeping you busy since the Frontier Days."

Bill leaned back into the settee and put an arm around Dorothy's shoulders. As she leaned back into his embrace, he set his coffee mug on a stump masquerading as an end table.

"After the rodeo was over in Cheyenne, me and Dot, here, as you know, 'the Ladies Buckin' Horse Champion of the Whole GoldarnWorld,' started makin' our way across Nevada headed up to Pendleton. Good thing there're trains goin' just about anywhere. Stopped over at the fair in Reno for a couple a days. Me and Harriman and Johnson come in fourth in the three mile relay race. Not much to tell about that."

Dorothy's eyes sparkled mischievously as she took up the story.

"Skeeter Bill Robbins of Douglas, Wyoming, and Marry Robbins of Cheyenne, two very well-known cowboys checked into the Bowman in Pendleton a few weeks ago."

Bill hooted.

"That's how the paper reported our arrival. Made Harry kind of mad. You know how guys are, Mum. He never heard the end of it the whole time we's there."

106

Dorothy added, "And Skeeter Bill Robbins got one of his poems published in the paper, as well," grinning slyly up into Bill's face.

"Oh, that is so nice, Roy," Sue said, before adding a little wistfully, "I wish your grandmother was still with us to hear this news."

Bill grinned, not at all uncomfortable with the story that now had to be told. He leaned forward and pulled his billfold from his hip pocket and took a folded piece of newsprint from it. Slowly and carefully, he unfolded it and smoothed it across his knee, all the while enjoying being the center of attention - as if he could be even more so than he had been for the last few hours.

He cleared his throat, squinted at the paper as if he actually had to be able to read it to recite it, grinning first at his mother and then his sisters and brother, Billy and last but never least, Dorothy.

I am from Wyoming, Skeeter Bill is my name.
I am six feet in my socks and slim as a crane.
I came here from Cheyenne to ride in the contest
Where they offer big purses to the one who rides best.
I drew old Happy Canyon of Oregon fame,
I mounted to his middle to world renown my name.
I said to Henry Webb, "Now raise up the blind,
Keep out of his way and let him unwind."
He blinked at the sunlight, tied his back in a knot
Stuck his head low and went up from that spot.
His mouth was wide open, his neck it was bowed,
By the way he went at it, I was due to get throwed.
He went up facing the east, came down facing the west.
To stay on his middle I was doing my best.
He jumped fast and crooked, he sure was a peach.
I had to pull leather, but I stuck like a leach.
He turned his old belly right up to the sun,
He jumped backwards two yards when he went forwards one.
He went high in the air and came down on his feet.
I will tell you at bucking he cannot be beat.
I lost both my stirrups and also my hat.
I was sure pulling leather and blind as a bat.
He lit on one foot and turned on his side.
I don't see how he kept from shedding his hide.
But I did my best and I have not lied,
I grabbed the horn and was disqualified.
But never, oh never again, will I say,
That the bronk I can't scratch ain't living today. *

Dorothy loved watching Bill's family as they listened to him tell the story of his infamous ride. Josie and Julia giggled when Bill compared himself to a crane, and Sue clapped her hand and threw her head back in laughter to think of a bronk shedding its hide.

Most cowboys would have been cussing and swearing for days after pulling leather, or as the paper had so ungraciously headlined: *Skeeter Bill Who Nearly Pulled the Horn off the Saddle.* She'd heard all kinds of excuses and defenses from disappointed cowboys, and cowgirls, too, for that matter. For anyone in the rodeo business, "pulling leather" was a sin right next to "thou shalt not kill" but for Bill, it was a reason to laugh, not only at himself, but with all the cowboys who had ever boasted that there had never been a horse born they couldn't ride.

The last light had now faded and the chill was beginning to be uncomfortable.

"Let's take this back to the dining table," Bill suggested as he stood and stretched.

Sue led the procession back into the house.

"What's next for you two?" she asked as they all settled into chairs around the dining table.

Bill answered for the two of them.

"We've got some offers for some moving picture shows. We're gonna check out an outfit in Salt Lake and if that don't pan out, we'll head on back to California. We gotta be back there anyway before too long."

Dorothy and Bill exchanged smiles.

"Yuh can take this one," Bill said.

"You've probably heard that San Francisco is hosting a huge celebration next year, well, actually starting the first part of December of this year," Dorothy explained, "though the 101 Ranch shows there don't start until February.

"Officially, the Panama Pacific International Exhibition is celebrating the opening of the Panama Canal. There's some say, though, that the powers that be are most interested in showing off how well San Francisco has recovered from that earthquake – eight, ah, nine years ago."

Bill continued the thought, "It's gonna be just like any other fair – only bigger. Lots bigger. No tents or big tops, though. They been buildin' what they like to call palaces an' halls an' towers – yuh name it – for displays and such from countries all 'round the world. Got theirselves their own Grand Canyon and Yellowstone Park in the part of the grounds that involves us – it's called The Zone."

"Hummm, yes," Sue nodded, "Yes, I think you told me that you'd been hired to do some kind of riding for it."

"All sorts of entertainment and concessions are in the Zone," said Dorothy. "Food and the like, just as you would find at county and state fairs, only much, much more so, I guess, being a World's Fair," Dorothy nodded across at Bill. "101 Ranch hired Bill . . . uhm . . . Roy and me both to ride in their afternoon rodeo shows in The Zone. It's a Wild West Show, only it's not touring or going anywhere. Afternoon and evening rodeos, parades through the arena. Indians play acting attacks on pioneers.

Cowboys play acting soldiers to the rescue. I'm looking forward just to riding! Bronks, not buffalo."

"Buffalo?" Sue shook her head in disdain.

"Oh, yeah, some do," Bill nodded. "Gads, Mum, it's crazy. Not only are they wantin' the Wild West Show but they're buildin' re-creations of all sorts a Pacific Island villages, Hawai'i and Jay-pan and who knows what else. Workin' model a the Panama Canal. I s'pose it'll be great for folks who've never been to those places.

"Me an' Dot, we walked through the grounds a couple a months ago. Lord, I cain't wait to see how they finish up a gawdawful contraption they're gonna call the Aeroscope. There's a 'car,' they call it, but it's like a two story buildin', little bigger 'n this house, built a steel and attached to the end of a bridge lookin' thing. For a couple a bucks a person, the bridge, or crane, rather, hoists the car an' about a hundred folks over 200 feet into the air."

The look of shock on Sue's face was priceless, Dorothy thought.

"I can't imagine which might be worse, ascending into the air in a steel box or flying in one of those flimsy looking kites they call aeroplanes," Sue said shaking her head.

Dorothy laughed. "Well, Bill and I took rides in those kites, as you say, both in San Francisco last summer and down in Douglas at the state fair last week. I've decided I quite like flying."

Sue nodded, trying to create a mental image picture of such a place - trying to picture the huge numbers of people who would be going to the Exposition - enough to fill the grandstands every afternoon? Every evening? And filling it for months? She shrugged and sipped her coffee as a mantel clock began tolling the hour.

"Oh, my!" she said startled, realizing how late the time had gotten. "It's high time you children all get to bed. No, go on now. Yes, you, too, Billy. Roy and Dot will still be here in the morning."

The girls reluctantly kissed their mother goodnight before making their way up the stairs to their bedroom, though Billy just muttered, "Good night" as he started for the stairs.

"Now, Roy," Sue smiled across her coffee cup at her son, "I hear tell that Mr and Mrs Skeeter Bill Robbins were staying at the LaBonte Hotel last week while in Douglas for the state fair."

"Yes, ma'am," Bill answered his mother. "Telephones in every room."

"No! In every room? Whatever for?" Sue was incredulous. Robbins Roost was miles from the nearest electric lines, let alone a telephone wire.

"I s'ppose so yuh could ring up anybody yuh wanted in the privacy of yer own room. Don't need to go down to the lobby or nothin'."

"And did you make a telephone call to anyone?" Sue was still in awe the situation. "Do Dorothy's folks have a telephone?"

"I'm sure they don't," Dorothy replied quickly, uncomfortable discussing her family back in Winnipeg. "It's little beyond their means."

109

Sue nodded in agreement and understanding. Suddenly she remembered she'd been interrupted in the middle of her line of questioning.

"All right then. You two stayed at the LaBonte. Why haven't I heard any wedding bells?"

Before Bill could start in, Dorothy said, "There are a few complications in Canada we need to sort out before we can officially tie the knot."

She blushed and reached for Bill's hand across the table. Since that the postponement of their marriage plans had been because of her situation, Dorothy felt that it fell to her to explain.

"I'm proud when folks have called me Mrs Robbins, though," she said, smiling across the table, looking Sue in the eye. "After a time, it seems useless to keep correcting them, especially since it won't be long now before it'll be a matter of fact."

"Well, then," Sue hesitated, weighing her words carefully.

"Roy, since half of Converse County – well, the half that reads the *Enterprise*, already thinks you're on your honeymoon, will it be any trouble for the two of you to settle into Grandmum's little cabin for the duration of your stay?" Sue asked, smiling as she noticed the relief on her son's face.

Bill beamed across the table at his mother.

"I'd say that's no trouble, no trouble a' tall," before adding, "Better'n what I was expectin'. I was thinkin' I'd have to be bunkin' with Bird an' Billy – they still upstairs? Or they out in a bunkhouse somewheres?"

Before his mother could answer, Bill went on, "And Dot, here, I's 'fraid she'd hafta be snuggled in between those two girls. Not that she'd a minded, but might a got a little crowded. Probably would a had a tussle or two over who got the blankets."

"Tss." Sue laughed softly and shook her head. "Just don't let the pastor hear about it."

"Hear 'bout what?"

Those at the table were unaware that Dub had walked into the kitchen coming in the back door.

"We don't need the pastor worrying that Roy has not been to church services in a very long time," Sue answered smoothly, irritated to be walked in on, interrupted and questioned all in one breath.

"Humh," Dub snorted, clearly doubting but not willing to insist on further intrusion into the conversation. "Just thought you should know that Bird is goin' to go with me down to Deer Creek with the sheep. Leavin' in the mornin', we are. Got the sheep wagon packed and ready this afternoon."

Sue closed her eyes and took in a deep breath before turning to speak with her husband.

"I believe we discussed that Billy would be accompanying you the next time you went to move the sheep to new pasture. He's anxious to go. He's ready to learn. It is high time he begin learning the business."

"No-ah, Mrs. Kimball, not this time," Dub retorted quickly. Firmly. "First, I don't need any flighty little kid runnin' around and spookin' the flock. Second, young Bill needs to stay right here and attend to his schoolin'. He's only 'leven. His education is his first concern at this age."

"I believe that when Bird was that age, he spent the summer following the flock on his own."

"This was different," Dub blustered. "Bird and myself will be gone for the entire winter, not just a few weeks. And Bird is a different cut of cloth from Little Bill. He's been serious minded since the day he was born. Never have to tell him more'n once the hows and whys of doin' things. Why, I give him a job and by Gawd, he gets it done. Don't have to spend all my time tellin' him every single thing or every little step of the way. He thinks things through without havin' to come runnin' to me to tell him how to get the job done but as I said before, we'll be gone for the winter, not just a few weeks."

Dorothy could see the color rising in Sue's face.

"You'll be gone for the winter? When did you decide this?"

"I've said my piece," Mr. Kimball said, "I've made up my mind, woman. Don't waste my time arguin' with me."

Dorothy heard Bill's sharp intake of breath as he stood to face his step-father. Undaunted, Mr Kimball drew himself to his full height, which was still a half-head shorter than his wife.

"Good night to you, Mr Robbins. I'm a-thankin' you for your visit to your mother for you must know that your absence, as well as those of all her sons, breaks her heart."

He turned to Dorothy. "Good night, Mrs Robbins," he said stiffly.

Dorothy's embarrassment was more for Mr. Kimball's rudeness and sharpness than in his reference to her as Bill's wife.

Mr. Kimball turned to his wife and simply nodded in her direction.

"Good night, Mrs. Kimball. Bird and I will be leavin' before dawn so we'll be sleepin' in the sheep wagon. Don't want to be disturbin' your sleep." And with that he stepped out the front door while slamming his battered gray felt hat on his head.

Dorothy sat in stunned silence looking from Bill to his mother. Bill was furious while Sue's face was a mixture of both anger and embarrassment.

"That pig-headed prig!" she fumed. "I swear he is the most gawd awful contrary man who was ever born to walk this earth. If it had been his idea to take Billy to the lower pastures, neither hell nor high water nor a mother's tears could have stopped him! On the other hand, since I'm the one who brought up the notion, nothing will convince him to take him."

Bill suddenly let loose terse laughter as he swept his mother into a bear hug, swinging her off of her feet, surprising both Sue and Dorothy.

"Mum, yuh got spunk an' a mouth that would make any cowboy proud! Give yuh that!" he said as set her gently set her feet back down on the floor.

Sue's mood brightened a little before she went on, "He never interferes with neither how I am raising the girls nor keeping house and garden. I must say, he does right by Bird, but I am afraid that the school of life will have a few hard knocks for Billy as he grows older."

She laughed now and added, "Though thinking on it, Billy will be under the direct instruction of his mum for the next three or four months. No interference from Himself!"

They all laughed in agreement to her logic.

"Let's check out Grandmum's cabin," she said as she lit a lantern before stepping out into the darkness of the yard.

Bill wound his fingers gently through Dorothy's, leaned over to kiss her and whispered, "Welcome to our little patch of heaven," as they followed Sue through the darkness of the yard and up the short lane to the tiny homesteader's cabin.

XV – 5 OCTOBER 1914 – AN HOUR SHORT OF BEING BURNT

Apples. Cinnamon. Cloves. Dorothy closed her eyes and inhaled deeply as she stirred the gently simmering pot. Aromas of autumn, promising comfort in coming winter evenings. Sue and Bill were coring and peeling another peck of apples to begin again the process of another kettle of apple butter. Fingers flew through the task as questions and answers flew back and forth. Dorothy marveled at the sense of serenity and calm that filled the kitchen.

This morning before dawn, Dorothy had awakened in darkness to the sound of sheep bleating, harness chains jangling, and horses snorting. All that hustling was just outside the windows of Grandmum's one-room cabin - it almost sounded as if she were in the middle of the muddle and surrounded by sheep and horses. For a brief moment, she couldn't remember where she was and she reached across the bed for Bill, and found his side of the bed to be still warm but empty. She sat up, rubbing her eyes, and then squinting to try to see anything at all in the dankness of the pre-twilight. Above all the else, she could hear whistles and calls from Bird and Dub, as the team of horses leaned into their collars to pull the sheep wagon and the dogs got the flock of sheep moving across the valley. She could tell, though, that all the noise really was outside so she relaxed a little.

The cabin was chilly. Dorothy wondered if the fire Bill had built in the small parlor stove last night had burned down to coals and was maybe even out. She curled back into the featherbed and pulled up the quilts, thankful for their warmth. Like a nest, she thought, a nest of comfort and security.

Contentedly, she sighed and closed her eyes as the sounds of the two men and their animals got further and further away.

"So much for not disturbin' our sleep," Bill said drily, his voice cutting through the stillness of the cabin.

Eyes wide and following the sound of his voice, Dorothy could now make out his silhouette next to one of the windows.

"Good morning," she said. "Did you sleep well?" How many times had her mother asked the same question?

Bill chuckled softly. "But a course, I did. Had me a little heater to keep me warm."

Dorothy was thankful for the darkness covering her flusters. Sharing their bed was now a matter of fact, but she still felt shy talking about it.

"Looks to me that Mum was up hours ago, cookin' breakfast and gettin' ready for the rest of the day. Lamps're lit over at the house."

Indeed, Sue May's kitchen had been warm, inviting and full of smells not only of breakfast, but of the beginnings of supper as well. The girls and Billy had finished their breakfasts and were packing lunch pails getting ready for school. Their chatter and laughter was missing now that they had gone for the day.

"Dot, come sit and have a cup of coffee with us."

Bill's invitation brought her back to the present as he and his mother washed the apple juice from their hands.

"Roy was telling me all about Cheyenne - now that stories can be told without interruption," she snorted. She pulled the coffee pot from the back of the stove and poured three mugs of her hot strong brew.

Dorothy carefully set the large wooden spoon onto a saucer being used as a spoon rest before sitting at the kitchen table.

"Pretty cozy here in the kitchen," Dorothy observed, stirring sugar and canned milk into her coffee. "Is there a secret to your apple butter?"

Sue's laugh sparkled, delightful and welcoming.

"No secret, as that would imply only I own the recipe. Fact is most every recipe I know is thanks to a good-hearted woman in this valley who felt sorry for Frank and my kids."

"Yer *kids*, Mum? I thought only nannies had kids." Bill grinned, teasing his mother's words.

"Go on, Roy! If I can use my neighbors' recipes, I can use the way they talk. No harm in blending in a little.

"So, Maria Heiser, she's been our neighbor for years," she continued. "She's a German-born lady and bigger hearted woman I've never known. She lives up the road just a little ways and she came by one afternoon years and years ago. She was bringing me a big mess of apples and I made the comment that we would never get them eaten before they went bad, even if I put them in the cellar.

" 'Vat?' she said, 'Dey vill go bat? Ach! Dere's pies und cider und butter you can make from dem. Und after all dat, den you slice da rest, sprinkle first vid sugar und den cinnamon und den you dry dem.' She was horrified that even one apple would go to waste.

"Needless to say, she was in my kitchen many afternoons that fall. So, if the apple butter recipe is a secret, then it is Maria's."

"So Maria is still your neighbor?" Dorothy asked.

"Oh, yes! We'll walk over one afternoon. You'll like her, I'm sure. According to Maria, it's an easy recipe to remember. 'Funf, Vier, Drei, Zwei, Eins,' she'd say. Five, four, three, two, one."

Sue counted down on the fingers of her left hand.

"Five pounds of apples, peeled and cored, four cups of sugar – sometimes less, sometimes more – three teaspoons of cinnamon, two pinches of salt, and one pinch of ground cloves."

The first homesickness she had felt in years crept over Dorothy as she remembered her mother counting the ingredients in her Oma's borscht recipe. She was surprised. She hadn't missed them at all for a long time. She wondered if her father or mother ever worried about her, ever wondered where she might be, what she was doing.

Bill cleared his throat as he reached across the table for her hand. She looked up at him. He was watching her expression with concern.

"Ever'thin' all right?" he asked, raising an eyebrow. "Yuh look worried. Yuh shouldn't be. It's just cooked down applesauce, an hour shy of bein' burnt, Dad used to say."

Sue reached across the table and covered both of their hands with hers.

"What is it, darlin'?" Sue was clearly concerned.

Dorothy half-smiled and shrugged.

"I've been gone from home a few years now and most days there is not one thing I miss. Not one, but listening to you talk about your neighbor and her recipe, well, it must be that I miss home and especially my mother more than I realized."

Sue nodded.

"Many was the day in the first years we were married, I wondered if my parents had gotten over me marrying Frank, if they'd approve of how I was raising their grandchildren. Come to realize after a time, it's only myself I need to worry about. Couldn't have changed them or their minds if I'd tried."

Silence settled over the kitchen as Dorothy listened to the slow bubbling of the apples simmering in their kettles. Now and then, a stick popped in the fire of the wood cook stove. Dorothy realized she could even hear the cackle and clucking of the hens out in the farm yard.

Sue got to her feet and dished up some apple cake for the three of them.

"Just something to tide us over until dinner," she explained.

She set the plates on the table, poured more coffee and asked once again, "Now, Dorothy, what did you think of Cheyenne?"

Dorothy laughed as she stirred her coffee. Cheyenne was something she could talk about forever, or so it seemed and all the while take her mind off of a tiny kitchen back in Winnipeg.

"From the minute Bill and I stepped off of the train at the Union Pacific Depot on the evening we got there until we boarded again heading back to Reno, everything went by in a blur. So much to do. So much to see. So much happened." She stopped for a bite of cake. Black walnuts, chopped fine, were a delightful surprise.

"First off, the depot. It looks more like a castle than a train station. There I was, trying to take in the grandeur of it all, the clock tower, the beige sandstone wings, the gorgeous arches built of russet colored sandstone, when all the sudden Bill started hollering down the platform.

"'Hey, Harry! Down here!' and here came this tall, lanky cowboy hurrying to greet us. No doubt whatsoever in my mind that he was anything but one of Bill's brothers.

" 'Roy! You old cuss!' Harry shouted back. 'You been away too long!'

"There they were, the two of them were pounding each other on the back, practically dancing on the platform."

Dorothy's own eyes were dancing as she looked over at Bill. He was nodding in agreement, while enjoying his own cake and coffee.

"'But I'm home now,' Bill says to his brother, 'least till the rodeo's over.'"

"Then Harry caught sight of me, I swear the cat got his tongue. Still grinning, his look toward Bill said it all, wondering just who I was.

"So Bill asked Harry if he read the papers, but Harry shook his head and said he didn't have time for such stuff.

"Then Bill introduced me to his 'little' brother, Mr. Harry Robbins, top bucking horse rider of Glenrock, Wyoming."

"Yeah, an' then I introduced 'im to Miss Dorothy Morrell, moving picture actress and famed bronk rider formerly of Winnipeg, Canada. More recently California," Bill added, grinning at the memory.

"Oh, and remember what you said next?" Dorothy asked.

"The part about Harry being top rider just 'cause I ain't around?" Bill answered and Dorothy and his mother laughed with him. "Though truth be told, Harry can outride me most any day of the week . . ."

". . . and twice on Sunday," his mother finished, smiling broadly. "Though, you two really should learn take the Lord's Day off."

Dorothy's face softened as she went on with her story.

"Sue, just watching them, anyone could see how much they cared for each other, how they'd missed each other's company. Though the two of them reminded me of school boys – pushing, joking, laughing, all the while trying to outdo each other. It was good to have Harry come to Pendleton last month. Your boys are easy to be around. You raised them well."

Dorothy suddenly realized there was hint of tears gathering in Sue's eyes which she quickly blinked away. Dorothy quickly went on, changing the subject.

"First thing we had to attend to after getting a good night's sleep in Cheyenne was to talk to the newspaper men and get our pictures made."

"Oh, shoot," Bill added. "I thought the only thing to making a picture was settin' or standin' still while the camera man flashed his powder. Little did I know!"

Dorothy added, "A few years ago, a reporter from a California newspaper made what I thought was a really big fuss over just how I was to stand, how to tilt my head, where to hold my hands, but he had nothing on Mr. Joe, the man in Cheyenne."

"Yup, this Joe fella had Dottie standin' in front of a 'backdrop.' Least that's what he called it. Looked like a dirty sheet to me. Then he begun to arguin' with himself. 'We shall have you stand just like this . . .' He took her by the shoulders and squared her to the camera. 'No, no, that'll never do,' he mutters to hisself. He quarters her and then runs back to his camera and squints through the 'view finder.' Didn't know the view was lost. 'Oh, no . . .' he says again. Bustled hisself back over to Dottie and started all over agin. He finally throws his hands in the air and sets her down on the floor. Had her cross her ankles."

"Oh, goodness!" Dorothy interrupted, shaking her head. "All I could think was what a fit my mother would have had if she could see me sitting like that even if I was wearing one of those split skirts."

"You looked mighty fine. Always do." Bill winked at her and then continued.

"'You, mister,'" he says to me, 'we need yer rope and hat for this lady. Pronto! Step lively now!' He snatched up my rope and begins to fuss about just how her hands is to be holdin' it and whether it's to draped acrost her lap or over her knee. Gawd, what a fuss-budget."

Dorothy smiled, remembering the day.

"The photographer was so busy attending to the rope, that Bill took the business of setting his own hat on my head. He leaned down and whispered to me that it was a ten-gallon crown any Buckeroo Queen could be proud to wear."

"That Mr. Skeeter Bill Robbins surely does have a way with words," Sue chuckled, picturing in her mind the comings and goings, the rounds and abouts in the photographer's studio.

"I had never laid eyes on that man before and he had the nerve to call me *sweetheart*," remembered, Dorothy fuming a little.   She pointed a finger and mimicked the fussy little man's voice.   "'Okay, sweetheart, chin up, no, don't look at me - look away from the camera - ahh, no, chin down - that's it!   That's it! Much better!   Perfect.   Just perfect.'   All that work and for just one picture!"

"So then I gave Bill his hat back and now it was my turn to stand back and watch. As Joe turned and arranged Bill, pacing back and forth to peer through his viewfinder, Bill became quite bored, I'd say.   'Mind if I smoke?' Bill asked Joe. 'Not at all.   Not at all,' Joe said watching Bill for a few seconds.   All of the sudden he quickly stepped back behind his tripod and camera and started snapping an image of Bill as he began the process of rolling his cigarette all the while continuing to talk to himself.   'Easy now.   Easy does it.'"

"Inside the building?   You know better than to smoke indoors!" Sue was as indignant as if he'd just been caught smoking in her kitchen rather than some place in Cheyenne months ago.

"Now, Mum!   Joe, hisself, was puffin' away on a cigar that stunk so bad I figured the tobacco musta come from a skunk farm.   Rollin' my own was next best thing to self-defense," Bill justified himself.

Dorothy laughed at the two bantering good-naturedly across the table at each other.

"Joe was as pleased as he could be.   I would have thought the way he was carrying on that Bill's picture was the best picture of his whole career. Then he was shooing us out of his tiny, cramped so-called studio, all the while muttering about developing and printing before his deadline.   All that fuss and feathers about rushing - Bill's picture didn't appear in the paper until a week later, the opening day of the rodeo."

"Yeah, but, Dottie, darlin', don't forget, yer picture an' story beat mine to print!"

"Only by a day or two," Dorothy countered, turning her attention to her apple cake while Sue got up and went to the stove to bring back the coffee pot.

"Dorothy, I've got something for you," she said as she topped of their mugs.   "Well, the two of you.   No, no. Sit tight," she continued as she gathered the empty plates from the table and set them into the dish pan. "I'll be right back."

When she returned from her bedroom, she was carrying a medium sized flat bundle wrapped in butcher paper and tied with string.

"Supposed to be a wedding present, but now is as good a time as any to give it to you," Sue said, almost shyly as she offered Dorothy the package, laying it on the table in front of her and Bill.   "You two be sure to send me word when the day comes you've officially tied the knot."

Dorothy was surprised and overcome.   Here she had just met Sue a day or two ago, and yet the giving of the gift showed Dorothy clearly how pleased Sue was to include her into the Robbins family.

"Why, thank you!" Dorothy murmured as she pulled on the end of the string to loosen the knot.   As she unwrapped the paper, inside she found a large flat box which contained a book, a strange looking book, bound in faux-leather containing pages of heavy black paper.   Beautiful gilt patterns were embossed into the front cover, as well as the words "*Mr. and Mrs. Roy 'Skeeter Bill" Robbins.*"   Puzzled, she looked to Sue for an explanation.

"Haven't you seen a scrapbook before?" Sue asked.

"No." Dorothy wondered why anyone would need a book for scraps, and what kind of scraps would go into it.

"Dottie, you mean your mum didn't have a scrapbook she kep' little bits of this or that in?" Bill jumped into the conversation.

"Scraps of what?" Dorothy asked, still puzzled.

"Not really scraps," Sue began.   "Here let me show you."

Sue was beaming like Christmas morning as she opened the book to its first pages and turned them to face Dorothy.   Carefully attached to the first page were side by side photographs, actually postcards, of both her and Bill.

"Oh! Oh, my," Dorothy exclaimed, amazed and surprised at the picture postcard of herself.   She hadn't even been aware that picture had been taken though she remembered the moment quite clearly.   In the picture, she was standing sideways to the photographer, whoever he had been.   It had obviously not been Ralph Doubleday.   The neatly written inscription at the bottom of the picture had none of the characteristics of Mr Doubleday's back-slanted block-style printing, but reading the words brought back again the thrills and joy of the day.   "*Dorothy Morrell And Her Prize Saddle Won at Cheyene, Wyo 1914.*"

Never mind the spelling, Dorothy smiled to herself as she studied her face in profile.   She clearly remembered smiling as she carried the heavy saddle with both hands, nearly tripping over its stirrups as she had made her way across the open area to Bill.   She slowly traced the edge of the photograph with her fingers, remembering the smell of the fine tooled leather, the squeaking as different parts of the saddle rubbed against one another, the weight of it in her arms as the realization of what she had accomplished sank in.   She had laid claim to the title *Ladies Bucking Bronk Champion of the World* – at least in the opinion of the folks at the *Daddy of 'em All.*

"However did you ever come by this?" she asked Sue, still fingering the smooth surface of the postcard.

Bill laughed, enjoying his part in Dorothy's surprise.

"Mind you, I had no idea Mum would be giving this card back to you, but look at this," he said as he carefully maneuvered the postcard out of the black corner tabs.   Instantly, Dorothy recognized Bill's handwriting before she even read the inscription.

"And I ask again, however did you come by this? I haven't seen one like it," Dorothy repeated.

"Let's just say, I know how to shop," was all Bill would say.

Next to the picture postcard of her, was one of Bill. The photographer had caught the bucking bronk mid-buck, both forelegs high in the air looking like a boxer ready to punch out his opponent. Bill was sitting straight backed in the saddle, almost standing in the stirrups and true to form, holding his hat high over his head in his right hand. Dorothy nodded, thinking back to how she had watched Bill take this ride. She didn't need to read the inscription which read *"Skeeter Bill on Tanglefoot"* to remember this ride, dust kicked up and scattered to the summer breeze by this horse, grunting and snorting, as it had battled through its dangerous duel with Bill.

"I believe ol' Joe, who brags hisself as 'The Official Photographer' for Frontier Days, did a damn fine job with this here photograph," Bill mused, wrapped in his own memories of the day. He had placed second in the Amateur Bucking Contest. Not bad, not bad, he thought to himself, considering the caliber of bronk riders attracted to the contests in Cheyenne.

"So this is what you put into a scrapbook?" asked Dorothy. "Picture postcards?"

"Yes, and anything else, really, that catches your fancy," Sue replied. "Me, I'd be making sure that newspaper clipping of Skeeter Bill's famous leather-pulling ride got included in here, and every other mention of the either of you in the newspapers, postcards, or on fair bills - if you can come by them," she added as she turned to the next page in the scrapbook. Newspaper clippings from the Cheyenne paper were pasted onto the page. Dorothy laughed as she sat looking at the very photographers she and Bill had just described to Sue.

"I guess one last thing that amazed me about Cheyenne was the incredible number of people who came to celebrate Frontier Days," Dorothy said, pointing to one of the paragraphs in one of the newspaper clippings. "Here it predicts that 25,000 tourists were expected to show up. That doesn't even include all us cowgirls and cowboys!"

"And the Indians," Bill added. "Town a Cheyenne was bustin' at the seams with all a us and then all them Cheyenne an' Arapahos who was invited down to play act battle scenes for the crowds." He was quiet for minute. "Too bad them fellers always had to lose. Didn't always turn out that way back then."

"All too soon, the rodeo was over." Dorothy's voice was almost sad as she remembered the crowds of passengers waiting for either the east or west out of Cheyenne.

"This year was golden. Bill and I had the best time. We'll go back again, but it will all be different. It'll never be the same."

Dorothy sighed as she turned yet another page. A newspaper clipping had been carefully pasted onto the middle of the page. Dorothy read the title out loud, "Wyoming Boy Making Good."

Bill ducked his head and lifted his coffee cup, forgetting though to take a sip as Dorothy skimmed down through the article.

"Hmm," and then she read aloud, "*During the Cheyenne Celebration he will be married on horseback to a charming young woman from the coast, they afterwards spending their honeymoon in this section with the groom's mother at her ranch.*"

"And here we are!" Bill said with a grin. "Must be our honeymoon."

"You!" Dorothy grinned back. She closed the album to return it to its box.

"What is this?" She lifted a small glass bottle labeled *David's General Mucilage* from the box.

"Oh, that's to put onto the back of anything you want to glue into your book and then this envelope has picture corners. Here let me show you how they work."

Sue opened back to the first page and pointed out the tiny black triangles at each corner of the postcards. "You slip them onto postcards or photographs. They already have a coat of mucilage on their backs so you just moisten the back." Her eyes twinkled. "I usually just lick them and then you can arrange them onto your page."

"Ahhh, thank you!" Dorothy was moved with the gift from this lovely woman, Bill's mother and someday soon, her mother-in-law. "This is such a treasure."

"You just keep adding to it. It'll grow! You be sure to bring it with you anytime you come back to visit."

"Of course, of course," Dorothy assured her, once more turning her attention to stillness, not a lack of sounds but a lack of busyness.

How peaceful, she thought. So far from the hustle of the arenas, the shouts of the riders and wranglers, the snorting and pawing of horses and cattle. The solitude enveloped her, the miles and miles of forested hills and mountains created an insulating rampart, keeping the world at bay. Her world, she mused. At this moment, her own struggles were the ones far away.

But not Sue's. She shook her head. She guessed that for Sue the barrier might be reversed, an almost impenetrable barricade keeping her from the world in which she had been born and raised. Far from the expectations of her father and perhaps even her mother. Creating challenges in maintaining the homestead she and her first husband had carved from the sagebrush and rocky ground. Hard to tell, even harder to talk about.

* * *

All too soon the time to spend in Boxelder was gone.

The weeks had flown by in whirlwinds of activities. Community dances with homegrown musicians at the school house, celebrated with potluck suppers, breaking up just in time to watch the sunrise, any leftovers from supper turning to makeshift breakfasts. Other mornings, horseback rides, just she and Bill, through frosty pastures and then into the hills blazing with golden aspen and scarlet sumac behind the homestead house. The quiet afternoon spent at the solemn final resting places of Benjamin Franklin Robbins and his dearest daughter, his only daughter Frances Pearl. A stark stone monument served as the marker for both graves.

Before long, a morning dawned that held no promises of lazy luxury, had no supper leftovers with which to celebrate the new day, no enticing promises of explorations or excursions. Neighborly visits had come to an end. Bill's and Dorothy's bags and trunks had been packed and were now carefully loaded into the automobile.

In the chill of the morning air, Bill folded his mother into his arms. Sue clung to him in silence for long minutes, silent tears streaking her face as she hid it in Bill's shirtfront. Dorothy stood watching in awkward silence, wondering anew if her own mother had ever cried such tears in the past few years since she had left home.

Bill tenderly stroked his mother's head and shoulders until at last she stepped back and out of his embrace.

"You take care, son," was all she said as Bill tried to assure her that he and Dot would be back, perhaps in the fall of next year. If not the coming year, then surely the next. She simply shook her head and repeated, "Take care, now. Take care of you and take care of Dot."

Bill sighed as he stooped to give her one last kiss upon her cheek. Dorothy embraced her as well, quickly kissing her on both cheeks before climbing into the passenger seat of the car. Bill took his seat as well and put the car into gear.

No more words were needed, none were said, as the car slowly left the farmyard and Bill steered their way passed potholes and rocks. After the first mile or so had passed, they crested the hill that would take them around the bend in the road and out of sight of the Robbins homestead. Bill braked the car and he and Dorothy turned for a last look across the valley.

Dorothy was startled to realize that Sue had not moved from the spot at which she had been embraced and kissed farewell. Dorothy raised her hat and waved good-bye.

Good-bye for now.

XVI – 14 APRIL 1915 – HELL BENT FOR LEATHER

An afternoon ride that had started as so many others. Settling into the saddle. Finding her stirrups. Hat down tight. Rope gripped firmly in her left hand. Right arm up. And then the gate burst open – the bronk charged head down out of the gate into the arena, kicking hind legs high.

Gritting her teeth, she leaned forward as the bronk's forelegs punched its front quarters up off the ground momentarily only to come down hard. Twisting beneath her, the bronk kicked first one hind leg and then the other in quick succession as Dorothy leaned back, keeping rhythm with her mount.

But now a stirrup lost. Then suddenly off-center. Desperation clawed her guts. Flailing fingers. Harried right hand grasping for a hold on the saddle, closing on thin air. Twisting. The horse below, her body above. Now her free leg - the right one free from the stirrup - tangled with her left one as she desperately kicked, urgent in her efforts to be free herself from being hung up. Cross-wise, still clinging to her rein, wind knocked from her as her chest and abdomen bounced off the seat and the cantle.

Up - for a split second up. Almost flying - floating. Hanging midair. Tangling. Falling face first. Gagging. Dirt. Gasping. Dust.Grinding. Hooves. Piston. Hammer. Pain. Hammer. Bones snapping. Screaming. Hooves. Oh, God, the hooves.

Dorothy pulled her arms over her head, still face down as she tried to roll away from the hooves. Instantly pain screamed through first her legs and then her torso and she collapsed back down face first into the dust, dirt and dried manure of the arena floor. Slowly the pounding and hammering moved away from her as men rushed to her side.

She moved her hands under her chest to try to push herself up, but other hands quickly soothed and held her shoulders firmly.

"Shhhhhhhh, be still. Still now. Don't try to move. Shhhhhhh!"

Dorothy relaxed for a moment aware that somewhere someone was still screaming.

"Shhhh, baby, shhhhh." Was it Bill? *God, what was he doing in the arena?*

Hardened, calloused hands tenderly stroked her shoulders, calming the desperation still burning in her belly. 'Oh, God! Let it be Bill,' she prayed. 'Let it be Bill.'

"Shhhhhh, baby girl, be still, now."

The screaming had stopped but now she could feel the slick of muck coating her face. Dorothy turned her head to spit. She coughed and cleared her throat and spit again.

"That's right, that's all right. Shhhh, still now. Still." A different voice had joined the first. "You'll be all right. Shhhhh."

"Shhhhhh, girl. They're sending out a stretcher," yet another voice joined in.

Oh, God! This is worse than I thought.

Dorothy cringed at the thought of being carried from the arena.

"No!" She was surprised to find her throat raw and sore.

"No," she repeated still face down but trying to push up again with both hands. "I can walk off by myself."

"No, darlin', yuh cain't." She was sure now it was Bill. "Yuh be still now and wait for the docs to do their work."

Now his face was near the ground, even with hers. "Yuh just had a goddamn bad wreck there, Dot. Scared the shit right outta ever'body. Yuh just gotta trust us and just be still."

"Bill, oh, God, please, Bill! Can't you just hold me up? Can't you just help me out of here?" she whispered through tears and gritted teeth. "I promise I won't scream any more. I'll just lean on you. We'll get out of here."

"No, baby, you don't understand." Bill's eyes were misting now and his voice hardened. "Dammit! I ain't no doc, but even I can see plain as day that you ain't gonna be walkin' anywhere for a while. Especially not outta here!"

He stroked her hair.

"Please, Dottie, just trust that we'll getcha outta here!" Bill was pleading now as Dorothy struggled to reach for one of his hands as he sat back on his heels.

"Can you at least roll me over?" Dorothy begged, turning her head the best she could to look Bill in the eyes.

"No, uh - no," Bill shook his head and rolled forward to kneel, then hunched down next to her. Face to face, nose to nose.

"Dottie, nobody's gonna move you 'less it's the docs," he whispered. "Dadgum, girl, it's that bad. Yer one tore up cowgirl."

Dread began to cloud Dorothy's mind. She'd been thrown before. She'd had plenty of awkward landings, but never had she been wracked with so much pain. Never had she been told not to move.

She closed her eyes and laid her forehead onto her hand. It seemed more than she could bear, the pain racking her body, the humiliation of being carried out of the arena, Bill's worry. No, not his worry. His fear.

"Give me room, folks," ordered a new voice. "Careful now. That's it. Easy does it."

Dorothy felt herself finally being rolled over carefully and slowly to her back. She gasped and grimaced as the new pair of hands began to carefully examine her right leg.

"Can we get these chaps off?"

"Just unbuckle 'em here," Bill answered as he stood and stepped back for the doctor.

Who cares about the damn chaps! Dorothy thought. *Just get me out of the middle of this god-awful arena!*

And just when Dorothy thought nothing could get worse, her skirts were being gently pulled away from her leg and she felt cool air running up her skin from her shins to her thigh. *What in the hell are they doing to me now?*

In desperation and humiliation, she kept her eyes closed, not wanting to see what was going on.

"Hooo, boy!" The medic's voice was tight with disbelief. "We have got to get her to a doctor and a medical center. Right now!"

"Get on over here as fast as you can," he yelled over his shoulder. He mumbled to himself. "Shoot, if I'd have known it was going this bad, I'd have had the ambulance just drive right on out here."

Dorothy opened her eyes to look into the face of a middle-aged man, obviously the medic. The urgency in his voice brought a new wave of fear.

"Bill! Bill, what is it?" Dorothy cried, looking around for him. He was standing just behind the medic, his face ashen.

"May I?" Bill didn't wait for an answer before he stepped forward and knelt next to her again. He took her hand as several men with a stretcher arrived and set it onto the ground next on the other side of her.

"You gotta be tough, kiddo," he said quietly as the medic and the men placed their hands underneath her. Quickly they lifted her just far enough off the ground to move her to the stretcher.

"Stop treating me like I'm gonna break and tell me just what the hell is going on!" Dorothy demanded through gritted teeth, determined not to start screaming again. Tears were again rolling down her cheeks.

"I'm thinkin' yer leg is broke. Yup, purty sure," was all Bill would say, still holding her hand and taking long steps next to her as the stretcher was hauled off the field led by the medics and surrounded by the curious, the determined and as always the newspaper reporters.

Later she wondered how much was memories and how much was dreams. Being enclosed in a small dark box. Or was it a room? Only this room swayed and bumped along, surrounded by the sounds of automobile traffic, the clang of street car bells, the hustle and cries of pedestrians. Moving sometimes forward, stopping at other times. Automobile horns honking. Blaring. Bill's voice far away at times, other times so close she could feel the breath of his whispers. Cold, so cold. Shivering, crying for blankets.

Lifted and carried, brought back into the light. Voices loud. Doors opening. Closing. Echoes, moving down hallways. Hands, fingers, prodding, pushing, pulling her leg. Pulling. Pulling. Screaming. Crying. Bill's voice. Had he been here or was she remembering other times, other whispered endearments? Shhhhhh, always, shhhhhhhh. A lullaby, Bill's lullaby.

And then silence. Almost silence. Whispered conversations swallowed up by corridors, muffled by doors, lost in the hum of the overhead fan.

The weight of her blanket embracing her body brought her to her senses. Twilight filled her room. Dusk or dawn, she couldn't tell. How long had she lain here?

Dorothy struggled to plump the pillow beneath her head, flattened by endless time spent lying on it. To her horror, she found that she could not move from the waist down, hampering her efforts to turn and reach behind her head.

"Here, darlin', let me do that fer yuh," Bill's voice was warm and husky. Likely he'd just woke up. Morning, then. He slid an arm under her shoulders to lift her while shaking the pillow back to shape.

"Morning, cowboy," Dorothy said. Bill nestled her back into her pillows and still bent, kissed her. Kissed her full on the lips, tenderly and gently. She closed her eyes and kissed him back.

"How yuh doin' this mornin'?" He grinned down at her. She smiled back up at him before answering.

"Give it to me straight, Bill. What's going on with my legs?"

"Still attached." He grinned his goofy Skeeter Bill sideways grin as he enclosed her hands in his. Was it her imagination or did he quickly glance away avoiding looking full on into her eyes?

"Goddammit, Bill! That's no answer."

"I know it ain't, but it's all I got fer now. Doc'll be around in a bit to check yuh over again."

"What all did they have to do for me?"

"Yer leg is broke, like I figgered," Bill began hesitantly. "B'fore they tried to set it, doc said they had a purty big mess to clean up. Lotsa scrapes and gashes. Dirt, mud. You know."

Bill seemed to be searching for words.

"You said 'tried to set.' Didn't they get that done?"

"Oh, well, yeah. It's been set but it's gonna be a while before yer on yer feet again," Bill answered vaguely.

"Mrs. Robbins, if I may."

A deep voice cut into their conversation. A sturdily built, gray-haired man stepped into the room, an unlit pipe clenched firmly between his teeth. He offered her his hand.

"Please, make it just Dorothy," she said reaching to shake his hand. Horrified, she realized her hands and arms were bruised and raw with freshly scabbed scrapes and cuts lacing their way up her forearms. She tore her eyes away from the carnage and tried to focus all her attention back on the doctor's words as he began his visit.

"Doctor Johannsen," he replied, introducing himself. "You are one lucky girl."

Oh, God, when was she ever going to get past being a girl? Was womanhood so hard to acknowledge, or was referring to girlhood a way to wield power over a woman? To remind her of 'her place' in life? Of the importance of taking heed to those perceived to be wiser than she?

Dorothy smiled wanly as she released his hand, mulling over her supposed luck while she nodded her assent.

"So I have been told," she hedged, while reminding herself that she had always worked damn hard for her luck. She slipped her hand back into Bill's fingers.

"Glad yer here, Doc. Glad yer here," Bill said perhaps a little too enthusiastically.

"Yer better 'n me at tellin' Dottie how things is," he quickly added.

"Now, Dorothy, both of the lower leg bones in your right leg – we call them the tibia and the fibula – were fractured, though not as badly as it would seem given your circumstances."

"Not as badly?" Dorothy asked, raising an eyebrow.

"Your situation would have been far more grave had the ends of your broken bones come through your skin," explained Dr. Johannsen. "We were able to manipulate the ends of the breaks back into position so they can begin their healing process. We have a temporary splint on your leg for now. We want your cuts to heal over somewhat and the swelling and bruising to go down before we cast your leg in a more permanent type of cast. Then if all heals well, you'll likely be able to be back on your feet in six to eight weeks."

Dorothy's spirits rose at the prognosis.

"More than enough time to get healed up for Cheyenne?" she asked.

"Cheyenne, Mrs. Robbins?" The doctor frowned as he pulled the pipe from his mouth. Dorothy looked up at Bill for support. His gaze was firmly fixed on a spot on the far wall in front of him.

"The rodeo at Cheyenne, Frontier Days," Dorothy explained, hope rising. "It's not until the middle of July and that's three months off. I'll be ready for Cheyenne."

"My dear young lady!" the doctor exploded, reinforcing his position of power and authority. "You are lucky, I repeat, lucky enough to be looking forward to walking again, but it is my professional opinion that you should *never* sit on a horse again, much less take part in that risky, daredevil, tomfoolery nonsense that has brought you and your health to this point."

Her delight was shattered. She swallowed hard, a lump in her throat and the beginnings of tears smarting her eyes. She blinked quickly as Bill now looked down into her eyes and the sadness in his face told her everything she needed to know.

She was not going to be riding in Cheyenne – not this year anyway! she told herself. But *never* is a long time, time enough to heal, to strengthen muscles again, to regain the rhythm of her life. Time enough to once again get back into the saddle and let 'er rip.

The doctor's demeanor softened slightly. "Mrs. Robbins, I understand your way of life has been on the back of a horse but things have gotten to the point you need to make some changes."

Dorothy gathered her gumption. "Truly spoken and I suppose that at this moment, some might expect me to say something ridiculous like I don't particularly care whether I live or die, but I do care. I care a lot. I care to live. On or off a horse, I care."

She squeezed Bill's hands in hers and fiercely repeated, "I care to live."

"Good! Good enough!" Dr. Johannsen nodded. "That is the attitude that will get you well on your way down the road to healing. That is your number one concern for now. The best care you can give your leg is to rest and recover. Soon enough, you'll be able to sort out a new direction for your life."

With a curt nod, he lifted his pipe and clamped it between his teeth as he turned and headed for the door. Just before leaving, he turned and repeated, "Mrs. Robbins, you truly are a blessed woman."

Bill gently squeezed her hand as the doctor finally made his exit. Dorothy listened to the sounds of footsteps as they faded down the hall before she turned to Bill.

"They shoot horses that break their legs," she said ruefully.

"You ain't no horse, and we're gonna get yuh back on yer feet before yuh know it," Bill replied.

Back on my feet in no time, but when will I be back in the saddle? Dorothy closed her eyes to shut out the uncertainties of the world. No amount of worrying was going to change things now.

XVII – 15 APRIL 1915 - "TUNE OF YOUR OLD LOVE SONG"

Dorothy's eyes sparkled, smiling first at the self-important looking reporter from a San Francisco newspaper who now sat at her bedside, pencil in hand, notebook open and then at his counterpart from Oakland. How the two of them managed to show up here at the same time was more than luck, Dorothy decided, it was divine providence. Two for one.

This was far more to her liking, being back in control of the story line of her life, instead of listening to her doctor preach doom and gloom.

She straightened up as best she could among her pillows, careful to keep her hands tucked under her blankets, bandages over the worst of the scrapes and cuts across her knuckles, while the cuffs of her long-sleeved bed jacket were hiding the bruises that covered the backs of her hands and made their way up her arms.

She hoped that the bouquets of flowers at her bedside were framing her to her best advantage. She had already sternly warned the reporters there would be no photographs taken today. The invincible Dorothy Morrell would never be caught on film with a shiner over one eye and bruises across her cheek and jaw, much less tucked into bed like a toddler ready for a nap.

"Hello, Mrs. Robbins, I'm Henry Davis. How are you?" Mr. San Francisco started out with the usual pleasantries though he seemed uncertain whether he should offer to shake her hand.

"And I'm Harold Metcalfe, from Oakland."

Metcalfe hung back a little, letting Davis take the lead for the moment. Dorothy smiled at the man, cuffs of his shirt rolled twice, stub of a pencil tucked over one ear; even from across the room, Dorothy could see that it was sharpened and ready.

"Please, I'm Dorothy. Dorothy Morrell. Feel free to call me Dorothy."
Is there an echo in here?

She stood firm on her decision to sabotage any thoughts of engaging in the hand shaking protocol by keeping hers out of sight.

"And, I'm doing as well as or even better than expected," Dorothy replied brightly, maintaining eye contact with Davis, her smile continued.

How in the world did this man expect her to reply? Surely not with complete honesty?

I'm layered with bruises from the soles of my feet - or at least that is how they feel - to the top of my head! In my right leg, the bones are cracked or broken in several places and it's wrapped like a mummy from the waist down. I'm sitting on a bedpan and that stuffy, self-righteous doctor 'believes' I've had enough laudanum 'for the time being.' Furthermore, his fellow doomsday doctors are telling me I should most assuredly never ride again and Joe Miller is beside himself with a half-dozen schemes to keep me in the spotlight - his spotlight. Not that he gives a damn about me, mind you, but I am on contract and by, gum, I had better be bringing him a return.

She shook off her self-centered, negative thoughts and nodded first at Mr. San Francisco, rather, Mr. Davis, still standing halfway between the doorway and her bedside. She noticed though that Mr. Metcalfe of Oakland had pulled up one of the several chairs in the room and was seated near the foot of the bed.

"Even so, they do tell me no matter what, I'm not to be out on any afternoon strolls down the Esplanade through the heart of the Exhibition, not any time soon."

She winked at the two as though inviting them to be a part of a grand conspiracy.

Davis shrugged off any invitation at being any part of dry humor as he casually flipped open his notebook, searching for a clean page on which to start his notes.

131

Metcalfe smiled, more kindly than indulgently.

"As you may know," she continued sweetly, practically gushing, "Mr. Robbins, ahh, Skeeter, here, was first to sign on to ride for the 101 Ranch Real Wild West Show during the Exposition here in San Francisco."

Joe Miller would be sure to appreciate that one, emphasis on *Real* and *Wild* and *West.*

"Bill brought me along to San Francisco to share in the applause from the Grandstand."

Bill ducked his head while shaking it with silent laughter. They both knew better. Both knew full well that, well, wild horses could not have kept Dorothy away from the Exposition whether she was a paid rider or simply sitting on the edge of her seat watching Bill or the many others ride. Metcalfe nodded encouragement, his sharpened pencil already busy.

Davis evidently had finally found a blank page and began to make a few notes. There really wasn't much to this story he thought. Not much more than a busted up, bruised up, probably washed up, soon-to-be has-been rodeo rider.

"It's been a great thrill for me to be riding for the folks who come to see the 101 Ranch in the Zone," she said, continuing to smile, all teeth, working her magic to try to pull Davis into her story - she could tell she already had Metcalfe hook, line and sinker. "As they like to say, *Near the head of the Zone - At the head of the List!*"

She nodded sagely, hoping that would get into the final copy as well. Metcalfe chuckled while he made notation. He had heard the Colonel - as Joe Miller prided himself in being called - use those very words. Davis, on the other hand, seemed to ignore the blatant plug and said nothing as he continued to scribble his notes.

Was he even writing about her, Dorothy wondered. It would be disappointing to discover lists of errands or other possible interviews or story leads instead of her well-practiced publicity plugs rehearsed over and again for one reporter after another.

Dorothy decided to change tactics.

"Can you believe the name of that horse?" She shook her head and frowned as if in great bewilderment. "The one that I tangled with? *Blondie* it was. *Blondie!* Such a dear name for such a wicked outlaw."

The memory of her disastrous unseating sent an unplanned, unpracticed and sudden shudder through her. Mr. Davis was still too busy scratching away on his notebook to notice.

What kind of reporter did he think he was? Or more importantly, just who was he to act as though interviewing the Canadian Cowgirl of Moving Picture Fame was some sort of a second rate story?

She forged on, wishing he'd at least glance up from his note taking now and again.

"Makes one think of the girl next door, I'd say," Metcalfe said, finally deciding if Davis wasn't going to chip in and help the conversation along, then by gum, it was up to him.

"I should think that *Hurricane's Hustle* or *Demon's Delight* would have been a better name," Dorothy added.

"Ah, yes.   Of course, Mrs. Robbins," Davis replied, hastily finishing a word or two before finally looking up.   He cleared his throat, mustering his courage before going on.

"I understand your doctors have announced that it is imperative that you never ride again."

Dorothy's gaze hardened as she sized up the pompous, arrogant know-it-all.

"That's what they tell me," she coldly replied, her smile frozen in place.

Davis stood and folded up his notebook.

"My sincere condolences, Mrs. Robbins.   Mr. Robbins," he added, nodding absently in Bill's direction.

Dorothy smiled wanly and replied, "It's been a pleasure, Mr. Davis."

Without so much as a backward glance, the man strode from the room. An awkward silence started to settle over the room, only to be quickly broken by Metcalfe.

"So, really, Miss Morrell?" he asked, cutting to the chase as well as recognizing her individuality.   "How long until you'll be riding again?"

Dorothy put on her practiced quizzical frown.   "Riding?   Well, those plow horses like the ones back home on the family farm hardly count, do they?"

Metcalfe's laughter was robust and hearty, melting away the lingering icy specter of Mr. Henry Davis.   Even Bill, who had been scrupulously careful to stay out of the conversation, chuckled aloud while shaking his head as well.

"No, ma'am," Metcalfe answered, "I'm sure they don't."

She took a deep breath, and sighed, genuinely this time, working to keep any worry out of her voice.

"They do tell me I'll never be riding again at all, not a plow horse, not a mail delivery horse, and not even on a prancing show horse for a grand entrance at the show," she sighed again, now for effect, "but, oh, well, I still have Skeeter, and that's enough."

She heard Bill snort beneath his breath from across the room but she ignored him.

Damn it, Bill!   I may sound like a dreamy-eyed school girl pining after her best beau, but for right now you are all I've got - and, truly, having you is enough.

Metcalfe, busy again with his notes, didn't notice Dorothy's wistfulness, but picked up on her cue.

"I understand that you, Miss Morrell, are the muse behind Mr. Robbins adding a verse to 'The Life and Battles of Skeeter Bill'."   He flipped to the back page of his notebook and cleared his throat, smile as wide as a Wyoming sky as he read.

"The riding of the bronchos, the throwing of the steers,
The shouts from the grandstand throng;

Not any of these can compare, my dear,
To that tune of your old love song." ∗

"You have really done your homework, sir."

Dorothy was amused with Mr. Metcalfe. Here was a man who seemed to understand that in the here and now, any story about Dorothy Morrell was incomplete without Skeeter Bill Robbins, and in turn, she now completed any story about him.

"Ah, well." Dorothy, her smile no longer practiced, was still determined to keep steering the interview in the direction of her choosing.

"There are, no doubt, many school children who have been saddened by the news of my" – she paused for dramatic effect – "unfortunate accident. As you know, I'm sure, everyone under the age of 18 is admitted free of charge to the 101 Ranch shows, but there are ever so many thrilling riders who will be providing for their enjoyment."

She paused to gather her thoughts, to compose the final punch to close this interview.

"The Miller Brother's 101 Real Wild West Show mingles education, sports, science and wholesome fun."

Yes, she was sure those were the exact words the Colonel, Joseph Miller, often used to promote his family's business, their bread and butter. She nodded again, thankful that at least this reporter was as interested in her theatrical performance as well as his notes.

"Yes, yes, I have heard Colonel Miller's description of his business," he said in an unusual tone of indulgence; better to maintain neutrality, he had learned.

"I'll be sure to include the name of the hospital here and the address so your fans and well-wishers will know how to get in touch with you," he said as he stood.

"Is there anything else you'd like to add?" Metcalfe asked before he folded his notebook closed and returned his pencil to its perch atop his ear, clearly hoping for more, reluctant to be on his way.

"Just thank you again for coming to check in on me." Dorothy kept her smile bright as Metcalfe turned to shake hands with Bill before turning to nod his farewell to her.

The sound of his footsteps echoed down the empty hallway.

"*Ach, Gott!*" Dorothy grimaced and sighed as she slowly sank back into her bed pillows, closing her eyes, glad to end her facade of endless cheer, her face of bravado, exhausted from her efforts even with someone as genuine and interested as Metcalfe.

"I don't think I could have kept up all that happy chatter one more minute."

"Yuh done alright," Bill said as he unfolded himself from the stool where he'd been listening to the interviews. He moved to the now vacant seat nearest to her bedside and sat himself down on it.

He carefully lifted her left hand, now out and free from the blankets. He cradled it with both of his own and carefully caressed her wrist through its bandages with his thumbs, slowly shaking his head, trying to keep his worries to himself.

How quickly and completely life had changed for Dorothy – for the both of them! What had been just recently stressful and anxious, the hustle back and forth through the crowded streets of San Francisco and worry about getting to the Exposition Grounds and through the crowded Zone on time for their afternoon and evening performances, now seemed carefree and lighthearted; he and his Dot joking about the days when bronks were ridden to a standstill, quite a change to their 8–second rides. Eight seconds kept the show moving more quickly, it seemed.

After a few long moments, he lifted her fingers and gently kissed them.

"Dot," he quietly said, not waiting for her to open her eyes, "yer a charmer – one woulda thought you wuz one of Joe Miller's own publicist for sure, but I'm thinkin' they come to talk to yuh about *you*."

Peering through slitted eyes, Dorothy groaned and shook her head.

"Agreed. Metcalfe did come to interview me and was glad to be here, but as for Davis, I am sure he came because the city editor gave him no choice in the assignment – it sure seemed to me he was already thinking on being on his way back out the door before he even said hello."

Bill reluctantly nodded his agreement, cradling Dorothy's fingers against his cheek.

Dorothy frowned and shook her head, overwhelming weariness and anxiety flooding through her. Her breath caught as worry and confusion became overwhelming.

"Bill, what in heaven's name am I going to do if I can't ride?"

She gritted her teeth, refusing to cry.

"Riding is all I've done since I left Canada, whether I was opening a show, or riding bronks for the grandstands or for the cameras. It's how I've been pulling my own weight for years."

Bill met the fierceness of her challenge with his ever crooked smile and shrugged.

"What was it yuh just told that reporter fellow?" Bill asked. "I b'lieve yuh told him yuh still got Skeeter, and that's enough! Well, girl, yuh *do* still have me and believe me, Dottie, that *is* enough."

"*Ach, Gott!* Be serious!"

How could he see humor in the face of despair?

"Worse yet, what if I never even get my feet back underneath me? Look at the long run. I can't expect you to be playing nursemaid for me for the rest of my life."

"Hey, all this talk ain't doin' neither of us no good. All it's doin' is pullin' down yer spirits and worrin' the hell outta me. No need burnin' bridges we ain't even got in sight yet."

He sighed and searched her face for any sign of her agreeing to his logic.

"Ever since I left Wyoming and that's been a lot more than a few years ago, I always found a way to put food in my belly and stay outta the cold. Ain't no difference now. Only now, it'll be even better. We'll be standin' our ground together."

Once again, he gently pressed her hand between both of his own. She squeezed back.

"Yer more than just a day rider, miss," he grinned, hoping to continue to lift her mood.

"By gum, yer Dorothy Morrell, Movin' Picture Star, the Canadian Cowgirl, the Ladies Buckin' Bronk Champion of the whole goldarn world. Yuh got more in yer back pocket than them ridin' gloves. Long as I got a breath, I'll be makin' sure the world don't forget it neither. Yuh just get to feelin' better. Stop yer worryin'."

He kissed her fingers again as she giggled.

"Love the way you tell it, Bill," she said.

"Oh, by the way. I b'lieve Joe Miller's is already talkin' about runnin' you for 'Queen of the Zone.' 'Backin' yer candidacy' he likes to call it. Just as yuh done for Griffin, yuh kin do fer the 101. Bring crowds in fer the show whether yer ridin' bronks or not, is what you do. "

"Queen of the Zone?" Dorothy questioned, not sure if she understood what Bill was talking about. "I thought that all the candidates had already been established weeks ago. Isn't it a little late, isn't it?"

"Ah, no! Not at all to hear Joe tell it. He's already got plans to print up votin' coupons in the Oakland newspaper for the kiddos to clip so they kin vote fer you.

"Why, to hear him tell it, you gettin' busted up broke all their hearts – all them school kids who clipped all them coupons to earn season passes just to watch you, Miss Dorothy Morrell, an' none of us other durn bronk riders," he chuckled. "All a them kids'll surely be pullin' for yuh to win the title 'Queen of the Zone.'"

"I should have known that he'd make sure the buttered side of his bread landed face up," she sighed, closing her eyes to the world wishing she could drift off to sleep and wake to realize the last two days had just been a horrid nightmare.

"Now, yuh do yer part by gettin' better, gettin' stronger, and me an' Joe Miller, we'll be doin' our parts thinkin' a ways to keep yuh in the spot light."

Bill caressed the back of her hand, watching her face relax. He gathered his courage, wanting to finish sharing his thoughts with her before she slipped into the sleep she needed so desperately, hoping sleep would ease her worry, even if for a short while.

"Carlina," he said softly.

Dorothy's eyes snapped opened wide and she locked her gaze with his.

"Yes, Roy?"

She answered hesitantly and lifted an eyebrow, waiting for his question. Using their given names deepened the intimacy of the moment.

"I was thinkin'," his voice fell to barely a whisper. He cleared his throat but held her gaze.

"Hell, I'm thinkin' it's high time to finish tyin' the knot. Get it done official like."

Dorothy nodded and hesitated only a moment before replying.

"I wrote to my sister a little while ago. Finally got a letter back from her just a few days ago."

She frowned trying to remember through the chaos of the last few days, just how much time had slipped away since the letter addressed to *Miss Carlina Eichhorn* had arrived at General Delivery. "She wrote the Mister remarried a while back."

Bill raised both eyebrows waiting for her to go on, not sure of her hesitancy.

"This may seem ridiculous to you, Bill, but now isn't the time."

She searched his face for any sign of impatience or annoyance before quickly adding, "Bill, I want to be able to walk beside you the day we marry."

Bill drew a breath to argue her point.

"Now, Bill," she continued, cutting him off. "It's not an aisle that I'm looking to walk down. None of all the fuss is necessary, not at all important or what I want. But I want to be able to walk at your side wherever it is we say our 'I dos' whether at a church, courthouse, or back forty at the Zone."

Bill's crooked grin spread across his face. He stood and leaned over to kiss her.

"God almighty, glad to hear it! In the meantime, we gotta getcha well."

Dorothy put back on her practiced, showgirl smile. "You better get going, cowboy. It's getting close to show time."

"Yup, an' yuh try to sleep some and I'll be back after the evenin' show. Sure as the world, I'm always gonna be comin' back home to yuh. Wherever you are!" He settled the her covers up over her shoulders.

He grinned and picked up his hat. He kissed her again before turning to leave.

As his tall frame disappeared from view, Dorothy was finally free to let go of her tears, long denied throughout the day. Tears that silently and slowly trickled down into her ears.

Dorothy listened until the sharp staccato of Bill's boot heels faded down the hallway. She listened until she could hear them no more. If only she could feel the same hope that Bill had, but barring that, his hopes had to be enough for the both of them.

XVIII – 2 JUNE 1915 - AT THE CONVENTION

L adies," Dorothy began, looking across a sea of women's faces, "and gentlemen." A few islands of both bewhiskered and clean-shaven male faces were scattered through the ballroom of the Inside Inn here on the Exposition grounds.

"Thank you for your kind invitation to address the California Branch of the Congressional Union for Woman's Suffrage." Being thorough always paid off. She was rewarded by a polite hand-clapping, restrained and short.

The California Branch was now in its second day of meetings here at the Panama-Pacific International Exposition. While yesterday's meeting at the Civil Auditorium had been dedicated to being addressed by women whom Skeeter Bill Robbins called The Big Wigs - women representing the on-going state and national struggles for women's suffrage, today was the day to hear from women from "all the states and countries . . . by which the feminine touch has been accepted as part of the various governments ranging from Iceland to China."

What a stretch! It had already been a long, long day.

Dorothy supposed that many of today's featured speakers were staying here on the grounds of the Panama-Pacific International Exposition, perhaps staying upstairs in the rooms and suites of the Inside Inn – a play on words that the developers must have come up with after a long evening in their cups, she supposed, returning her thoughts to the crowd before her.

"It is an honor to represent women from many different walks of life. I am both housewife and businesswoman. I am voice for immigrants and the native born. I speak for sisters, daughters and mothers.

"I hail from Winnipeg in faraway Manitoba."

She wondered if the women from New Zealand, Denmark or the Isle of Man would consider Manitoba to be far away from San Francisco. No matter. For Dorothy, Winnipeg might as well be on the far side of the globe as removed as she now was from her mother and sisters. Her father and brothers, too, for that matter.

"My own mother, and father, for that matter, were born on the steppes of Russia, among windblown wheat fields along the Volga River, of German heritage. My ancestors went to Russia at the invitation of Catherine the Great, but the time came that my parents became determined to better and restart their lives. To realize their dreams meant removing themselves from under the thumb, even the strangle hold of a great oppressor," *no need to draw unnecessary battle lines in the sand,* "I doubt they had a full vision of the changes that would come to their lives. They came to Canada with the dreams of being full recipients of the rewards of their lives' labors, to enjoy the freedom of being at their helms of their own ships of destiny."

A smattering of applause allowed Dorothy to catch her breath, to inhale deeply, and relax a little into her crutches, relying on them to keep her standing upright, taking the weight from her right leg still in its plaster cast.

Dorothy smiled a little to herself. When rehearsing her "no more than five minutes of address" to Bill, he had laughed, declaring her speech to be plumb full of four-bit words. Maria, her faraway mother, might have listened while shaking her head at all of "Carlina's pretty words;" the pretty words carefully penned and folded in the front pocket of her leather split skirt adorned with silver conchos. The written words were there for moral support only. She knew them all by heart.

"For some time now, my father has exercised his civil right to vote in both the provincial and national elections of Manitoba and Canada."

Dorothy imagined a slight chill now beginning to emanate from the politely frozen faces of the delegates and participants, and so she hurried to make her point.

"My father, a goodly man, who works hard for his daily bread, is but one half of the partnership that keeps the home fires burning back in Winnipeg."

A slight warming as she watched many women start to nod in agreement to her implied reference to her mother.

"There are few women who know and speak their minds as well as my mother, Maria."

More nodding and a wave of murmuring agreements.

"Even now, in Manitoba, an endeavor–" Dorothy had chosen her word carefully hoping to bring to mind the Icelandic Women's Suffrage Society founded in Winnipeg in 1908 that was called the Tilraum, or *Endeavour*, "– an essential and sustained endeavor is being fought, the battles now many years long, to bring the same rights, responsibilities and opportunities to vote that are enjoyed and employed by my father and the rest of the men of Manitoba.   Hopefully in the near future suffrage will also be afforded to the women, the wives, mothers and sisters not only of Manitoba but all over the world.   Women are surely entitled to political, social, legal and economic equality with men."

The ice was clearly broken now, and a grand applause filled the hall. Dorothy smiled, nothing private or personal now in this smile, beaming across the grand gathering of women from every corner of the globe – she laughed and then shook her head at the thought.

"Now, ladies," she quieted her audience for her last point while pulling her crutches forward from beneath her arms to showcase them, "as many of you can see, I recently came out on the short end of the stick in a rodeo arena.   While I may never be able to sit a bucking horse again, as a woman now calling Wyoming home, I will always be able to handle the ballot, and so will every other woman in my state, just as we have for almost a half century now."

She was pleased with the audience's final reaction, the applause still polite but warm and unrestrained, as she turned to carefully make her way down from the speaker's platform and return to the table where she sat with the representative women from Idaho and Washington, happy to know that everyone's attention had returned to the lectern, and was not focused on her painful slow progress. She cautiously sat herself down, laying her crutches under the table the best she could.

Her breathing slowed, she relaxed into her chair, and the high excitement of being front and center performing, faded, being replaced with familiar doubt and the depression which had plagued her for the past two months.   She wondered just what in the world she was going to do with herself next. Despite Bill's optimism, she had no idea of what the rest of the month of June would bring, let alone the rest of her life.

"Miss Morrell," came a quiet whisper.   She looked up surprised into a familiar face.   Showtime.   Again.

"Mr. Larkin!" she almost forgot to whisper.   "What are you doing here? How did you find me?"

"As if you have to ask!" Mark Larkin chuckled. "I follow the people who make the best stories, not necessarily front page news – and it was no effort to follow you to your table."

"I'm pretty sure this shindig *is* front page," Dorothy countered, leaning in to whisper. Mrs. Idaho cut her a withering look, while Mrs. Washington pointedly ignored the pair, fluttering her fan to try to ward off the closeness that the hundreds of people in the ballroom added to the mugginess of the afternoon.

"Perhaps, perhaps," was all Mark Larkin would say, as he slid his chair closer to hers, to better carry on their conversation without disturbing their table companions.

"But how are you? I mean, really! How *are* you?"

Dorothy shrugged, knowing that she would not be able to brush off Mr. Mark Larkin, human interest reporter extraordinaire, with a smile and wave of her hand.

"Well enough, I suppose," she cautiously began. "As you know, since we visited a few months ago, I've been a little laid up. No longer the feature attraction of the 101 Ranch show."

She drew circles with her finger on the linen table cloth. "I've had to own up to the reality that I won't be returning to Cheyenne as a contestant, at least not this year."

Mark Larkin nodded, raising an eyebrow in an invitation for her to continue.

"But even without being in the arena, I've had a quite a few things to keep me . . . "

She let her words fade away. Busy? Occupied? Walking – rather crutching – from the kitchen table to the front room sofa wasn't being busy. Reading newspapers from front page to last, even the classified advertisements. Occupied, perhaps. Preparing simple suppers while waiting for Bill to return home at the end of his evening shows. Those were the things that kept her busy these days. Brooding, she hardly noticed when Mrs. Idaho and Mrs. Washington, one at a time, quietly stood and moved to another table. This late in the afternoon, the crowd had finally thinned somewhat.

She suddenly brightened, pointing out the brooch pinned to the broad sash she wore over her blouse, both white in support of the suffrage movement. A gold watch hung from the ribbon shaped pin.

"I may be gone, but I'm not forgotten," *yet, she thought to herself.* "I was guest of honor just last week at a dinner hosted by Miller Brothers. Attended by all the muckety-mucks of the Wild West Show. The Colonel himself presented this watch to me."

She quickly unfastened the brooch and turned it over in her hand. Mark Larkin squinted as he leaned over the watch to make out the inscription.

To Our Queen, Dorothy Morrell, from her associates with the 101 Ranch Show. PPIE, 1915.

He nodded and smiled up at her. "I read that Joe Miller had backed you as a candidate for the Queen of the Zone."

"A late entry, I might add," Dorothy replied quietly. "It seemed to me that it was an afterthought by Colonel Miller, put into motion after my accident, not really a chance of pulling off a victory, but that's the business of show business."

Mark Larkin nodded, for as a freelance reporter, he was more than familiar with the power of the press in providing publicity for those whose livelihood depended on the spotlight focused on them.

Dorothy continued, "Stay in the limelight as long as possible. Don't let people forget who you are. What you can do. Keep them coming back for more." *More what now though?*

She suddenly wondered what had really brought Mr. Mark Larkin to her table.

"What about you, Mr. Larkin? Who is being highlighted in *your* limelight?"

"Not important, Miss Morrell. Not at all. That's not why I am here." He sighed before continuing. "I suppose you noticed that the full version of our story didn't print here in California, though a paper in Santa Cruz did pick up and print the part about Skeeter Bill daring you to ride your first bronk."

To Dorothy's surprise, she realized she hadn't noticed at all. She felt a little guilty that she had never even thought back on her visit with Mark Larkin or his interview with her which had been just days before her injury in April.

"Well, you did say that it would be hard to predicate when or where it might be published," she replied. "'*We'll just let it go and see where it lands,*' I think was how you put it. I have been so wrapped up with my recovery, I'm sorry; I didn't even think to look for it.

His face brightened.

"Well! Here it is the full version!"

With a look of pride, Mr. Larkin laid a neatly folded copy of a Wichita newspaper onto the table in front of her.

The austere front page heralded the number of deaths from the sinking of the Lusitania with sobering statistics. She blinked in surprise, the realization of events far more tragic and worse than being pitched from a horse, sobering her.

Larkin was quickly unfolding the paper and opening it before her.

"Page 15!" he said, pointing with a flourish.

Dorothy smiled in spite of herself as she read the headline blazed across the top of the three columns at the top of the right hand side of the page. "BECAUSE SHE LOVED HORSES AND HATED NURSING MISS MORRELL BECAME CHAMPION BRONCHO RIDER."

She smiled back at herself, at her photograph smiling up off the top of the page, remembering the excitement of the day. The fuss of sitting at just the right angle to the camera, tucking the fingers of her left hand along the side of her face while holding to her tall black cowboy hat with the other.   Her longest set of curls making their way to her waist.   A tingle started up the back of her neck just as it had then.   A flip of her stomach.   An excitement not at all different from facing that bronk or the sea of an expectant crowd of suffragettes, or mounted at the ready to gallop into an arena, steadying the flag pole into the top of her boot.

Mark Larkin tapped the tabletop, no longer whispering as he got to his feet, "Excuse me, Miss Dorothy, but as I said, I have stories to chase."

She realized the presentations and speeches were over for the day and Mark Larkin had responded to the siren call of the promise of the Next Great Story. He was half way across the ballroom before Dorothy could form a reply.   No matter.

She returned her attention to the printed page before her. It stretched across three columns, as close as one could get to half as the page was seven columns wide.   As for the printed words, she could see that once the half of a page of advertisements was discounted, her story was about a third of the printed text.   Well, her story and her picture.

All the details rang familiar, but Mr. Larkin had added his own twist and spice to her already colorful story.

Two years ago, the world's champion ladies broncho buster didn't know a martingale from a bridle.

Dorothy nodded, chuckling soundlessly.   Though true, she didn't remember saying such, and *nightingale* was still the first association that came to mind when she heard the word.

Today she is the feature attraction at the of the 101 Ranch show on "The Zone" and for the entertainment of the world's people she is riding the most fractious horses available – horses that have bucked off some of the best and loudest howling cowboys in the country.

She couldn't wait to read this to Bill.   "Fractious horses" and "best and loudest howling cowboys!"

The lady loved horses.   She pined for life in the open, for the creak of the saddle and the clink of the spur.   To watch the ripple of muscles that played beneath the saddles of a galloping horse thrilled her until every vibrant fiber echoed the resounding hoof beats.

Maria would like these *pretty words*.   A shame Mark Larkin had only left one copy of the newspaper.   Dorothy might have sent a clipping to her mother.

Before she became champion woman buckeroo Miss Morrell was a movie star and vaudeville actress.

"But I like being a cowgirl infinitely better than being a movie star, perhaps because I love horses; horses and babies.   I sometimes wish I could be a horse.   Of course, I have been a baby once and therefore have no desire to be a baby again. But I would dearly love to be a horse!"

Maria's favorite expression burst through her thoughts – 'Ach, Lieber Gott im Himmel!'   Had she really said all that?   "I've been a baby once . . ." She quickly skimmed over those sentences to the last paragraph.

"And besides, there are many movie stars, but there is only one champion lady broncho buster - and I am the lady."

He got that right!

The ballroom was slowly clearing, people leaving, some slowly, some more purposely as they moved toward the doors to depart.

She noticed a tall man carrying a gray cowboy hat shouldering his way into the ballroom as best as he could. Dorothy's heart skipped a beat. This man, her man, was worth pining over; more important than open skies or creak of the leather.

She stood and waved to be sure he saw her but he immediately waved back. He knew. He already knew.

She was only a couple of steps into making her way to his side when she realized she hadn't even thought to retrieve her crutches and so she returned to fold the newspaper and then fit the curved arches of the tops of the crutches under her arms.

". . . only one champion lady broncho buster - and I am the lady!"

That she was, broken but mending, out of work but not for long. She may be down but never out. She had picked herself up and dusted herself off. All that was left was to wait for her leg to strengthen and, by gum, she'd be back in the saddle again.

XIX - MAY 1924 - THE VOYAGE

Dorothy closed her eyes, finding calm in the slow breezes washing over her face. She pulled up the collar of her coat against the chill of their first morning at sea. Feet shoulder width apart to better brace herself against the slow shift of the deck beneath her, she breathed deeply of the air freshened by thousands of square miles of the northern Atlantic Ocean. Though the sun had been up for some time, there was still time before breakfast would be served.

Opening her eyes to scan out over miles upon countless miles of open sea, her spirit found renewal as the uncertainty, the confusion, the struggles, the anger, the frustration of the past few weeks melted away just as the fog on the far horizon. Without even turning around, the sound of sure measured footsteps let her know that Bill had joined her. He slipped his arm around her shoulders and she returned his embrace by slipping hers around his waist. At this hour, she and Bill had the second class deck all to themselves.   For now.

"Mighty purty out here," Bill began as they watched the foam swirling away from the hull of the ship.   Sea birds dipped and whirled above them.

Dorothy nodded, not wanting to break the peaceful spell of their comparative solitude.

Bill was quiet for a few minutes, waiting for the reply he was sure was coming.

"Bill, were there times you thought we'd never get here?"

Dorothy was pretty sure that Bill's optimism had never failed him, even on the roughest days or the longest lines.

"Nope, but not sayin' it was smooth sailin' cuz it sure wasn't," Bill replied with a lazy grin.   "I'm sorry it was hard on yuh, gettin' all them details ironed out."   He snorted, and then teased, "All them secrets yuh had to tell."

"Hush you!"   Dorothy quickly retorted, though smiling.   "That's all behind us now."

"We gotta keep thinkin' back to the beginnin' when we first got the invite to join up with this hellacious opportunity."

"Humm, you're right," she replied. "I could have spent more time remembering how excited we were instead of worrying that we would never get everything ready."

Easy to say after all was said and done.

From the day last November that the first telegram arrived – the siren's song that quietly transformed itself into a clarion call – until they had finally boarded the *SS Lapland*, their lives, or at least her life – Bill kept his attention on the business end of each day – had been overwhelmed with hustle, hurry, bustle, worry, plan, pack, plan again, pack some more.   And excitement.   And pinch herself anticipation.   And eagerness.   Dreams not yet dreamed coming true.   For Dorothy, returning to the Europe she hardly remembered, for Bill, a journey past the furthest horizon of his imagination.

She thought back to the telegram.

The invitation to the "First International Rodeo" had arrived in the usual way, no fanfare at all, delivered by the "boy on his bicycle" to their front door.   Dorothy had tipped the boy and started to set the telegram on the kitchen table until she took a second glance at it and realized who it was addressed to.

Mr. and Mrs. S B Robbins.   Not just *Skeeter Bill Robbins* but to the two of them together. Without hesitation, she quickly opened it.

MR AND MRS S B ROBBINS. BAKERSFIELD CALIF. ANNOUNCING INTERNATIONAL RODEO.   LONDON ENGLAND.   JUNE 1924.   EVENTS ROPING RIDING RACES STEER WRESTLING. QUALIFIED CONTESTANTS INVITED. CONTACT TEX AUSTIN. FORKED LIGHTNING RANCH. NEW MEXICO IF INTERESTED.

England! Dorothy caught her breath. Leaving the country had seldom crossed her mind, but England? This would be more than just a border crossing!

She looked at the clock. Nearly suppertime. Bill would be in before long but Dorothy absolutely could not wait. She exploded through the back door and barreled through the backyard.

"Tell–u–gram!" she yelled at the top of her lungs, waving it in the air, even as she realized there was no way Bill could hear her. Even if she had a voice like that rodeo announcer, Foghorn Clancy, her voice might not have carried. As it was, she threw caution to the wind and picked up her pace as best she could as she gathered her skirts and charged down the short lane to the stock pens and corrals where she could see Bill was pitching hay to some of the horses.

From Bill's look, Dorothy knew she had startled and surprised him. The memory still made her smile even after all these months.

"Got a snake on yer heels?" he asked, planting his pitchfork into a pile of hay as he tried to read her expression.

Bad news traveled like wildfire and seeing her running toward him triggered worry.

"Oh, no! No, no, no!" she laughed. "Not a snake! Much better than that!"

Her eyes sparkled and danced as she quickly handed the telegram to him. She watched carefully as he read it for himself.

Surely, surely, he would want to go as badly as she did.

His eyebrows rose as he looked up, grinning wide.

"What do ya think?" Then he laughed and corrected himself. "No doubt a tall what yer thinkin'! Yuh look like a kid on Christmas mornin'. So, am I right in guessin' yer want to be counted in on this fer sure?"

"I . . . well, yes! I'm sure! All in!" Dorothy clasped her hands, finding it hard to contain her excitement. "I mean, I don't think I'd like to try to make a go of it on my own. But, if you want to be going, I'm going to be right on your heels."

"If I want to go?" Bill hooted and swept her into his arms, his embrace lifting her from her feet. "Yuh know what they say . . ."

"Wild horses couldn't keep you away!" Dorothy finished for him, wrapping her arms tightly around his neck as Bill spun on his heels, swinging her around, and then around again.

The 7:30 breakfast gong brought her back to deck of the SS *Lapland*, churning her way toward the port of London, England, at 17 knots per hour. She moved her hand into the crook of Bill's elbow.

"Ready for some breakfast?" She grinned up at Bill only to realize that he didn't look all that well. "What's wrong? You feeling all right?"

Bill cleared his throat before answering.

"Nope, cain't say as I am. I might jest have a cup of coffee with yuh. Maybe. Thought of eatin' anything right about now just ain't much to my likin'."

Dorothy frowned, worried.

"We could wait until the second seating at 8:30," she suggested.

"Nope, don't think it'll help a tall to wait. Let's just go on. Maybe the sight of food'll help."

Without further ado, they made their way around the deck to the dining area. Of the hundreds of passengers on board the *Lapland*, only eighteen were contestants sailing for London and the *Cowboy Championships*.

Dorothy noted that she and Bill were the only two competitors heading for the *Cowboy Championships* in the dining room this morning. And it seemed that if Bill had his way, he wouldn't have been here either. Dorothy thanked her lucky stars that she had escaped seasickness.

After being seated, Dorothy picked up her menu card.

"I'll just have fruit and oatmeal porridge, please. And a cup of coffee," Dorothy decided.

"Milk and sugar for both?" the steward asked.

"Yes, please," Dorothy replied.

"Only coffee for me," Bill added, as he brushed a hand over his forehead, grimacing.

"What do you suppose the morning is like on the *Menominee* right about now?" Dorothy wondered. Many of the rest of the other contestants, over 120 of them, were sailing to England on the chartered cargo-turned-passenger ship which was scheduled to arrive in London a day or two after the *Lapland*.

Bill groaned a little. "Whatcha think is happenin' on a ship one hundred percent plumb full a cowboys? The boastin' and braggin' more'n likely is knee deep by now."

"There are a few cowgirls, too," Dorothy reminded him.

"Not all that many. Not enough to make a difference in the number a tales bein' told," Bill answered, and then his face brightened slightly. "Just think on this fact for a minute. We don't hafta listen to all that bull and we ain't settin' over hundreds a head a livestock, neither!"

Dorothy laughed. "If we were there, you'd be right in the middle of it all, telling your stories with the best of them!"

After her fruit and oatmeal was served, Dorothy studied the layout of her silverware. One spoon, one knife, one fork. Simple, but this was only breakfast. The challenge would come later, perhaps at lunch or dinner. She wasn't worried though. "Lady Bob" had primed her well on what to do; they had practiced more than once.

"Bill? You remember Mrs. Aubrey Montgomery?" A rhetorical question.

"Of course," Bill looked up somewhat startled. He seemed to be worried that the self-proclaimed Grand Dame of San Francisco society was even now descending upon their table.

"Now, Bill, she wouldn't be traveling second class," Dorothy assured him.

"What about her then?" Bill groused.   "Surely she ain't gonna be in on this Rodeo?"

As Dorothy shook her head in disbelief, Bill quickly added, "Oh, I remember back to them 101 Ranch days.   Seems she had a' opinion for the Colonel every time he turned around.   '*Oh, I am so interested in horses and anything else that is wild,*' she sez.   Only question'd be, would she be for this rodeo or agin it?   Seems as if there's no end of the crusades she grabs by the horns."

"I'm sure she doesn't care one way or the other," Dorothy replied. "But it's not that at all."

"What then?"   Bill was beginning to look a little more chipper, whether it was to coffee or the lack of high-brow company, Dorothy wasn't sure.

"You remember the dinner party she had for us a few weeks ago," she began.

"Too damn bad I wuz outta town and couldn't go, no way in hell," Bill replied, as Dorothy laughed – laughed into her napkin, as the "Lady" had instructed.

"I was just thinking on the hints she gave on when to use certain forks or spoons or knives."

Bill looked a little perplexed, but winked at her.   "Yuh mean she had to tell you not to eat with your fingers?"

Dorothy laughed again, not even bothering with the napkin.

"Breakfast is not a good example of multiple utensils," she explained. "But 'Lady Bob' explained what she called the 'Outside In Rule.'   You don't have to worry about choosing which fork or knife to use, you just start at the outside and work your way in."

"Seems like an awful lotta dishwashin' for not a lotta reason," Bill answered in his usual practical way.   "So how wuz it anyway?   Her little dinner party at the Whitcomb Hotel?   We been so busy, haven't had time to tell me much."

"You really want to know?"

It was Bill's turn to laugh.

"Why, sure!   We got ten days a just you and me.   Bring it on."

"As you can be sure, her guests were the crème de la crème."

"Why don'tcha just say cream a the crop?" Bill asked.

"Because I am telling you this in the manner of Mrs. Montgomery."

"Ts!" Bill snorted as he signaled the waiter to top off his coffee cup.

"She was pretty proud of her guest list.   Beforehand she kept going on and on about how nobility was going to be in attendance and such a wonderful opportunity to become acquainted with the expectations of high society."

"Jeez!   She coulda just said 'get yer feet wet by hobnobbing with the muckety mucks.'"

"Shhh," Dorothy giggled.   "Anyway, I kept wondering just who her 'nobility' might be.   Turns out her guest of honor was as near as I can tell, a business man 'from one of the leading noble families in Great Britain.'"

"Whatever the hell that means!" Bill hooted.

"And get this!" Dorothy went on. "He didn't even sound British - he haughtily explained that the 'education of his youth was directed by a Yale graduate' who insisted on American enunciation.'"

"Sounds like a maverick tryin' to run with the main herd, if yuh ask me," Bill said.

"Could be," Dorothy agreed, "but she called him *Sir Charles* all evening long."

"This comin' from the *Mining Queen of Nevada*, ol' 'Lady Bob' herself," Bill added. "If yuh ask me, she's a just gadabout livin' high off a the sale of her husband's mine."

"Now, Bill," Dorothy protested. "Half that mine was rightfully hers and she certainly drove a hard bargain when they sold it. She held out signing the papers until she got what she wanted. So I suppose in that sense, if she's 'living high,' as you say, it's off of her own money!

"Besides she's worked to do wonderful things with her time and money. She is quite the proponent of education and children. And she was Vice President of the planning committee for the San Francisco Exposition."

"Or so she claimed." Bill grinned across the table at her. "Yuh don't hafta keep tryin' to sell her to me. I ain't buyin', besides I already got me the best darn partner ever."

Dorothy smiled across at Bill but took it that he wasn't really all that interested in "Lady Bob" and turned her full attention to her oatmeal.

The rest of breakfast time was a quieter affair. Dorothy noticed that Bill was finally doing less stirring of his coffee and more actual drinking it. When finished, they made their way back to the open decks where Bill surprised Dorothy by asking a deck steward if he could get them two deck chairs and steamer rugs.

"Don't know why they call a lap blanket a rug," he groused, obviously still not feeling a hundred percent.

"Didn't expect you to want to be sitting in a deck chair," Dorothy said, somewhat surprised.

"What else is there to do?"

"We could play one of those deck games. Like shuffleboards."

"How's about that ring toss game? Like them fellers over there?" Bill pointed to a group of young boys throwing rope rings onto a target painted on the deck. "I'll go see what I can get for us."

Watching Bill make his way to the short line forming at the deck steward's office brought back a sudden fresh flood of harsh memories.

Instantly Dorothy was back on Chambers Street in downtown New York. Towering columns loomed high overhead supporting the portico three and a half stories overhead. Clutching Bill's arm, she was climbing the broad staircase, overwhelmed with the magnitude of not only the building but of the importance of acquiring the necessary passport to travel to England.

Mr. Tex Austin had been clear in his instructions to the future contestants of the *Cowboy Championships* on how to apply for a passport.

Have on your person the following: birth certificate or if none can be attained, bring the required affidavit from relative or 'other than relative' attesting to knowledge of your birth since your native birth proves your citizenship. Bring two photographic portraits no larger than 3 inches square – head shots only. Wives will be included on their husband's passports. Women traveling unaccompanied must provide the above information attesting to either husband's or father's nationality. Please arrive at the Courthouse in the company of one who can vouch for your identification.

His side instructions were words of dire warning: *Under no circumstances, should an applicant provide information that might harm or hinder his chance at being issued a passport. Such information may include volunteering that oneself or one's parent was born in a variety of enemy states such as Germany or the Soviet Union. Avoid embarrassment or confusion when traveling with a wife by supplying accurate dates and places for their marriage. And for gawdsake, be married!*

Well, now, come to think of it, Mr. and Mrs. Austin were celebrating the first month's anniversary of their marriage. Better yet, Buck and Tad Lucas were now just into their first week of wedded bliss as well.

Among the throng of hopeful contestants in New York City preparing to travel to Wembley Stadium, Bill had found Frank Carter from back home in Wyoming, to vouch for his identification, though still grumbling and grousing that "if a man ain't as good as his word, he ain't good fer much. Why do I need somebody to tell them folks that he knows who I am?"

Frank had been through the cumbersome process just a few days earlier, and assured them he could easily walk them through the tangled bureaucratic web. As they finally reached the top of the wide granite stairs, Dorothy, Bill and Frank made their way through the gleaming hardwood doors into the courthouse.

Frank led the way down the halls to the counter where the Passport Agency was located, only to be overwhelmed at the line already formed in front of it. The passport clerk was standing behind the counter, typewriter at hand, clacking away at the keys, loudly asking for the applicant's personal information over the din of crying babies, and the chatter of many voices, as each person was trying to be heard over the chaos.

The lines slowly moved but at last Bill and Frank were laying out documents, answering questions and supplying dates and places as Dorothy did her best to melt into the background. Days ago in the quiet of an evening, Bill had assured her that there was no need to worry.

"Come on, now, gal, relax. Yuh ain't got *Russia* plastered on yer forehead."

He tried to calm her queasiness and worry. "Besides, anybody who's ever read a newspaper kin tell any old clerk in any old courthouse in any old town, that Miss Dorothy Morrell hails from Winnipeg, Canada."

"But, Bill, there's that record from the last census. I told the census taker I was born in Russia as well as Mutti and Papa."

"Ain't nobody gonna spend precious time lookin' up a census record. Besides, where the hell would yuh even go to read such a thing?" Bill shrugged and shook his head. "Just smile and nod. Leave the talkin' to me and Frank."

As Dorothy listened to Bill's slow talking answers to each of the clerk's questions, she thought back to Mutti and the census taker so long ago in Winnipeg. So much more was at stake today than then.

After finishing typing the first side of the application, the clerk turned it over to finish filling out the back by hand. In spite of having photographs attached, a physical description also had to be included. Grey eyes. Black hair. Scar on left side of chin. For Bill, not her – she was just a woman traveling on her husband's passport.

Frank – Franklin E Carter – then signed the statement attesting that he had known Roy R Robbins for 20 years and knew him to be a native born citizen of the United States and that the facts in Mr. Bert Maddox's affidavit were true to the best of his knowledge.

Good to know they would soon be finished and on their way.

"Well, now, Mr. Robbins, will you kindly look over the information on both sides to assure accuracy."

Dorothy watched Bill's face as he began at the top of the first page. He had only read down to the third line, before he stiffened and pointed out an error.

"Sir," Bill began hesitantly. "There was a misunderstandin' here. My birthday's listed here as my wife's birthday as well."

"Ahh, I see," the clerk reached for an eraser to rub out the typewritten date. "And just what is the correct date of her birth?"

Dorothy was horrified to think that anyone, everyone in earshot, but especially Frank Carter, would be aware of just exactly how old she was. She had never divulged her age publicly to anyone. She tugged on Bill's sleeve to get his attention. As he looked down, she pleaded with her eyes and shook her head violently.

Standing on her tiptoes and leaning over the counter, she hissed, "Sir, are you absolutely sure this is necessary? Can't we just say 'over twenty-one?'"

The clerk sighed in exasperation and impatience. "No, ma'am. We cannot be so imprecise."

Dorothy's mouth tightened into a thin line and she narrowed her eyes at the man across the counter.

"May I at least be afforded the privacy of a whisper?" she demanded angrily, though in a low voice, not wanting to draw any more attention to herself.

"But of course, ma'am. As you say," the clerk replied quickly to try to appease her.

Both Bill and Frank were suddenly very interested in the dirt under their fingernails and were doing their best to dislodge it with their thumb nails, not with much luck, either.

"October 27," Dorothy began. "Uhmm, Eighteen, uh" her voice sank lower, ". . . eighty-eight."

"Yes, ma'am." The relieved clerk blew the eraser dust from application and reinserted it into his typewriter.

Dammit! Dorothy's eyes filled with tears but she refused to blink.

One other fact had been a thorn in her side. She and Bill had argued over it several times prior to their trip to the Passport Agency.

Almost ten years had passed since October 15, 1915. An over-the-moon and then back again day. A day for just the two of them. No reporters. No cameras. A day in Marysville, California. A railroad stopover between Oakland and Pendleton. A quiet place where two rodeo stars could walk the streets completely unnoticed.

No need that day for tall hats, leather chaps or split skirts. There was no one in Marysville on that Friday morning to recognize either Roy Robbins or Carlina Eichhorn as they bought their marriage license in the tiny courthouse. Hand in hand, they then made the short walk from courthouse on 5th Street to the ME Church on D Street – less than three blocks away. October 15, 1915, Mr. Skeeter Bill Robbins and Miss Dorothy Morrell tied the knot.

But that had been a good year after they'd showed up at Converse County Fair and checked into the LaBonte Hotel as a couple. A good year, a great year, and a full twelve months. And it was nobody's business, Dorothy insisted, when they had officially married.

"I don't know why yer so set on keepin' this on the down low," Bill had said time and again when Dorothy pouted and argued with him over the date.

"I am a . . ." Dorothy sputtered. What? *A good woman? Ein gute Deutscher Frau? One who still hoped for her mother's approval?*

"I do not need the whole damn world to know that I wasn't married to you the first year we were together. My God! All of the newspaper reporters who made sure to write 'the wife of Skeeter Bill Robbins' in their stories will have a hay day screaming about being misled. There is enough scandal in my life without adding to it."

"Scandal? Girl, you ain't never run off with yer husband's best friend. You ain't never divorced one bronk rider just to marry another. You ain't got the faintest idea of scandal."

"Oh, my hell!" she yelled back. "You have never met my mother! She could spell out scandal for you if you'd like."

"Listen. Don't make no difference to me. Sorry I cain't see this yer way, but if you wanna say we was married in August of 1914, it's no never mind to me. Just simmer down a bit."

Dorothy had wanted to do anything but simmer down and so had stewed about their differences in opinion for a while longer. She finally decided she'd had enough of trying to give Bill the silent treatment.

"So, we can say we were married on the 15th of August? 1914?" Dorothy asked. *Never let facts get in the way of the truth. That's how Dolly had put it.*

"If that's what floats yer boat, it's fine by me," said Bill, still bewildered that it made such a difference to Dorothy.

Floats yer boat! Dorothy smiled as her reminiscing was interrupted with Bill's return to her side.

"Look at these rings here," he said, showing her the quoit rings made of rope. "Shall we find us a target and see what we kin do with a short rope?"

Dorothy laughed, shaking her head, and took Bill's hand ready to follow him to the ends of the earth. Barring that, to the closest quoit targets. No more officials prying at her age, squinting at her photograph, no more worrying about the questions that had no right answers.

This week on the *Lapland*, courtesy of Mr. Tex Austin, was going to be one of peace and joy.

The honeymoon they had never had, never missed, never even guessed they'd have wanted.

Prelude to an adventure of a lifetime.

XX - 14 JUNE 1924 - OPENING THE SHOW

How yuh doin', Dot?" Bill called as he grinned at her from his saddle, reins in hand.   Knee to knee.   Side by side.   Almost shoulder to shoulder.   He was now standing tall in his stirrups, craning to see over the hundreds of horses and riders that were assembled in the tunnel opening into the arena.   Close as he was, Bill still had to raise his voice to be heard in the crush of the crowd.   All were waiting for their moments to arrive to take part in the Grand Entrance into Wembley Stadium.   The opening day had finally arrived.   The hour had arrived as well.   2:30 p.m.

Each day for the next two weeks, except for Sundays, there would be two shows per day, the afternoon and an evening program at 8:30.

Dorothy took in a deep breath of excitement and nodded, keeping tight rein on her horse. Like so many others, it danced in place, picking up on the high energy of the excitement that filled the crowded, dimly lit tunnel.

This was like no other opening ceremony Dorothy had ever ridden in. Even the 101 Ranch at the Panama-Pacific Exposition, with all its stagecoaches, hired-on soldiers of fortune and Native Americans, could not hold a candle to this "fine mess" of teeming horses and riders. And that wasn't all.

Ahead of the crowds of mounted horsemen and women, the Royal Irish Fusiliers were lined at the mouth of the tunnel on the stadium side of the gates separating them from horses and their mounts. Chills went through Dorothy as she heard the pipe major barking orders, immediately followed by the sharp staccato of snare drums and the booming cadence of both the tenor and bass drums.

"Shhhh. Easy girl." Dorothy patted her horse's shoulder as the skirl of bagpipes began. She wasn't familiar with the tune, but it didn't matter, no doubt a marching tune that had led countless warriors into battle in the past centuries. Standing as tall as she could in her own stirrups, she could just make out the regiment. Over the heads of the horsemen and women, she could make out the green hackles adorning their caubeens - fancy word for beret, Dorothy thought - that signified them as part of the Irish Regiment. Clad in saffron colored kilts, the pipe and drum corps, complete with standard bearers, the colors of the Empire snapping smartly in the slight breeze, began its dignified and carefully measured march into the arena. The band playing its stirring marching tunes, would traverse the length of the stadium floor, a good 150 yards, then turn to march back, still piping, to its place on the western stand.

Grinning, she glanced over at Vera McGinnis, who grinned back and waved.

"Gonna take this place by storm," Vera shouted over the din. Dorothy nodded in her excitement, hardly able to be any more still than the horse beneath her.

At last, the gates to the tunnel were opened for the rodeo people, and just as they had practiced earlier, the horses and riders exploded into the arena, led by an Oklahoma cowboy, a Creek Indian of the Five Civilized Tribes, Riley Burgess. He had put aside his cowboy garb for the time being and was dressed as brightly as any drug store wooden Indian, complete with striped blanket and a souvenir headdress.

Following right on Burgess' horse's heels were the cowboys and cowgirls of the First International Rodeo, a mighty wave of brilliantly colored shirts, blouses, silver studded saddles and bridles blazing in the sun. On they came, a huge shining serpent, advancing to overtake everything in its path, forming a long double and triple file cantering around the outside edge of the huge oval arena, thundering over the tan bark and peat duff that separated the turf of the exhibition ground from the tall wire fencing. Each and every contestant saluting as he or she passed the judges' stand.

The last riders out of the entrance tunnel were met by the first who had already completely circumnavigated the arena. At that point all the riders turned to gallop toward the center of the arena, forming a line with their backs to the judges' box, facing the crowds seated in the better seats of the house on the northern side of Wembley Stadium, facing the welcoming twin domes of the front entrances standing tall and clearly seen from within the arena.

Heart pounding, Dorothy slowed her horse to join her fellow riders in the line down the center of the field, as the booming voice of the rodeo announcer filled the stadium, his words being broadcast over a sound system the likes Dorothy had never seen. *Actually,* she corrected herself, *the likes she had never heard!*

After being surrounded by and listening to so many Brits in the last two weeks, it was almost comforting to realize the announcer was also from the United States, though the slow cadence of his words and careful enunciation guaranteed that the Brits should be able to understand him.

"Lay-deez and Gent-al-men!" the announcer began, his amplified voice echoing throughout the stadium. "The cowboys and cowgirls – assembled now before you – have come from the far corners of the world – at their own expense."

The announcer paused as loud applause burst from the assembled audience of over 90,000 drowned him out even with the aid of the electric speaker system.

"They work for no one but themselves – they are not salaried performers" - more applause - "They have come to your fair land to take part in the greatest – international – cowboy contest ever held – and to compete for the largest prizes – ever offered."

Dorothy wondered just how many of the spectators had the slightest inkling what was about to unfold before them. This was no Wild West Show, carefully choreographed down to the last minute. The unexpected had to be expected. This could get gritty.

"You have met the contestants," the booming voice continued; " - they are mounted before you - in great anticipation - of the contests in the coming days –

"Now I take great pleasure - in introducing the judges - upon whose very capable shoulders - the great responsibility rests - of deciding the winners of the coming events - in the coming days - and weeks."

Another surge of applause and cheers.

"Misss-terrr Add-i-son Perry Day - of Medicine Hat – Alberta - Canada!"

The roaring cheers from the crowd evidenced their pride and approval of Mr. Day as one of their own, a fellow citizen of the Empire, unaware he was a Texas-born and passport carrying citizen of the US.

AP Day's beautiful stocking-footed stallion trotted, proudly high stepping to the center of the ring, as Day removed his hat and bowed from the waist to the still cheering audience, calling and shouting from the tiered seating above him. Dorothy thought how smart, but almost out-of-place, he looked in a business cut suit in sharp contrast to the chaps and colored shirts of the cowboy crowd.

"Cap-tain Tom R Hickman - Company B - Texas Rangers" intoned the announcer as Hickman lightly touched his spurs to his tough mustang, Tejano, to canter to center ring, reining up next to Mr. Day. Dorothy could easily imagine the square-jawed, clean-shaven Captain Hickman sporting a thick black handlebar mustache, but this was 1924, and the days of old time bristle faced lawmen were in the past.

"And rounding out our esteemed trio - Captain G -   M - Jones - Las Vegas - New Mexico!"

A polite smattering of applause greeted Captain Jones; they were clearly ready for more exciting action than introductions. Captain Jones first ceremoniously saluted the announcer before he also cantered across the arena to join Day and Hickman. Some of the riders knew that Captain Jones was also Doctor of Veterinary Medicine Garrett Jones, handpicked by Tex Austin to attend stock if necessary, especially trick riders' horses trained to maintain a smooth, even gait, with never a misstep, or the working cow horses running full out to carry the steer wrestling cowboys to their targets.

"Without further ado - we now introduce - the world's greatest - exponent - of cowboy contest - Missss-ter Texsssssss Ausssss - tin!"

From the far end of the long line of riders, a huge black stallion stepped proudly forward, but no more proudly than the tall familiar figure sporting an equally impressive tall white Stetson. Once clear of the line, Pilot sidestepped and cavorted even as the rider lifted his reins. Instantly Pilot broke into a full gallop circling the entire arena, ending up in center ring. There he reared back, a carefully practiced move, as Tex Austin waved his hat in a salute to the thoroughly approving and excited crowd who increased their applause and heightened their cheers.

"Watch the chutes, folks - our first contest - special to tonight's program - Red Sublett - Rodeo Clown Extraordinaire - on a wild steer."

Immediately, Dorothy with the rest of the entire company of riders split their line in the middle and each half cantered to the opposing far ends of the arena. The central gate of the heavily timbered chutes, specially built for the rodeo event here at Wembley, swung open and a huge white-faced steer leaped into the arena.

Clinging to its back was rodeo clown, John "Red" Sublett. Dressed in his usual castoff ragged clothing, he looked more like a hobo than a cowboy, but he could ride with the best of them. The steer, bellowing, leapt into the air, twisting and jerking, intent on dislodging the tenacious rider on its back.

Dorothy followed her fellow riders into the makeshift waiting area and swung down off her horse and turned to watch Red. His signature bowler hat stuck squarely on the top of his head, its crown punched down for a flat top. Dorothy gritted her teeth as she realized the steer had turned and was charging straight for the unfamiliar woven wire fencing on the outside of the ring that provided a cushioning zone between the exhibition grounds and the stadium. The steer ran head on into the fencing and immediately dropped to its knees, rolling over onto its rider, raising a thick cloud of dust.

A collective gasp erupted from the stands followed by anxious muttering. *Baptism by fire,* Dorothy thought, not sure if it were for the crowds or the clown.

The steer quickly regained its feet and turned to face Sublett, lying still and prone on the ground.

A fearful silence fell over the arena, as the most of the spectators held their breaths. A few shouts and calls from a small number of the onlookers could be clearly heard, the crowd unfamiliar with the scene before them. Would a goring be the opening act of the International Cowboy Championships?

Before the steer could lower its horns, cowboys poured into the arena, shouting and hooting, waving their hats at the steer, which lifted its head, bellowed, sniffing the air before nonchalantly trotting across the ring to the now opened exit gates. Ambulance men took to the field, trotting out with a stretcher to remove Sublett from the ring.

Damn! Not the best way to open a show, Dorothy thought remorsefully.

"Give him a hand, folks! – Let 'im know yer here for him!" directed the announcer. Hesitantly the crowds put their hands together, not sure why a fallen rider should be applauded.

Quickly, the announcer redirected the crowd's attention to the first event on their programs.

"Numm–ber One E–vent for the evening – Bareback Bronk Riding – names of the riders listed on your colored programs."

Dorothy turned to unsaddle her horse. For this first show, her part was over. She joined others, both those watching and those waiting to go on where they were gathered under the canvas awning of the temporary stables. Bill would be competing in the Fancy Roping event, the second on the program. He was nowhere to be seen. Chasing one of the many irons he had in the fire, no doubt.

First bareback bronk rider of the night was Charles Johnson, a slow talking, quiet man from New Mexico who usually kept to himself. His horse crow hopped and twisted before throwing its rider. The crowd roared its disappointment as Johnson picked himself, slapped the dust from his hat and waved to the fans, still clapping and cheering the fallen cowboy. Meanwhile, the men in the chutes were busy getting the next horses and riders ready.

160

Dorothy found a seat with Vera McGinnis, Bea Kirnan, Tad Barnes, and Olive Tegland who were on deck to compete in the Cowgirls' Bronk Riding Event a little later in this show. Olive was pacing the tent nervously.

"Oh, come on, now, girl," Vera called. "Come have a seat. You're going to wear yourself out before you even get started."

"I know, I know," Olive replied. Then she grinned at them all. "I know this isn't any different than any other rodeo, but I feel like it's my first time out of the chutes."

"You're going to do great!" Dorothy reassured her.

Her pretty face framed with thick bangs and short bobbed hair, Olive stepped over some of the cowboys' bronk riding saddles and sat down next to Dorothy. Dorothy was surprised to see tears starting in Olive's eyes.

"What's wrong? Surely, this isn't about your ride," she asked. All eyes turned to Olive.

She shook her head. "You girls are so good for me. I think I would go crazy if I didn't have you to talk to."

"What are friends for?" Vera laughed, still confused. Cowgirls didn't make it a practice of crying before their rides.

"It's just hit me harder today than most. Here I am in London, England, on the ride of a lifetime and all I can think about is my baby boy back home!"

Dorothy put her arm around Olive's shoulders. Once she had wondered how a girl could divide her time between rodeos and a husband. It was beyond her imagination on how to add a baby into the mix, let alone leaving a young son in the care of another for over a month - maybe closer to two months.

"Will he even remember me?" Olive's tears were now making their slow way down her cheeks as she tried valiantly to keep her emotions in check.

"How old's your youngster," Tad asked.

"He's just six months old," came Olive's teary reply.

A hush fell over the group of women. Though none of the rest of them was a mother, they all understood the worry of leaving family behind.

Tad gently broke the silence. "You know, Olive, I'm the youngest of twenty-one kids. Yup, I said twenty-one. Tell you this. I don't remember back to the days I was only six months old, but I bet my mama does. That's the part that counts. When you get back home to your baby, you just make up for lost time and by the time your kid is my age, important thing he'll know is that his mama loved the dickens outta him!"

Everyone in earshot laughed as Olive dried her eyes.

"You got it!" she told Tad. "Say how'd you come by that name anyway?"

"Oh, well, they say I never learned to crawl. Slithered around on my belly so my dad took to calling me Tadpole. Maybe it was easier to remember than my given name."

"Which is?" Olive asked.

"Barbara," Tad replied. "Barbara Inez Barnes." She blushed. "Well, Barbara Inez Barnes Lucas. Been married now – let's see – three weeks!"

"Well, now, ladies," Vera put in, "now that that's settled, there's only one thing to do at a time like this!"

They all laughed. England was "wet" and they all knew there had to be a bottle of something "mighty fine" hid out when a single – hell, a double – shot of courage was needed to carry on.

"Cheers!"

They toasted each other from the bottle Vera produced from her war bag not even bothering to wipe its lip as laughing, they passed it around.

XXI - 17 JUNE 1924 - AFTER THE RIDE

The muggy heat of the afternoon was finally giving way to evening coolness. The first rodeo show of the afternoon was behind them and the second was still an hour or so away. Two shows daily, 2:30 and 8:30.

Now was time for reflection, for camaraderie, relaxing a little - reliving the rides, comparing the bronks, remembering the echo of the cheer of the crowds.

The crowds! The colossal crowds. When they were impressed, their roars sent shivers up Dorothy's spine and lifted the hair on the back of her neck. When they were pleased, their applause boomed across the arena shouts of "blimey," "blinking" and "bloody" echoing through the air.

When they were disappointed or angry, as they often were when it came to steer wrestling, the air was filled with boos, hisses and taunts. Cries of outrage filled the stadium. Not as the cowboy chased down the steer while aside this horse.   Not when the cowboy's horse was shoulder to shoulder with the steer so the cowboy could slide from his saddle to grasp the steer by its horns, slowing its all–out run across the arena, but as the cowboy dug in his heels to slow the critter, twisting its head to knock it off balance and land on its side or back.   That was the moment that cries of foul were overwhelming.

As much as the Brits hated steer wrestling, though, their anger at steer roping could not be contained.   Long before Tex Austin had even sailed for England, early in April, solicitors had been petitioning the courts to disallow the event.   Extreme cruelty, they cried.   Unfortunately, during the first roping performance of the first day, the steer being roped had broken its leg, and the hisses and boos were devastating as it was announced that the animal would be put down.   It puzzled Dorothy that for a nation of people who in general saw nothing wrong with fox hunting – the quarry ultimately pulled to pieces by the hounds – the Brits were horrified that the cowboys not only roped steers, but then the steers were jerked off their feet, sometimes being dragged for some distance.   Dragged by its horns, the strain upon them very great!   Other times, rolling over once or twice as the lariat settled around its neck.   And then the race was on as the cowboy leaped from his horse.   The horse whose job it was to keep the rope taut, not allowing the steer to regain its feet.   After running to the steer, the cowboy must hog tie three of its legs to earn a scoring time.   *INHUMANE*, the headlines screamed and the crowds screamed louder, still.

Today's shows had been crowd pleasers, though, as the steer roping event was no longer being held in public. As one of the arena directors, Bill was sporting a grin wider than usual.

"We done good t'day!" Bill said to the clutch of competitors gathered in the stable tent, relishing the shade from the late afternoon sun.

Sea chests doubled as both seats for the company of riders and as places to set their saddles to keep them off of the ground.   Tex Austin had made it clear that it was every competitor's responsibility to bring their own tack – saddles, bridles, halters.

"Yup, purty much," Dave Lund replied.   Dave had been in the money today, taking first in men's bareback riding on the bronk called *Bootlegger*. Bill had made it to the end of his ride but hadn't placed.

"Not bad," Dorothy agreed.   "Not bad."

Dot had come into the money in second place on the horse Chalks Bluff behind Bonnie McCarrol who finished in first place and ahead of Vera McGinnis in third. It wasn't often anyone beat out Vera in a contest, so Dorothy felt accomplished.

Competing against the likes of Vera McGinnis, Bonnie McCarroll, Tad Lucas, and Bea Kirnan was hard.   Not only did she have a few years on them, but none of them had been through a "train wreck" of the magnitude she had in '15.   Not yet anyway.

164

In the shade of the tent, Dot sat on a rough plank bench and listened to the two josh and banter as Bill and Dave pulled the makings for cigarettes from their pockets and stepped out into the open to roll their own. The process always fascinated her. Tiny sheets of thin paper were in a small envelope attached to the back of the draw-string sack of crushed tobacco leaves, more thin than any other paper she'd ever seen anywhere else.

She watched as Bill pulled a sheet out and turned up the longer edges to create a trough by threading one end of it between his thumb, index and middle fingers, cupping it in his left hand. He pulled open the draw-strings of the bag with his right hand and gently shook some tobacco into the paper. She knew he was thinking of her when he stopped filling the paper with tobacco long before he would have if he'd thought he was smoking it all on his own.

Dot smiled to herself as Dave seemed to overload his own cigarette paper. Pulling the drawstrings closed, each returned the makings to their pockets. She watched Bill lick the longer edges of his paper and roll the tobacco and paper into it, finishing by twisting each end of the cigarette.

"How do you do?" An elderly looking gentleman called to Bill and waved.

He was striding long steps to approach them, his mustache grey and bristled. Even in the heat of the day, he seemed cool and dapper, buttoned inside his white dress shirt and vest, tie knotted precisely, though his jacket was open, unbuttoned. A watch chain looped across the front of the vest.

His eyes showed delight as he approached.

"Mr. Robbins, I presume?"

Absently, Bill handed Dot his yet unlit cigarette as he stepped forward to shake the man's hand.

"Yes, I am and how do you do?" Bill returned the man's greeting.

"Well, doing very well. Rudyard Kipling, here! Delighted to meet you!"

Bill glanced at Dot, surprise plain and open on his face.

"Your poetry, my good man! I've read some of it in the newspapers. Top notch, the best!" Kipling beamed as he pumped Bill's hand.

"Thank yuh, sir. And I've read many of yer pomes as well," Bill replied. "I especially like that one about the water boy, Gunga Din."

"Ah, yes," Kipling quickly accepted the compliment and moved on, "poets write of things just as we see them."

He reached inside his suit jacket to an inner pocket and pulled out a cigarette case filled with tailor-mades.

"Do you smoke, sir?"

"Thank yuh, Mr. Kipling," Bill replied as he fished a wooden match from his pocket and struck it on the pant leg of his jeans.

"Jolly good!" Kipling laughed as he leaned in for Bill to light his cigarette before lighting his own. The two men continued talking as they left the area near the stable tent and walked over to the eight foot wire mesh fence surrounding the arena.   Dorothy could no longer make out what they were saying.

"Dave," she asked, "do you have a light for a lady?"

Dave was watching Bill and Kipling and didn't seem to hear her.   She waited a moment or two, watching Dave dragging deeply on his own cigarette.   He breathed the smoke out through his nose, looking for all the world like a smoking dragon. The smoke curled up past the brim of his hat and faded away in the light breeze.

"Hey, David?" she began again.   Dave Lund had a faraway look in his eye and Dorothy realized he had never been interested in whatever Bill and Mr. Kipling were talking about.   She wondered if his thoughts were back in Alberta.   Was there a sweetheart waiting? A family?   She had never heard him mentioned either.

"Mr. Lund?"

Third time might be the charm, she thought as she again tried to get his attention.

Dave startled.

"Yes?" he replied.

Dorothy smiled before she asked, "Just what is your name?"

Dave's face melted into his usual smile, crinkles deepening around his eyes and dimples.

"And just what makes you ask that, Miss Also Known As?"

"Oh, and you think Dorothy Robbins also known as Dorothy Morrell is trying to hide anything?"

Her laugh was light-hearted and easy, but if he only knew, she thought, but the girl she had been - Carlina, the German-Russian immigrant raised in Winnipeg - was so far away.

"At least I'll always answer to Dorothy . . . or even Dot!" she grinned.

Dave took a last drag on his stump of a cigarette and finally noticed hers wasn't lit yet.   He reached over and held the glowing end of his cigarette to Dorothy's before pinching it carefully between his calloused fingers, rolling and scattering the last of the tobacco to the wind.   He tucked the scrap of paper into the watch pocket in his jeans.   Gone with the wash, Dorothy thought.

"Shouldn't tell you my name," Dave laughed.   "You just might write a letter to my good bishop back home.   I'd be in big trouble with all my rowdy ways."

"You?   Rowdy?" Dorothy shook her head.   The Canadian cowboys from Alberta seemed to be in a world apart from the cowboys from Texas, Oklahoma and especially California.   The hard drinking, big talking, swashbuckling men full of piss and vinegar.

Her father, Friedrich, with his thick German accent, would probably call the Canadians *Landmanner*, men who rode horses to make a living from the rich black earth, who husbanded the land and the hay and cattle it grew. Men who usually just battled bronks locally on summer weekends.

"Smoking is frowned upon back home amongst my good Mormon neighbors. And my family. They go back to the old days. Pioneering up from Utah. Brother Brigham and all that. As for drinking, if we make it ourselves, it doesn't seem to be such a sin."

"Hummm," was all Dorothy could think to say.

She didn't know much about Mormons. Didn't really care much either. She thought she remembered Bill telling her that one of his brothers, Will, in fact, had married to one. She frowned. Had she ever met him or his wife? She didn't think so, but she couldn't imagine anyone marrying into the Robbins family who would be bothered by smoking or drinking. Maybe it was just Alberta Mormons. Maybe just his Mormon family.

Dave shot Dorothy a sassy smirk, turned his head away from where Kipling and Bill were still deep in conversation, and muttered just loud enough for her to hear, doing his best to mimic a Cockney street thug:

It's moonshine an' never beer when yer ridin' clear out here
Spendin' all yer time a wishin' ya had penny in yer pocket
But when it comes to slaughter, ye'll do yer work on water
Cuz you know a barbeque is on the docket. ***

Dorothy snorted and shook her head.

"You should know," she whispered back.

Dave shrugged and wandered off to find something else to do with his time, most likely catch a cat nap before the evening show.

Dorothy stepped over next to Bill, slipping her hand into the crook of his elbow and smiled as she heard his reciting some lines of poetry he'd already penned while in London.

The cowboys are in London,
They took the town by storm -
The lads with shirts so gaudy bright,
And hearts so big and warm.

Tex Austin, with his merry smile,
Has come and brought his bunch,
With leather straps and jingling spurs,
The punchers with their punch.

The roper, Tommy Kirnan,
Is also with us here,
To hand us dope and spin the rope,
And wrestle with the steer.

There's Vera 'Ginnis and Ruth Roach, too,
The girls who ride 'em clean,
Dot Morrell, she is the one,

167

Dorothy shook her head and smiled.   *Queen of my heart,* Bill would say. Bill's heart.

"I say, chap," Kipling said, "have you ever considered publishing a collection of your poems?"

"Well, now, sir," Bill answered, "more'n a few of 'em have appeared in print, published as yuh say, in several newspapers 'round the West."

He didn't bother to explain just what "the West" was.   In Bill's mind, surely everyone would know, Dorothy thought.

"No.   No, sir.   That is not what I mean," Kipling explained.   "You should print them in booklet form at least, although hardbound books are more durable and command a higher price."

"Hmmmm," Bill rubbed his chin as he thought out loud, "a book a pomes."

"Your poetry is more than good, it is real.   You make it real because you write of things just as you see them.   Just as you know them," Kipling urged.

"*Rhymes of the Rodeo.* Has a nice ring to it," Bill nodded.   "*Rhymes of the Rodeo, by Skeeter Bill Robbins, Cowboy Poet.*   It could happen."

Dorothy could see the wheels turning in Bill's mind, plans already spinning into place.   Dorothy shook her head and sighed.   Where on Bill's docket would the publication plans be placed?   At the head, before rodeo cowboy, rough stock provider, cowboy suppers and dances, or at the end after clean the stalls and feed the stock?   Bill was a practical man.   Food on the table and roof over the head always came first; dreams were filled in where he could.

"Ah, Mrs. Robbins," Kipling nodded, turning to Dorothy, his eyes lighting in delight in recognition.   "Thank you for joining us."

Shoot, Dorothy thought, *he must have been quite delighted to be meeting Mr. Skeeter Bill Robbins in person, not to remember I was standing right next to him just a little while ago when he walked up to the little knot of friends about to share a smoke.*

"You are quite welcome," Dorothy smiled back.

"Oh, I nearly forgot!   You bring to mind another much more important reason I have sought out the company of the Cowboys and Cowgirls of the Cowboy Championships!"

Kipling laughed at his own expense.   He reached into another inner pocket of his jacket and withdrew a stack of printed cards.

"As a member of the planning committee, I have the distinct honor and privilege of bearing dinner invitations to your company from the President of the Committee which organized this Exhibition, even, Edward, the Prince of Wales."

Dorothy caught her breath.   Had she really heard correctly?

"As one of the arena directors, would you be so kind as to distribute these invitations for me?" Kipling smiled up at Bill's equally surprised face extending the cards to him.

"But of course," Bill replied, echoing the British expression of assurance, taking the invitations in hand.

"There are plenty of invitations for each and every one of your contestants," Kipling explained, "and the address of the hotel and time is printed on each, as well."

"Oh, before I forget," Kipling went on, "I am very serious about encouraging you to publish your poetry. I shall look forward to receiving a copy, fresh off the press. Here is the address to which you shall mail your *Rhymes of the Rodeo*."

Kipling took a previously addressed envelope from his pocket and handed it to Bill as well as the stack of invitation cards.

"Many, many thanks," Bill, the Poet of the Plains, humbly said to Kipling, the Poet of the Empire.

As Kipling turned to greet others and shake their hands, Mike Hastings stepped out from under the awning of the tent and walked over to where Bill and Dorothy stood.

"You better keep good track a that envelope," he said. "That autograph should be worth a pretty penny."

But Bill just laughed as he folded it carefully and stowed it into his breast pocket. "That ain't why he give it, and that ain't why I'll keep it."

Mike shrugged and the three of them began to make their way through the clusters of seated and standing contestants, Bill handing invitations to all.

So much to look forward to. So little time.

XXII - JUNE 1924 – A BRUSH WITH ROYALTY

B ill," Dorothy wailed. "I didn't pack anything even close to evening clothes." She stood dripping wet, wrapped in a bath towel that was larger than most of the blankets back home on their bed.

"Dot, my dear, nobody did!" Bill calmly replied from where he was seated across from her in their narrow hotel room, boot in one hand, and boot brush in the other.

"Yer problem is that yer seein' yerself as a guest of the Prince of Wales, but that ain't who he invited to his shindig.   He invited the cowboys - *and* cowgirls – of the rodeo to his party an' that's who he expects. Boots, hats, neckerchiefs, and vests."

Dorothy sighed but could not find an argument for that.

"Course, I s'pose cleanin' the horse manure off our boots an' applyin' a coat a boot wax could be appreciated," he said as he continued to brush the dirt and dried debris from his boots with a boot brush.

Dorothy watched with tired eyes, still not convinced that she felt up to being a guest at the Prince of Wale's dinner party in her working clothes. She should have started thinking on this the minute Rudyard Kipling handed the invitations to Bill.

"Come on now, Dot. Smile! Oh, and hand me them boots a yers over an' I'll do the same for 'em," Bill offered.

Dorothy shook her head, scattering water droplets all around her as she tossed her boots over the bed and to the floor at his feet. Though she could see the logic in what Bill was saying, she was beside herself wondering what she should wear to the Royal Shindig this evening.

She sank back into the comforting arms of the other stuffed chair gracing their somewhat Spartan hotel room. Spartan in comparison to some, she reminded herself. She apprized the room, calculating the measurements of the room and decided her first apartment back in Oakland would have surely fit into it.

"I just wish I had something better to wear than what I had on all day," Dorothy continued to complain, though she was realizing that Bill was right. Edward, Prince of Wales, was surely not expecting or even wanting evening gowns and pearls on the cowgirls, or bow ties and tails on the cowboys.

"Put on a clean blouse, and a smile," Bill suggested, as he applied black Kiwi wax to his boots. "This here boot polish is worth all that we paid for it. An' then some."

Dorothy watched, fascinated by the results she knew were coming. This British boot polish had won over most every rodeo rough rider or trick roper she knew. *No, Kiwi polish was an Australian import. So, Aussie boot polish!*

Bill was now using what looked to Dorothy to be either an oversized toothbrush or an extremely undersized hairbrush to carefully work the polish across and into the leather of his tall black boots.

"Yuh still wanna try that new color a polish on yer boots?" Bill asked, unsure just how her brown boots would look with a coat of cordovan polish on them.

"Sure! At least something will seem new," Dorothy answered, smiling now as she stood to start dressing for the evening.

"It'll be diff'ernt, that's fer shure," Bill agreed as he picked up her boots.

Minutes later, dressed in her layers of underclothes, Dorothy stood in front of their bathroom mirror and brushed out her damp, shoulder length hair.   She knew that as it dried, its natural soft curls and waves would pull it up closer to her head and crown her face.

She squinted, trying to decide if the fine lines next to her eyes were deepening or not.   *More than likely*, she thought as she frowned.   Then she remembered something Mutti used to say to her frowning daughter.

Be careful, Schautzi!   You do not want your face to freeze like that!   Dorothy smiled and nodded.   *Good advice, Mutti.*

She carefully smoothed a thin layer of facial cream up her neck and over her chin, cheeks and forehead.   All this craze about "vanishing" facial cream!   If it paid off, though, it would surely be worth the time she spent nightly putting it on.

"Yuh puttin' yer war paint on?" Bill called from the other room.

"Whatever!" she called back.

Her eyelashes, as was her hair, were dark and thick, so she seldom used the eyeliner that was so popular these days, thanks to the starlets of the silver screen.   Not that she had anything against using it, especially for dramatic emphasis.   *As might be in order for an evening hobnobbing with royalty!*   She pulled the kohl black eyeliner pencil and carefully traced the edges of her eyelids.

She smoothed her eyebrows with a tiny dap of cold cream and studied the results.   A touch of lipstick, something Bill also disliked but reluctantly abided, and she would be ready for the night.

"Yuh almost ready in there?" Bill asked.   Dorothy could hear the cadence of the shoeshine brush on leather boots.   She stepped to the doorway.

"Always amazes me how those boots go from a greasy looking dull finish to a mirror shine with that brush," she said.

"Well, whatcha think?"

Bill was smiling broadly as he lifted her boots, no longer dusty or scuffed, but shining brilliantly with a deeper, richer shade of brown, nearly oxblood.

Her eyebrows raised in delight and laughter trilled across the room.

"Oh, my stars!" Dorothy breathed.   "They look better than the day we bought them."

She pulled them onto her feet, and while looking down at them in admiration, did a few dance steps.

"They are beautiful!   Thank you, Bill, my dear!" Dorothy smiled up at all six and half feet of Mr. Skeeter Bill Robbins.   He leaned over and kissed her.

"Well, gal.   Purty as they are, I'm a-thinkin' yuh better git a few more clothes on!   Though truth be told, some a them evenin' gowns I seen cover up less'n what yuh got on now!"

"Oh, you!" she sputtered, buttoning herself into a freshly ironed blouse.

As she stepped into her leather skirt, she could see that Bill had done a little leather magic on it as well.   The dust of the day was long gone.   She sighed as she began the tedious task of fastening the side buttons she'd

172

undone earlier that day.   When it was laid out, the skirt looked like a pair of extremely wide legged trousers. Legs so full and wide that when she stood, their fullness fell into a pleasing allusion of a skirt.   The fringe at the bottom of the skirt swayed back and forth just about even with the tops of her boots.

She still wasn't ready for bloused trousers and especially not the jodhpurs that so many horsewomen had taken to wearing.   Made their backend look as broad a barn.   Vera McGinnis' satin trousers, on the other hand, pleasingly hugging her shapely legs.   One extreme to the other. Maybe one day she might decide to make a wardrobe change, but not now.

Silver conchos buttoned up both the left and ride side of the skirt, not unlike a pair of old time sailor's trousers.   *Why anyone needs two sets of buttons on a skirt or trousers, I'll never know,* she thought to herself.   She only ever undid the buttons on the right side as they were the ones easier for her to button up.

The cool of the evening greeted them as Dorothy and Bill stepped from the foyer of their hotel and onto the street.   Bill had already discovered that the hotel where the dinner party was being held was only a few blocks from theirs, so "just a good stretch of the legs," as some would say.   A few friendly pedestrians were still out and about this time of the evening. They smiled and nodded as Dorothy and Bill briskly walked along.

"Who ever heard of starting a party at 10:00 pm?" Bill had groused, surprised, after reading through the invitation card back on the day that it had been handed to him by Kipling.

"We were thinking that it would be foolish to begin the reception before the evening performance of the rodeo is over," Kipling had explained good-naturedly.

"Ahh, good thinkin'."   Bill quickly corrected his attitude.

"I guess that it won't be much different than those all-night dances up on the Boxelder," Dorothy added.   "Brings to mind those pot luck suppers that turned to dancing until dawn."

"When yuh put it that way, it makes perfect sense." Bill grinned down at her and winked.

"A woman's guess is more often more accurate than a man's certainty, I would say," Kipling added, grinning broadly as well.

In no time at all, Bill and Dorothy were walking through the gleaming glass front doors of a much more opulent and splendid hotel than where they were staying.   A greeter discreetly took in their outfits and with a nod of his head pointed to a hallway that would lead them to their destination.

Dorothy's heart was pounding as she and Bill walked down the gleaming corridor, following the pleasing sounds of stringed music.

Another greeter stood officiously at the doorway to a huge ballroom.

"Invitation, please," he firmly ordered.

"Yup, an' here yuh are," Bill replied, handing him both his and Dorothy's invitations.

"On behalf of the Prince of Wales, welcome." With hardly a second glance, the doorman put the invitations into one of his coat pockets and nodded, looking past them and off into the distance.

"Your hat, sir."

A liveried hat checker stood at the ready to take Bill's hat handing him a claim ticket in return as soon as they stepped into the cavernous ballroom.

"Oh, yeah. Of course," Bill gulped and Dorothy grinned. A cowboy and his hat seldom parted company. As they looked across the ballroom floor, the only hats in sight were those set at jaunty angles over cowgirls' faces.

Beyond the scattered groups of folks visiting, Dorothy saw that rows of round tables were arranged along the far wall. Even from where they stood, she could see that the tables were set with elegantly folded napkins and never ending rows of gleaming silverware. What was more amazing were the ice buckets, one on the center of each table with the three or four bottles of champagne being chilled.

"There's Tex," Bill pointed out and the two of them began to make their way across the yet uncrowded floor. "Bet this place'll be bustin' at the seams in no time a tall," he added.

"Sir? Madam?" A tall butler offered them champagne in crystal flutes on a silver platter.

"Thank you kindly," Dorothy answered as she and Bill each took a glass from the tray. Without another word, the waiter walked off to find anyone who was without a glass, and barring that, someone with an empty glass.

"Jumpin' jehoshaphat!" Bill exclaimed in low tones as he surveyed the ballroom. "Ain't no prohibition on this side of the pond!"

"And no limits, either, it seems," Dorothy added, pointing out the many bottles being chilled at the tables, as they approached the clutch of cowboys and cowgirls circling Tex Austin.

"Well, Bill. Dot." Tex nodded, welcoming them. Dorothy nodded and smiled brightly past her irritation.

You don't know me well enough, Mr. John Tex Austin, to be calling me Dot!

"How yuh, doin', Tex? Seems like a month a Sundees since last we met!" Bill joked, though it had only been a few hours.

"Isn't this something else?" Tex went on. "They say we're going to be dining most the night long."

"Dining, my eye," Bill teased. "It's the drinkin' that's got my attention."

He lifted his champagne flute and took far more than a sip.

"Not bad! Not a tall!" he proclaimed. "Sure, beats the hell outta that wine we had the other day."

Tex grinned.

"They tell me wine is an acquired taste . . ."

". . . and I sure ain't acquired it yet!" Bill finished.

Another waiter appeared with a tray of dainty canapés.

"May I interest you in any of these?" he asked, clearly expecting them to help themselves.

174

Rows of savory appetizers filled the tray. Dorothy thought back to the reception at the downtown San Francisco hotel, given by "Lady Bob" Montgomery, only days before she and Bill left California by train to New York City. These tiny delicacies were just the beginning. Lady Bob's instructions came to mind. *Canapés, my dear, are nothing more than hors d'oeuvres meant to be eaten with your fingers.*

Without even hesitating to weigh his choices, Tex Austin chose one, lifting it and the tiny paper napkin beneath it, and then turned to greet another group of cowboys who had just walked into the room.

"Don't mind if I do," Bill answered, though looking puzzled at the selection.

"Here's a nice little egg salad." Dorothy pointed out a cracker topped with chopped eggs and garnished with sliced chives, hoping to be helpful.

"Hummm," was all the reply she got.

Dorothy decided on one featuring smoked salmon over a buttery sauce on a tiny thin slice of toast, as the server was waiting for Bill to also make a choice.

Bill pointed to a very similar looking tidbit and asked, "What've we got here?"

"Gravlox," was the waiter's somewhat bored sounding reply.

"Grave locks?" Bill repeated.

"Yes, sir," came the reassurance.

Bill's eyebrows went up as he picked up what was obviously thinly sliced salmon, though it had a tinge of orange to it and seemed to glisten and shine compared to Dorothy's. Under it was cream cheese and a cracker.

Bill popped the entire thing in his mouth. He grinned, nodding as he chewed. Dorothy took a little bite of her own.

"Salty!" he exclaimed, "but mighty tasty. I'll have another, if yuh don't mind," he added, reaching for another just before the waiter turned to move on to find more empty fingers.

Bill seemed to enjoy his second treat just as much as the first.

"Makes yuh thirsty, though!" he said as he upended his champagne flute.

Before he could even wonder what to do with his empty glass, yet another waiter appeared at his side to exchange it for one that was filled.

"Wonder if we kin find another one a them guys with the tiny sandwiches," Bill said grinning down at her.

"We've got a lot of eating yet ahead of us," Dorothy reminded Bill.

"I s'pose I kin be patient," Bill grinned, "but I'm plenty hungry now."

Just then an excitement began to build in the ballroom which had nothing to do with the countless guests in attendance. Bill nodded toward the head table at the far end of the ballroom to a stately dressed younger gentleman who had slipped in unannounced.

"I b'lieve that's him, now." There was no doubt as who *him* was.

Throwing protocol to the wind, His Royal Highness, the Duke of Cornwall, even Prince Edward of Wales, tapped his own water goblet with a silver spoon and an instant hush fell over the usual rough and rowdy crowd.

"We are glad to welcome you this evening," he began.

"Come in, come in," he continued, waving in a small party of guests who had just now stepped through the door. "Come in and please be seated as you wish."

And with that, he stepped around the head table and began shaking hands with Tex Austin and Charles Cochran, together with the contestant judges, Add Day, Colonel Hickman, and Dr. Jones.

Bill took Dorothy by the elbow and guided her to the nearest table. As he slid her chair out so she could take a seat, he grinned down at her and said, "I believe it's suppertime!"

XXIII - JUNE 1924 - DINNER

D orothy and Bill found themselves seated with six other diners, some with familiar names and faces, the men all sporting the cowboy tan, or lack thereof, on their foreheads which had been in the constant protection of their hats.

"Mabry McDowell, here," said a thin but wiry, sunburned and windblown looking cowboy who took it upon himself to break the ice with the others, "from Billings, Montana."

"Or there abouts," laughed the identical looking cowboy sitting next to him. "Aubrey McDowell, from Bridger, Montana."

"Or there abouts!" Mabry argued, grinning from ear to ear.

"But we ain't the only set a twins in the McDowell family," Aubrey said.

"But shure as shootin', we're the last!" Mabry finished for him.

"This is my wife, Dorothy Morrell . . ." before Bill could go further, Aubrey finished for him as well.

"An' yer Skeeter Bill Robbins, in the flesh!"

Bill nodded. It wasn't often he had the words taken right out of his mouth.

"Ah, yup, from Bakersfield, California," he added.

"Or there abouts," laughed Dorothy. She decided she liked this dynamo duo.

"I'm Bonnie McCarroll, Boise, Idaho, and this is my husband, Frank."

"Yuh ride real good, Miz McCarroll," Aubry said as each of the McDowells nodded.

All eyes turned to the last two women who were seated at their table.

"Vera McGinnis." Dorothy thought that Vera's soft, drawn out vowels gave her away as not only an American but an American from the south, well, southern Missouri.

Vera continued, "This is our friend, Marie Gibson."

"We know Marie. She's a Montana rider like us," Mabry said. Marie smiled and gave a short nod at Aubrey and Mabry, before directing her attention elsewhere. They all turned to see what had caught her eye. She was watching Prince Edward as the royal made his way from table to table. Not quite hurrying, but wasting no time in his greetings as he moved one to the next. It was apparent that he intended to greet each of his guests.

"Seems to me Skeeter and Miss Dorothy here are outnumbered by the Macs at this table," Mabry joked, overlooking Marie Gibson.

At that moment, waiters descended upon their table, setting covered soup bowls before each of the diners.

"First course, Cream of Barley Soup," and without another word, the porcelain covers were lifted from their bowls and the waiters disappeared to ready for the invasion of yet another table.

"More eatin' utensils here than yuh throw a stick at," Bill announced. Dorothy quickly picked up her soup spoon and glanced toward Bill. He winked.

"They say that you just need to start with the spoon or fork the farthest from the plate and go from there," Bonnie laughed. "Heaven forbid you use a spoon or fork more than once."

"Yuh sure bring to mind the advice some ol' social biddy give recently. Somethin' about the 'Outside-In Rule' though I think it's a shame to dirty so many eatin' utensils. Makes a heap a dishwashin' for somebody," Bill added. Dorothy was horrified to think that Bill might start naming names, but he calmly and deliberately picked up his dessert spoon from nearest his plate.

"This'n looks fine to me," he said, winking again at Dorothy, hesitating for only a second before he placed it back to its spot and picked up the spoon on the outside as the rule of thumb required. She gave an inward sigh of relief as he picked up the beautiful silver soup spoon with its oversized and rounded bowl and quickly put it to use.

"Don't see no barley in here," Aubrey said. "This soup is so thin, you could . . ."

"Read a newspaper right through it," Mabry finished for his brother.

"Do you often do that? Finish each other's sentences?" Vera asked.

Aubrey and Mabry looked surprised.

"Didn't realize we was," Aubrey said.

Everyone at the table laughed as Bonnie explained. "I understand they cook the barley and vegetables together with a soup bone and then strain the soup. They simply serve the broth."

Mabry lifted both eyebrows in surprise. "Seems like a waste a perfectly good food to me."

Bonnie chuckled. "All those vegetables are just too filling. They offer them to their hired help as *Servant's Hall Soup*, or so I hear. Gotta save room for what's to come next."

"Don't matter what comes next, I think we oughtta open 'nother one a these," Mabry suggested, lifting a dripping very cold bottle from its bed of ice.

"You can do the honors," Vera smiled across at Mabry, who quickly obliged and their flutes were refilled.

The next course was served as bowls were exchanged for plates. Dorothy's mouth watered as the delicate aroma of poached salmon, smothered in a rich, tangy butter sauce. Deliciousness wafted upward to fill the air around her. Julienne strips of cucumbers were curled on the side.

"Where's the beef?" Frank McCarrol asked jokingly as he lifted a forkful of salmon. "We're cowmen not fishermen."

"I'm sure it's coming, Frank," Bonnie laughed, eyes sparkling up at her husband. "But, oh my goodness, this is tasty!"

Bonnie was clearly taken in with Frank and Dorothy could see the feelings were mutual. Chasing rodeos could be hard on a couple, and Dorothy hoped the best for the two of them.

"How did you get started riding?" Dorothy asked Bonnie.

"Oh, I grew up on a cattle ranch, my grandfather's ranch, back in Idaho. I started riding when I was about ten." Bonnie grinned up at her husband. "That was about how long it took me to convince my mother that a girl ought to be able ride along with her brother if she wants to. Her younger brother, to boot!

"I was about fourteen when I became acquainted with my first bronk. I mounted up, the boys let go, and that horse began to behave like a wild cat wriggling and writhing beneath me. I held for about five seconds and then all at once I seemed to grow wings. Up I soared, and turned a somersault, and the earth seemed about ten miles below. Next thing I knew I woke in bed. Nothing worse than a bad case of hurt pride."

"More champagne?" Aubrey had opened another bottle for the table. Dorothy was starting to feel the effects, but reasoned that the evening was going to be a long one.

"Ah, this is more like it!" Frank exclaimed as the salmon plates were finally exchanged out for a heartier course. "Beef!"

"And chicken," Bonnie added. Crispy chicken tenders, battered and golden fried, were arranged next to filet mignons topped with sautéed mushrooms.

"What do yuh s'pose this is?" Bill asked, dubiously studying the third item on their plates. "Looks like nothin' I ever seen."

Dorothy had noticed there were no menu cards on the table and so she wasn't certain herself.

"Bonnie here is the best little cook in the world," Frank said proudly, hoping Bonnie could solve the mystery vegetable for them.

Dorothy watched as Bonnie took yet another fork and knife from next to her plate, and cut herself a bite, studying it on her fork.

"Looks like zucchini stuffed with . . ." She lifted her fork and took a bite ". . . mmm! Tomatoes. Mushrooms, maybe. Sauteed with onions. Looks like the kit and kaboodle was baked in the oven with a light dusting of bread crumbs!" She smiled at herself before cutting another bite.

"Zoo keeny?" the McDowell twins said in unison.

"It's like a cousin to cucumbers," Bonnie explained.

"A long lost cousin," Frank added. "And one that should a stayed lost."

"Oh, come now. Try it before you give up on it," Bonnie encouraged.

Just as they were all cutting into whatever looked best on their plates – and Dorothy noticed for most it was the filet mignons – Prince Edward approached their table with a hearty hello.

"How are all of you?" he asked, a champagne flute in his hand as well.

Dorothy would have preferred to keep her eyes on her plate, but again one of Mutti's constant corrections came to mind. *Look a person in the eye when he or she is talking to you. Nothing is ruder than looking aside.* Dorothy had come to understand looking others in the eye was a cultural expectation not universally practiced. For instance, Riley Burgess, the Oklahoman, seldom looked anyone in the eye. It was just his way.

"Very well, and thank you," Vera answered for them all.

"No, no. Keep your seats," Edward urged as the men at the table started to rise. Dorothy noticed he was no longer shaking hands. Perhaps such formalities could be proffered to big wigs like Austin and Cochran, but were considered unnecessary for the likes of common cowboys and girls.

"Wonderful evenin', sir," Bill said easily, not in the least intimidated by His Royal Highness. "Cain't thank yuh enough for havin' us."

"You are more than welcome," came the gracious reply. And then, "Dear me!" The Prince of Wales seemed dismayed at the lack of any bottles left in their champagne bucket.

"Here, here!" He caught the eye of the nearest wait staff. "We need more champagne at this table."

"Please, please. Drink up!" he said even as he smiled and was moving on to the next table.

Dorothy was still feeling dumbstruck as Bill reached over and squeezed her hand.

"Relax an' breathe," he teased. "That didn't take much longer'n two jumps outta the chute. That maverick is long gone a'ready."

Dorothy quickly turned the attention to someone other than herself.

"Vera, tell us about your beginnings," she said, encouraging Vera to retell her story for the benefit of the McDowells.

"I didn't grow up on a farm or ranch, like you all."

Vera looked around the table, studying each of them. Dorothy sat still and kept eye contact.

"I sort of fell into rodeoing when Barney Sherry needed another girl to ride in a relay race at the Pendleton Round Up. Barney had brought a string of horses to the Round Up," she explained. "Did okay. Barney hired me on as a relay rider and we headed up to the Stampede in Winnipeg."

"So this was 1914?" Dorothy asked, knowing full well it had been 1914. The year after the first Stampede in Calgary.

"Humm, you're right," Vera continued. "In Winnipeg, in addition to the relay race, I started trick riding. What a thrill! When the Stampede was over, I went back to Missouri. My mother was beside herself with my 'wild-westing' but she was the one who had encouraged me to ride from the time I was tiny. My first baby-sitter was a burro named Croppie.

"Not long until I got an invitation to ride for Doc Pardee in his Wild West Show in Tulsa, Oklahoma. That was where I rode my first bronk. I've come a long way since then."

"Oh, gads!" moaned Mabry, surprised as yet another plate of meats and vegetables was served. Medallions of lamb in mint sauce, roasted ducklings in applesauce, a sirloin of beef surrounded by creamed carrots and peas served with new potatoes.

"We are not even close to being finished," Vera explained, though she noticed that Mabry was making short work of his beef and vegetables.

Dorothy wasn't sure how she felt about eating the tiny bird and so she decided to turn her attention to the beef and lamb. The rest of the diners at the table were also picking and choosing their favorite parts of the plate. The prediction she had given Bill about a long evening of dining was coming to fruition.

When at last, the knives and forks were laid parallel across their plates – Vera had explained that was a signal to the waiters that they had finished all they wanted from that part of the meal – Bill took his turn and uncorked yet another bottle of champagne.

"No, no thank you," she smiled up at Bill as he offered to refill her glass again. She noticed that none of the others turned him down, though.

"And what about you, Dorothy?" Vera asked.

Dorothy should have seen it coming.

"What's to tell? I ride horses. I'm a bucking horse rider."

Laughter burst from around the table. The champagne was doing its work well.

"What's to tell? You ride horses?" Mabry repeated, grinning as he toasted her.

"Well, that's a damn fine answer," Aubrey chided. "I think we're all goddamn buckin' horse riders!"

Another gale of laughter made its way around the table just as Dorothy was saved from further explaining when their plates were replaced with sparkling but squatty cut crystal chalices set on filigreed saucers. All eyes were on the frothy light orange colored contents wondering just what was in store for them now. Thinly sliced strips of orange peel embellished the cloud of whipped topping on each.

"Sherbet?" Vera guessed.

"Sorbet, perhaps," Dorothy wondered.

"It's a little too liquid for either of those," Bonnie announced.

"Well, hell, let's dig in," Bill said looking around. "Only we ain't got no spoons left b'side our plates."

"The dessert spoons are the ones up there past the tops of our plates," Dorothy said.

Each of them took a spoonful of the partially frozen concoction. Eyes popped open.

"Wow! Who'd thunk anybody could get that much likker into a dessert?" Bill exclaimed. "But what in tarnation is in it?"

A friendly discussion ensued as one and another claimed to know exactly what the contents were.

"Rum, I say!"

"You wouldn't know rum if it bit you in the . . ."

"Shhhh, ladies, present!"

"I'm pretty sure there's more champagne in this."

"Yes, well, that could be, but I'm sure I detect a hint of wine."

"Wine! Oh, my gawd! Not in somethin' this good! That crap's for the birds!"

"Not all wine is red and not all wine is horrid."

"What'd yuh s'pose this fluffy stuff is? Sure ain't whipped cream!"

"I'm thinking it's . . . mmm . . . maybe like raw meringue . . . beaten egg whites."

"Oh, gads! Not raw?"

All too soon, each and every crystal dish was emptied. In fact, after looking sheepishly around the table at each other, they lifted them in a mock toast and made sure not a drop of the wonderful stuff went to waste.

"Don't s'pose there'll be another round a this," Bill said hopefully.

"Oh, just let me top off your drinkin' glass," Mabry said, merrily, popping the cork on another bottle of champagne. *Merry* - a word seldom used for most cowboys, but there was a ballroom full of them tonight.

"Now for the final course," announced one of the waiters standing at the ready, "Eclairs and French ice cream."

"Which one a these ay-clares you gonna eat first?" Mabry boldly asked Dorothy.

"Hard to choose. Maybe both at once," she replied reaching for the dessert fork at the top of her place setting.

"Wondered why we had two a them spoons," Aubrey said as he retrieved the last one and dug into his ice cream. As he put the first bite of ice cream into his mouth, his eyes closed and he shook his head, humming to himself.

Don't sing to your food! Mutti's voice once again rang uninvited through Dorothy's thoughts, so just for good measure, Dorothy followed suit, humming with a bite of the chocolate eclair.

The mood was relaxed and jovial as the last crumbs of the vanilla and chocolate eclairs disappeared and the ice cream bowls were emptied.

"Well, folks," Bill said, gently pushing himself back from the table. "I b'lieve I just et a horrible meal."

"What?" Dorothy exclaimed.

"Oh, I meant, terrible. Yes, terrible," Bill floundered. "No, I mean tremendous."

"Oh, yes, I see," Dorothy said, "I believe we did just eat a tremendous meal of such delightful dishes as I have ever had."

"Not even atcher Lady's reception?" Bill guffawed.

"Not even there," she assured him.

The attention of the entire company in the ballroom was called for by Prince Edward himself.

"Ladies and gents," he began, his champagne speaking for him as well, "I have just been informed that the hotel is closing for the evening . . ."

Dorothy was startled to realize it must be at least two if not three in the morning.

" . . . and I for one am not sure that this party is ready to be over yet, however. Therefore we take pleasure in inviting you to join us elsewhere for the rest of this evening . . . erh, this morning. So before the police must be called in to evacuate us, let us get our hats and wraps." He then proceeded to give far too detailed directions for most of the guests to follow in their current states of mind.

Dorothy looked around the table. Aubrey and Mabry were hanging on every word of direction coming their way as if their lives depended on it. She smiled, thinking what wonderful stories of big old stone castles - without a drop of water to drink - they would be telling in the coming days. Looking at the others, she couldn't rightly tell from their expressions what their plans might be, but she was sure she and Bill would be holding each other up while making their way back to their hotel.

183

XXIV - 9 SEPTEMBER 1924 - "TOUR OF WEMBLEY CHAMPIONS"

C ertainly sitting at the window of her hotel room, looking across the Paris skyline, punctuated by the far off spire of the Eiffel Tower, was one of the highlights of her life; but to take it over the top, she would have been sharing it with her best friend, her lover, the sunshine of her day. She should have been. But she wasn't.

She sighed and picked up a couple of postcards from the small dressing table at which she sat. Hand-tinted close ups of the famous tower, looking for all the world like a bridge to the stars, brought back memories of the Aeroscope that had been just across the way from the 101 Ranch Rodeo at the PPIE.

So long ago. She sighed.

Picking up a pencil, she addressed the first one to Mrs. Aubrey Montgomery.

Dear Friend, We are in Paris, France, and we are a sensation here. I like the French people very much. Yesterday I visited the battle fields and the American cemetery. I placed a wreath to our boys from Bakersfield; also one for Los Angeles, and one for San Francisco. I shall be back in London within a fortnight. Regards to all, Dorothy Morrell

Now for Bill. She wrote their home address on the second card, wondering, though, if Bill would ever even be in town during the months he was stateside. She smiled ruefully. Stateside. She never would have thought she'd be using such a term.

Dearest Bill, We are in Paris. The people here are warm and friendly. Our shows are quite the sensation. I thought of your Cowboy Company yesterday at the American Cemetery. So many of our boys who will never come home. Hope all is going well with Mr. Texas Walker. Best wishes in that regard. Miss you and wish you were here, Yours Always, Dot

Damnit! Why had he let that smooth talking, big dreaming, second rate rope twirler turn his head?

She thought back to two and a half months ago. The 24th of June. Only a week of performances left. That morning, it was turnabout as the entire rodeo company, ropers, riders, behind the scenes livestock hands, had taken to grandstands overlooking the empty arena.

High Noon. The earliest time Mr. Tex Austin dared to call a meeting. As it was, there were glares from all quarters, and hats pulled very low over most everyone's eye.

Dorothy and Bill sat on the front row of the bleacher seats surrounded by a couple hundred other of the 'early risers.' Early compared to the time they'd gotten to bed the night before – earlier that day, rather.

Ever since the Prince of Wales had hosted his party, it seemed that the flood gates had opened and invitations for various soirees and dinner parties had been poured out among the performers. So many, everyone had the pick of their choice of their events. They were entertained, and wined and dined. The only request from their hosts or hostesses was that they wore their western clothes – boots, hats, spurs, vests, the whole regalia. And the nights had become shorter and the days longer.

"I'll be so glad when this is over," Dorothy whispered to Bill.

"Only got a few more days," Bill answered. "Then the championships'll be awarded and we'll be packin' up to head home."

"I am exhausted," Dorothy said. "And I know I'm out of the running. These girls are great riders."

"Yuh ain't goin' home empty handed, though.   Yuh done good!" Bill grinned down at her through bleary eyes just as Austin stepped up to the front of the crowd.

Austin lifted a megaphone to his mouth and began.

"Good mornin', all!"

A few *good mornings* were called back, but for such a large crowd, it was unusually quiet.

"I don't need the whole north side of London hearing what I've got to say, to I won't be using the loudspeaker," he explained.

"We've done pretty well here in London, but not as well as I hoped nor not as well as needed, so there's going to be a slight change in plans."

Dorothy could hear the crowd stirring as many sat up to lean forward to better hear.   She looked up at Bill who shrugged.   This seemed to be news to him as well.

"We are going to end the competition performances as planned on the 28th of June.   Championships will be awarded that evening just as planned; however, at the end of the awards ceremony, I will be announcing an encore week of rodeo performances from June 30th to July 5th.   Except for July 5th, the encore shows will only be held in the afternoons.   You are all expected to be available to ride or otherwise perform as scheduled – as per your contracts," Austin sharply drove his point home.

A muttering began which grew louder by the second.

"What the hell?" came shouts from the grandstands.

Tex raised his hand for quiet which the crowd begrudgingly gave him.

"As you know, the rodeo has been earning a cut of the gate receipts.   To date we haven't brought in enough to even cover expenses.   I – well, Cochran, Britton and I, – have talked it over with the board of directors for the Exhibition and they have agreed to let us continue the afternoon performances for one week, as the stadium is needed for other events already planned for the evening.   We will continue to get a cut for the first 5 days of performances, but will get the entire gate receipts for both performances on July 5th which will be divided equally among the all of you here."

Someone from a few rows back stood and shouted down at Austin. "What about the plans everybody's got for seein' parts a Europe that week?"

"Hear! Hear!" came another shout before a torrent of complaints came pouring from the bleachers.

Again Austin held his hand up for attention, though Dorothy noticed it took longer for him to get it this time.

"You always have Sundays," was his only reply as he turned on his heel and left the crowd to grouse and complain on their own.

"Did you have any idea this was coming?" Dorothy turned and asked Bill.

"I knew that him an' Cochran's disappointed in how the money was comin' in but I had no idea it would come to this.   Makes sense, though.

187

We're here. The livestock is here, the bulk a the expenses ain't gonna to be any different 'cause he's shipping the main part a the crew out on the *Menominee* on the 8th, the same day as originally planned. This might just be the ticket for the rodeo to break even."

"What do you mean, the main part of the crew?" Dorothy asked.

"Ain't you heard the scuttlebutt? Or don'tcha women talk?" Bill asked.

"Evidently not! So what's going on?" Dorothy demanded.

"Well, Tommy Kirnan an' Leon Britton thought maybe they could take a scaled down version a the show on the road to Ireland an' France. Maybe some other places. More like a Wild West show than a rodeo. Just for entertainment. No competition."

"How long have you known about this?" Dorothy asked.

"I don' know. A few days maybe," Bill replied. It seemed that a spat might be brewing. Everyone needed more sleep these days – since there was little sleep at night.

"So you are not interested in joining with the Kirnans?" Dorothy asked, hoping to dissuade him joining into a harebrained scheme for trying to succeed where Austin had failed. Her hackles had been raised the minute Frank Walker had started in trying to persuade Bill to join him in organizing their own rodeo tour of Europe.

"Nope, me an' Texas Walker's still plannin' to get back to the States an' see what we can do 'bout roundin' up rodeo stock for that circuit we're puttin' together this winter startin' here in England. See if we can find a stock producer we can buy some critters from."

"I don't like Walker," Dorothy said for what seemed like the dozenth time in the last two weeks. "Why would anyone born in England call himself 'Texas'? I wouldn't trust him to help me across an empty street on a Sunday afternoon."

Bill laughed. "Good to hear yuh still got yer sense a humor about yuh. But it ain't just my money he'll be burnin' through, it'll be his. Sometimes yuh gotta spend money to make money."

Dorothy tightened her lips, not able to think of a single thing of support to say to Bill.

"I don' s'pose I gotta ask what yer thinkin' right about now," Bill said, almost as if he were challenging her to say something. Anything. He raised an eyebrow to punctuate the dare.

"By God, Bill! We do not have that kind of money to spend!" The dam had broken and once started, Dorothy made no effort to tone down her frustrations.

"And if this is such a damn fine idea, why aren't Austin or Cochran falling all over themselves to get into a piece of the action? That should be warning enough!" Dorothy said through gritted teeth. The grandstand of Wembley Stadium wasn't her idea of the ideal sparring ring.

"Now the way I see it, them two had a belly full of fightin' an uphill battle in the courts and in the press, but me an' Texas're startin' out a step ahead in this game. We already know what the folks here'll tolerate and what they wanna see. Texas done his trick ropin' all over the world, let alone England. He's been contactin' folks all over the place. Places like Liverpool, Newcastle, Edinburgh . . ."

"Oh, why can't you see through him? He is just a two-bit hustler," Dorothy huffed.

"Oh, come on now. He's at least a four-bit talker," Bill joked. It was damn hard to fight with someone who was constantly making a joke. "An' just between yuh an' me and the fence post, no matter how many times he says otherwise - yuh know, like openin' his rodeo in Leeds, the 'city of his birth' - his passport says he was born in New Mexico."

"Oh, my hell! Do you see what I mean? He is as slippery as a snake!"

Bill studied Dorothy's face. The set of her mouth. The snap of her eyes. The tilt of her head.

"By gum, gal. I think I see what's goin' on in yer head. Yuh wanna go with the Kirnans, don'tcha?" He grinned as she tossed her head and glared at him.

"Goldarn, that's a first rate idea. Yuh go on the road with 'em whilst me an' Texas run up the livestock for his shows."

"And just how is that going to work?" Dorothy asked, reminding herself not to be surprised at how well Bill knew her. "I'm traveling on your passport."

"Women don't have to travel on a man's passport," Bill began. "Look at Vera an' Marie Gibson."

"But they got their passports back in the States. How I am going to get a passport over here?"

"I don't know right off, but I betcha we can figger it out. Gotta be a way to do it," Bill assured her as they stood to follow the last of crowd out of the grandstands.

"Wait, wait!" she protested, "this is too much. Let's go back to the week we, you and I, were going to spend on the Continent, as they like to say. Together. Austin jerked that rug right out from beneath us."

"One disaster at a time, Dot," Bill said, using one of her favorite expressions, "one disaster at a time. Right now, we better git down to them stable tents and git ready for this afternoon. First things first."

Dorothy took his elbow as they walked together to a set of stairs that would take them to the arena floor. As they walked, she thought over the last two weeks.

How she had looked forward to seeing Paris with Bill between the time the rodeo ended and they sailed for home. Ah, well, such is life, she thought, remembering back to Bill's philosophy on life. If there was nothing she could do about it, she had better just get on with it.

And now, here she was, in Paris without Bill, still thinking back on the events of that day.

"Damn it," Vera McGinnis had growled, out of sorts and out of character, as Dorothy and Bill stepped under the stable awning, her mild manners lost in the anger of the moment. "I had my heart set on Paris. When in the hell am I ever going to get this kind of a chance again?"

"I've been thinkin' on it," Marie Gibson interjected. "We do have Sundays off. It's just an hour or so by air! We can charter us a plane and a bunch of us can fly over Sunday and back on Monday by show time!"

Vera's eyes lit up as she said, "You really think so? Hot damn! Just what the doctor ordered!" She turned to Dorothy. "You and Bill want in?"

"Thanks, I'll talk it over with Bill," Dorothy replied.

Not likely, though, she thought. *There were already plans for Sunday. Sleep for one! Finding Tommy Kirnan for another.*

Tommy Kirnan and his wife, Beatrice, were no strangers to the rodeo circuits nor to putting on the shows themselves. Why couldn't Bill have connected with them instead of that fly-by-night, couldn't-even-remember-where-he-was-born, damn Two-Bit Hustler, Mr. Frank Texas Walker?

It had taken Bill and Dorothy a while to track Tommy and Bea down that Sunday afternoon. Even longer to make their case.

"Have a seat," Bea smiled up at them from a table in front of a sidewalk café.

"Thank yuh, kindly," Bill answered, helping Dorothy into a chair. "We come t' talk t'yuh 'bout the show yer takin' on the road in a few weeks."

No sense in beating around the bush, or making small talk.

Tommy laughed. "Bad news travels like wild fire."

He looked from Bill to Dorothy. "But I thought you were teaming up with Walker on some shows of your own."

"Yup, that's *my* plans," Bill explained, "but Dot, here, she's taken a fancy to the idea a stayin' here till me'n Frank git back from the States. The two a us got our work cut out for us the next couple a months makin' the arrangements to git them rodeos off the ground."

Tommy took in a deep breath, looking across the table at his wife. She gave her husband a slight nod though she knew she would have little to do with a final decision.

"You need to know this is a very small show," Tommy began, patiently explaining the plans to them. "Leon Britton and I thought we'd keep the number of performers low, a dozen or even fewer. Everyone will have to be pulling double, maybe even triple duty, every day. Steer wrestling and riding. Bareback and trick riding. Fancy and trick roping. Fact is, folks'll be outnumbered by the livestock. In each venue the shows will be three to four weeks long. Unlike here, Sundays will not be off."

"I've always pulled my weight," Dorothy promised.

Tommy then began to look uncomfortable and avoided making eye contact with her. Bea stepped in with her gentle matronly manner. "Leon Britton, our producer, is headlining this as a Tour of Wembley Champions. We know the championships won't be awarded until Saturday, but we've got pretty good indications."

Bea smiled in not an unkindly way, but certainly not in an encouraging way across at Dorothy, holding eye contact steady.

"Tommy and Britton had already spoken with the cowboys and cowgirls they've decided to put into the show."

Not a breath stirred at the table.

Dorothy held her own gaze steady as she searched Bea's face for the slightest sign of haughtiness, of disdain, of dismissal. There was none. Dorothy tried to refrain from taking in her own deep breath before presently her case, wanting to appear calm and steady, nonchalant, as she gathered all her reserves and began.

"I will be the first to acknowledge that I am not in the top ranking as bronk rider here at Wembley. Vera and Tad have outridden me, it is obvious."

She wondered about bringing up her 1914 Goldarn Lady Buckin' Horse Champion of the Whole Damned World title, but it seemed far away and somewhat unimportant in the bright light of the others' more immediate successes.

"I did not compete in trick riding here, but I believe I can hold my own. As for the relay races, getting up and down quickly out of the saddle is hard." She didn't want to bring up further explanations fearing she would sound like she was trying to make excuses.

Dorothy looked from Bea to Tommy who had relaxed a little and resumed eating his lunch.

"I am willing to pay my own travel and lodging expenses, just as I would for any rodeo competition, but I should like to sign a contract for . . ." she hesitated for a split second ". . . whatever daily appearances, whatever responsibilities, whatever it is you may want me to do for your Rodeo Shows."

There it was. Daily appearances. It seemed every time she thought she was finally finished with them forever, immediate needs raised their hungry heads and demanded to be fed. When the chips were down, they put food on the table and roof overhead.

Tommy seemed to be studying the Sunday strollers who were casually making their ways around them, but Dorothy knew better. He was mentally making a checklist of pros and cons of adding one more person to an already well thought out plan. Calculating the adjustments. Adding up the balance sheet, weighing the possible changes in the final profits.

"Since you put it that way," he finally said smiling across at Dorothy, "I bet we can add you to the show."

He reached across the table to seal the deal with a handshake.

"But you need to understand that in consideration for the focus for the Rodeo Show, to know right up front, you won't be headlining in our advertising, though, of course, you'll find yourself in all the printed programs for the daily shows."

"Fair enough," Dorothy replied, hiding the sting while celebrating her success.

"Come around sometime in the next little while and I'll have a contract ready for you to sign," Tommy said, concluding what had become an interview.

"Welcome to the tour, Dorothy," Bea smiled across at Dorothy as well as she and Bill took their leave, walking hand in hand down the noisy, crowded sidewalk.

XXV - 23 DECEMBER 1924 – REUNION

Dorothy pulled her hat further down over her head and her scarf higher over her ears. The December weather here in Southampton was nothing like London's when the *SS Lapland* had sailed into harbor last June. Today the fog was so thick, she could hardly make out the outline of the *SS Majestic*. The sea breezes of summer had long since turned to gusts that tore through those waiting at the docks to greet the incoming passengers. First class had finished disembarking an hour ago and now second class were making their way down the gang plank, but Bill had sent her a wire letting her know that for this trip, he was traveling in third class. Dorothy hoped it was not an omen of things to come.

The Tour of Wembley Champions had broken up after its last shows in Brussels, and most had sailed for home back in October. Dorothy had rented a flat on the outskirts of London and counted the days until Bill's return. When she learned that Frank Walker would be returning to England the end of October, she let her hopes be raised that Bill would be traveling with him, but no. Walker had returned on the supposition that he had to be nailing down final arrangements here in England, while Bill was left to bring up the rear bringing the livestock they needed to ship into the country for their rodeos.

When at last, she could make out the tall, familiar figure coming down the gangplank, she was surprised at his demeanor. Slow stepping and bent as if in deep thought, Bill had not yet started looking for her through the thick misty fog. Perhaps in this weather, he hadn't expected her to make the trip to meet him. She wasn't sure where Walker was. He seemed to be making a point of staying clear of her – hadn't heard from him in weeks, nor even read a word about his 'upcoming rodeo' shows. She was tremendously glad he wasn't around to be part of the welcoming committee.

"Hell–ooooo," Dorothy called, raising an arm to wave. Bill's head immediately snapped up and found her in the thinning crowd.

"Hey, girl," he called back, his steps quickening as he cleared the end of the gangplank and strode across the dock.

Dorothy didn't even have time to move to meet him before he leaned forward to scoop her up and gather her into his arms. She found herself lifted high off of her feet, but no matter. It made it easier to throw her arms around his neck and hold tightly as she breathed in the warm, sweet, familiar smells of soap, and boot polish and tobacco, and returned his kisses.

"Oh, Dottie," he whispered, continuing to hold her tightly. "I missed yuh every minute of every day."

"I know, I know," she whispered back, clinging to him. "Let's never do this again!"

"Deal!" he agreed, finally setting her back down on her feet.

He breathed a great sigh of relief.

"It is so damn good to be back with yuh," he said, shaking his head. And then he laughed. "Don't see no sharra–bangs waitin' to greet us. What? No triumphant parade into the streets a London?"

"If I'd known you wanted a charabanc, I would've hired one, but don't you think it would have been a little bit of overkill?" Dorothy replied, joining Bill in laughter, looking up into his face, studying his familiar features trying to discern any differences. Were those new lines around his eyes? Was there more gray in the hair below his hatband?

He looked down into her eyes, saw her concern, but chose to save his report of the last four months for later.

"Overkill? Not by a long shot. But I s'pose this ain't June an' I ain't Tex Austin an' me an' you're only two, not two hundred."

He stepped back to look her up and down.

"Besides, we ain't dressed in our rodeo duds. An' since there's no brass bands 'r keys to the city, a train'll do fine. How 'bout it?" he asked, and arm in arm, they found their way to buy tickets and board their train.

As they settled into their seats, Bill pulled Dorothy close, his arm around her shoulders. Dorothy held his other hand in both of hers and decided to carry on as if she had never seen the shadows behind his eyes.

"I rented a flat in Battersea, as you suggested," Dorothy began, "but I haven't seen hide nor hair of Mr. Frank Walker."

"Ain't likely, to neither," Bill said, cautiously. Dorothy waited for an explanation, but none seemed to be coming. Yet.

"You did say he had a place rented here, too," Dorothy asked.

"We don't need to be talkin' 'bout him right now," Bill said, changing the subject. "Tell me everything. Start in London and don't quit until yuh git to what yuh had for breakfast this mornin'."

Dorothy laughed.

"Oh, my word! First off, the Kirnans were the nicest people I've ever had the opportunity to work with. They were as concerned for all of the rest of us as they were for themselves. Never expected anything out of us that they didn't do themselves many times over."

"All the while yuh was with 'em, I never worried that yuh'd be all right," Bill agreed.

"Next of all, Cochran is just as full of himself as most any of the producers and promoters I've ever met. He was quite nasty in his public opinion of Kirnan's tour. Got himself quoted in the London newspaper saying how Tommy Kirnan had no business calling our show a 'rodeo' and he made it clear that he had made arrangements to transport 'all' of the contestants back to their homes."

"I imagine he'd wanna downplay anything that might a seemed to compare to the Wembley Rodeo," Bill said before adding, "Didja know how good yer hair smells?"

"What?" Dorothy asked even as Bill kissed the top of her head.

"Oh, go on. Didn't mean to change the subject." Bill grinned past the shadows in his eyes.

Dorothy mustered herself and went on with her story. She let go of Bill's hands and moved out of his embrace. She turned to face him as she straightened her shoulders and deepened her voice to mimic the famous British showman.

"It would be quite impossible to hold any sort of rodeo performances in such a confined area as the theater. I, myself, would strongly disapprove of any such foolish attempt at such a reproduction."

195

Dorothy stopped to clear her throat, and frown in a pompous and exaggerated way up at Bill.

"Don't you laugh, young man!" she ordered as Bill chuckled at her impression of Cochran. "This is serious business. Not to be taken lightly! This type of light-minded stage entertainment should never be advertised a 'Rodeo' for to do so is entirely misleading to the public, and it belittles the magnificent sport that the rodeo actually is."

Bill nodded in agreement with the sentiment, though still grinning.

"I see what yer sayin', sir," he playfully answered Dorothy. "But yuh gotta do what yuh gotta do to keep the wolf away from the door."

"Young man," Dorothy said as she glared up at Bill who was laughing harder than ever, "there are no wolves in London, or in any of the loneliest, wildest, most far-flung crags of dear old Britannia. But I digress.

"Indeed, I have heard there may be two, perhaps three cowboys who are wishing to stay in England to provide rope spinning exhibitions or horseback riding demonstrations and other suitable performances for music hall displays, but again, no such entertainment should ever be called a 'Rodeo' and certainly is not sanctioned by either Mr. Tex Austin nor myself. I can assure you that no bucking horses remain in England and that all the cattle, all of the cattle," Dorothy repeated for emphasis, "have been sold to farmers."

"Music hall? Is that what he's callin' the London Coliseum these days?" Bill asked.

"You better believe it," Dorothy answered slipping back into her own persona, "though before we opened, I was pretty unsure how any type of riding or steer wrestling was going to be pulled off. It was just strange to be inside a building.

"Here, let me show you," and she pulled a program from her handbag and read:

"'A Stage Triumph! Tommy Kirnan presents Wembley RODEO Champions and Prize Winners . . . A performance rendered possible for theatrical presentation only by the unique resources of the wonderful Coliseum Stage.'

"Wonderful resources – 100 square feet of grass matting!"

"Wished I coulda seen it," Bill said. - Instead a wastin' my time chasin' down rabbit holes.

"We were there at the Coliseum for a month before we moved the whole show to Dublin," Dorothy nodded. "It was good to get passed the feeling like we were doing 'theater' and really back in the cowboy business.

Bill smiled and nodded, agreeing with her.

"Oh, my, but how it rained on us and rained on us and rained. We'd get to thinking that the show for the day would have to be cancelled and then all these wonderful Irish people stood in line under their umbrellas and filled the seats in the stands and huddled together never budging an inch. They were there to see us and so whether we liked it or not, the show had to go on!"

196

"That's my girl." Bill grinned and scooped her back into the seat next to him with an exuberant embrace, his arm cradling her shoulders.

"The rodeo shows were great. Nowata Slim did a great rodeo clown act and you know the others. They all know how to please a crowd, and the show always went on, no matter what. Like when Vera got busted up after her bronk went over backwards."

"I didn't hear 'bout this," Bill said, sobering at the possible outcomes of Dorothy's tale.

"His name was *Wasp Nest*. He went over backwards on her in the chute, before they ever even got out into the arena. But by the time the gate was opened, he was back on his feet and she gave a good ride, though she said she was all out of starch by the time the pickup men got to her. After that, she took to riding steers for the remainder of the tour. She said something about all it takes to be a good bronk rider is a strong back and a weak mind."

"Oh, is that so?" Bill laughed and groaned at the same time. "Well, I s'pose there may be some truth to it, but, goldarn, it stings!"

Dorothy curled into his side before going on.

"I'm not even going to try to tell you about Paris. The city, I mean. You and I are going to go there together come hell or high water and then I'll show you all the best out-of-the-way places to find the most wonderful food - and drinks. And it won't cost us an arm and a leg, either."

She smiled at the memories of late night suppers of savory onion soup and crusty baguettes.

Bill folded his other arm around her and rested his cheek against the top of her head.

"Never lettin' you loose again," he said, "I felt like a maverick calf, lost without a friend in the world all the time I was gone."

"Hummm," Dorothy murmured, listening to the beat of Bill's heart, short inches from her ear, wanting to press Bill for more details, but knowing they would come in time. His time.

When they arrived at their station, Bill took Dorothy by one hand and his newfangled suitcase in the other and they made their way through the fog until Dorothy stopped in front of a wrought iron gate opening to a set of narrow concrete steps, three steps up to the front door.

"This," Dorothy announced, "is the building where our flat is."

Our. Had a nice ring to it, Dorothy decided. *No longer 'mine' but 'ours.'*

She pulled a set of keys from her handbag and unlocked the door.

"Our rooms are on the second floor."

"Lead on," Bill said, as he clumped up the narrow stairway behind her.

She unlocked the door at the top of the stairs and flipped on the electric light switch revealing a tiny hall opening into two different rooms.

"Ahead we have the kitchen and to the left we have the front room. The bedroom opens up from the kitchen," Dorothy explained.

"Reminds me a little a the basement apartment we rented that one winter back in Pendleton. Back in the cowboy-through-the-winter days," Bill said, "but I bet the view out this front window is better."

Dorothy laughed.

"Bet you are right, especially since back in Pendleton, we were in the basement. We didn't have any windows at all. On the other hand, you'll have to wait for the fog to be gone before you'll be able to see much."

"Dot, fer me, the fog is already clearin'," Bill said shaking his head. "I'm seeing life more clearly now than I did four month ago, and I'm sorry, Dot. I'm sorry."

XXVI - 24 DECEMBER 1924 - CHRISTMAS EVE

Dorothy awoke still curled into the circle of Bill's right arm. She could tell he was still sleeping as she listened to his gentle breathing. She wanted a cup of coffee. She wanted to start breakfast. She wanted to stay curled up in the warmth of the covers. More than anything, though, she wanted Bill forever right where he was, next to her.

She finally wriggled out from beneath the blankets and tiptoed into the kitchen. She opened a jar of ready ground coffee to fill the basket in her percolator.   Some sacrifices had to be made when one was so far from all the conveniences of home.   She turned on the gas under the coffee pot and began to plan the breakfast meal.   Then she shook her head and smiled to herself.   It wasn't going to be what she wanted for breakfast today.   It had been six months since last she'd made breakfast for Bill.   This was his day. Humming, she headed for the tiny water closet.

When she returned to the kitchen, Bill was sitting at the table, frowsy haired, in his long johns, first cups of the morning already poured, his and hers.

"Got two real chairs here, I see," he said.   "Best thing a feller could ask for."

Dorothy giggled and shook her head.

"What'll it be this morning, mister?" she asked.

"Whatcha got?" Bill asked, "I mean, besides yerself," laughing as Dorothy's cheeks brightened as he had known they would.

"Eggs, bacon, toast, potatoes, pancakes.   You name it," she replied good-naturedly.

"How 'bout toast an' jam an' a listenin' ear?" Bill asked, pushing his hair back off of his forehead.

Headache? Dorothy wondered to herself.

"Coming right up, my good sir," she replied trying to match Bill's high spirited comments.

She piled the toasted slices of bread onto two separate plates and set out strawberry preserves and butter.

Dorothy watched as Bill carefully buttered a slice of toast and spread jam on it.   Sometimes it was maddening to wait for Bill to decide to get around to speaking his mind.

"I can tell this here is bread yuh baked yerself," he finally began.

"It is," was all Dorothy replied.

"An' better to have baked bread than a cooked goose," he soberly went on.

"Oh."   Dorothy steeled herself for the unknown, the yet unshared.

"Gawd a mighty, but that man is a son-of-a-,"

"Wretched excuse for mankind," Dorothy finished for him.

"Yup, yuh got that right," he continued, shaking his head.   "Now, Dot, if yuh wanna say 'I toldja so,' I can take it, just so long as I don't hafta hear it more'n 'bout a couple hunnert times."

"If that's how you're feeling, Bill," Dorothy said, shaking her own head, "then I don't have to say it even once, and so I won't!"

That broke the ice for the both of them.   Dorothy reached across the table to take Bill's hand and just as he had asked of her the previous day, he started at the beginning and ended with toast and strawberry jam.

"That man is the most self-centered piece of dirt I ever run acrost in my entire life."

"How so?"

"For starters, he never had an eye on the prize. The prize being his own goddamn rodeo. Oh, he talked big. He dreamed big, but he didn't have the faintest idea a how to commit hisself to actually git from the start to the finish. Hell, he didn't even know where to start. I think that's why he wanted me in on the deal.

"Worse'n that, he seemed to think that just cuz he was callin' hisself a rodeo producer, that entitled him to go first class on everything. For starters, I could not believe that I, Skeeter Bill Robbins from the middle a nowhere, was sailing in a damn first class cabin on our way back to the States. Worse'n that, I was sailing in a first class cabin all by m'self. It was the most ridiculous situation I ever been in. Well, no, take that back. Bein' in his spur-a-the-moment 'rodeo demonstration' in the middle a the goddamn ocean, in front a couple hundred first class passengers, me bein' the only performer. That was the most ridiculous. It wasn't that the fancy ropin' was all that bad, it was the idea that he could tell me what to do an' I better do it. Felt like one a them monkeys back in San Francisco. Remember the ones them organ grinders had trained to beg for pennies? The ones at the end of a leash? Well, that was when I begun to b'lieve I was the one bein' played.

"So, we get back the States and headed west, all in hope's a findin' more damn fools willin' to buy into his crazy schemes. We ended up in Nevada and he's writin' checks right an' left whilst we were at some oil company's big ol' summer shindig. Quite a rodeo show, they had there, though," Bill paused thinking back on the Wild West show. "Cowboy singers, comedians, clowns. It was a show, though, not a contest!"

"He musta knowed them checks was never gonna make good," he continued back on track again, "cuz all the sudden he's a high-tailin' it back to New York, leavin' me high an' dry with instructions to try to round up and buy livestock to ship over here. Like I had any money left by then!

"When I got to readin' in the papers that there's a warrant out for his arrest, yuh know, for all them checks, I decided there's only one thing left to do."

"And that was . . . ?" Dorothy asked.

"Git back over here to you, and see what I been missin' these last few months. I knew it was gonna take a month or so workin' here an' there to get the money for a ticket, so I set my eye on my own prize and here I am settin' beside her!"

He beamed across the table at her.

"An' I broughtcha a Christmas present!"

"But I didn't . . . well, I'm sorry, I didn't even think about it being Christmas," Dorothy sputtered, embarrassed. "I was just so glad to count down the days until you got here."

"That ain't the way gift givin' works, least not to my way a thinkin'. B'sides, yuh ain't seen what it is yet," Bill said, grinning and dismissing her worries.

201

"Well, it is Christmas Eve," Dorothy began, "and as children, we always opened our gifts on that evening. Of course, then later we went to midnight mass and came home to eat cold ham with hot mustard on Mutti's wonderful rolls - mine are nothing like hers. And in the morning, Mutti began cooking the Christmas goose . . ."

She suddenly stopped herself, and laughed at the look on Bill's face.

"No, no goose. We children hated it. No goose for us.

"I think I started this trip down memory lane because I wanted to know if I could have my present now," she said, eyes shining.

"Well, when I was a kid," Bill replied, "we had t'wait for Christmas mornin' and we had to be dressed an' our chores had to be done. But no midnight church. No mornin' church. Not that we was heathens. Mum saw to that." Bill nodded remembering days gone by.

"So, which way's it gonna be? Yer family 'r mine?" Bill teased.

"How about 'our' family? You and I. We can make our own rules!"

"Fair nuff!" Bill agreed. "How's about after the last piece a toast is gone?" he said, looking down at the already empty plates.

"How about after a kiss or two?" Dorothy replied.

"Now yer talkin'!" Bill said, as Dorothy jumped from her chair and waltzed around the table to sit on his lap. His arms cradled her close and she returned his embrace, relaxing as they held each other close.

"So, we really don't have any reserves to get the both of us back home?" Dorothy asked suddenly, not wanting to break the magic of the moment, but worried that they might not be sailing home anytime soon.

Bill chuckled as he nuzzled her hair.

"Well, I do got me two cents to rub t'gether in my pocket, if that's what's worryin' yuh. We can live on toast an' jam an' tea. Nothin' wrong with tea, mind yuh, bring back mem'ries a my grandmum.

"But I did learn one thing from that son-of-a-buck Texas Walker. He's made his way all over the world, twirling a rope. Well, him an' his rope and his whiny way a sweet talkin' folks. But, hon, anythin' he can do, I can in spades! Even if we gotta play them 'musical theatres' or stand on the street corners to twirl our ropes, we're gonna be able to git money ahead and git back home.

"An' I ain't gonna be whinin' nor askin' nobody for nothin' I didn't earn. B'sides, we gotta lotta sights to see. No hurry."

"All right," Dorothy answered, more than happy to have Bill all to herself for a while. "But what places are on your must see list?"

"Well, on my way back acrost country, I took me a detour to a little right a middle a nowhere . . ."

Dorothy giggled, reveling in the memory of a spunky, sass-talking woman.

"An' I vis'ted with Mum for a day 'r two. She wrote down a couple a places she remembers her dad talkin' about from he's a kid. Well, a child," he corrected himself.

"I got the list tucked away right next to yer present," he said, smiling into her face, nose to nose.

"Then we better get dressed and get our chores finished so we can look over your list," she said, kissing him once more for good measure before reluctantly getting to her feet. "We're burning daylight."

"Ain't no daylight t'burn," Bill said, not quite whiny, "ain't never seen fog hang 'round like this. But yer right. 'Bout time we got our day started."

Once they were dressed, Dorothy washed their few dishes while Bill opened his suitcase and began to unpack.

He brought with him back to the table two envelopes. Grinning he asked her, "Which one yuh wanna open first?"

There were no markings on either envelope, so Dorothy slid the one next to her from his hand as the two of them sat down at the kitchen table. She opened it and pulled out the familiar lined pages, folded neatly into thirds.

"Mum got all excited when I told her I was going back to England – though she was purty surprised at me for leavin' yuh '*all alone over there all by herself*,' by the way."

Dorothy shook her head, picturing Sue May lecturing Bill on her behalf.

"I understand her concern but I was not all alone nor by myself, well, not until October, I guess," she said.

"That's what I kep' tellin' her. Anyway, after she calmed down, she told me she'd write me a list of her dad's folks and where they's born just in case."

"Just in case of what?" Dorothy asked.

"She's sorta sentimental at times," Bill explained. "She likes to talk about the places she's been, 'specially before her mum an' dad come to the States. She and Gran'mum both. They'd click their tongues an' tell us they's speakin' the language of the natives of Africa. We kids wondered if they might a been foolin' us, but mostly we thought it was great. I tol' yuh Mum was born in South Africa, din't I?"

"I think so," Dorothy replied, beginning to appreciate the list before her. The list written in a tiny, neat script so unlike Bill's.

"One of Gran'mum's favorite cities in all the world was Paris. I forgot all 'bout that till Mum reminded me. I guess one a Mum's sisters was born there. I don't recollect Mum talkin' much about Eva – that was the sister born in Paris. She was still just a girl when Mum and Dad was married. I never met her.

"So, here's the list she give me," Bill said, reading and pointing out the name of each person while explaining his or her relationship to his mother. "This here's her dad, David Stephenson. He's born in Newcastle. Ain't that a kick in the pants? Newcastle's one a them places Big Talkin' Walker was sure he was gonna be puttin' on a rodeo."

He snorted his disgust.

"Her aunt Jessie, one a her dad's sister's born in Scotland." He squinted at his mother's tiny script. "Edinburgh, I b'lieve."

Dorothy nodded in agreement.

"An' her dad's mother was named Eliza. See this?" he asked pointing to the list. "Says she's born in Cork. Ireland, isn't it? Quite a name for a place, don'tcha think?"

"There's not a place on this list I wouldn't love to visit." Dorothy's voice, though, expressed doubt.

"Whatcha worryin' about?" Bill asked, though guessing. "Bet there's folks in every one a them towns that just cain't wait to watch us spin a fancy rope 'r two. Dressed up all cowboy like in our boots an' hats. Tell yuh what. I'll spin for the both of us and you can be the monkey collectin' the pennies!"

"I will not!" Dorothy cried, disgusted at the thought of passing a hat. "I will be your lovely assistant. I will announce all your fancy tricks. I will even cheer when you toss a loop, as you say, around my waist, but I will not be collecting the pennies."

Bill laughed at her indignation.

"Them folks'd better be givin' up shillings or pounds or . . ." he stopped, stumped at the intricacies of the British monetary system. "That oughta make it a little easier on yuh, if they fork out the big dough."

"Even after all these months, it's still pretty confusing. All those pennies, and half-pennies, even tuppence - that's a two penny," Dorothy laughed at herself. "I guess that since I want to get back home with you, I'll do my part to help any way I can."

"An' we ain't just gonna put every penny away with only gettin' home in mind. Long as we're already here, we're gonna make the most of it. We'll git home when we git there!"

"Bill, I've enough for at least one of our tickets," Dorothy said.

"Well, we'll keep it for a last ditch backup an' hope it never comes to that," Bill grinned at her. "Don't let no whiny cowboy sweet talk yuh outta it, neither!"

She suddenly remembered the other envelope. It lay on the table before her. Looking up at Bill, she pointed to it and lifted an eyebrow. He nodded and grinned, a little self-consciously, though. It wasn't like him to hold back.

Dorothy pulled the unsealed flap open and took out the same lined, familiar paper.

"*Queen of My Heart*," she read the title, glancing up at Bill who was watching her intently. He nodded.

"Go on," he said, before ducking his head.

Dorothy began to read aloud:

To see the world's cowboy contest that nowhere is surpassed,
With features wild and thrilling too that never was outclassed,

Tex Austin, on his black stallion, came and brought his 'boys,
With leather straps and wooly chaps - bronk saddles were their toys.

The tall and skinny roper, Skeeter Bill was also with 'em there,
With high hopes to spin his ropes at the London fair.

The dark haired laughing beauty, his darling Dot Morrell,
To London Town she came to ride wild bronks as well.

But now her cowboy ain't with her, and in his heart's a storm -
Missing her smile so cheery bright, her heart so big and warm.

The Queen of his heart with her tender touch, is far across the sea,
And he is here in the middle of nowhere, as lonesome as can be.

He sits alone and eats his grub, breakfast, supper, lunch
With worn out chaps and beat up hat, this puncher's lost his punch.

He's far from the best that's in the west, no memory is spared,
There's nothing he wants more now, a kiss, reminding him she cares. **

She looked up, surprised to see - what? Misty eyes? Surely not!
"So, yuh, see, Dot, I already got my dearest Christmas wish."
His voice was colored with tender feelings.   Then he pointed to the
bottom of the page, where he'd written a post script.

Let's never do this again, All my love, Bill

He stood and offered her a hand up.
"Amen, Bill, amen," Dorothy agreed, sliding her arms around his waist
as he held her face in his hands.   "The time with the Kirnans was great,
but no matter how good the good times were, the fun and laughs we were
sharing, there was always a hole in my heart.   My heart always expected to
turn around and find you there.   But that's behind us now.   From here on
out, let's do our best to stick together."
"Yup," he agreed, kissing her.   "Stick t'gether like cockleburs.   Yuh
remember them, I'm sure!"

XXVII - NOVEMBER 1933 - JACK OF DIAMONDS, QUEEN OF SPADES

F ear and dread writhed and coiled themselves around one another in the pit of her stomach.   She hated automobiles.   She hated their tight quarters with little leg room, their uncomfortable seats, the endless sitting in one cramped position for hours on end, or so it seemed.   Not being able to walk to the dining car, the smoking lounge, the goddamn bathroom at a moment's notice.   On a whim.   Whenever she wanted to.

But most of all she hated being in one on icy, snow covered roads. Hated the feeling of slipping sideways going around corners.   Hated the thought of fish-tailing on a downgrade.   Hated being blinded by the blowing snow, anxiously wondering how the driver could see to make his way at all over the roads.

Roads that lay between here and there, but especially the long stretch on the rugged, winding Mint Canyon along the Sierra Madre Highway passing through the southern end of the San Gabriel Mountains, or whatever the hell they were called.   God, the roads tomorrow would be hell on wheels.   She grimaced.   Why couldn't they just try to take the train? Trains.   Now that was the way to travel.

Furtively, she glanced up from her suitcase over at Bill busily packing his own - no need for a trunk for so short a trip.   His continued silence and undivided attention to such a mundane task - arranging and rearranging so few pairs of socks and undershirts - screamed at her in a way no words he could ever say.   Her fear and dread, great though they were, were overshadowed by the sorrow crushing her heart.

Twenty years.   Twenty years they'd chased each other's dreams. Together.   Twenty years through thick and thin, taking joy in each other's successes and pride in their own.   On the other hand, though, through those same twenty years, there were disagreements, differing opinions and difficult times, yet seldom had they ever raised their voices to each other. Even less often in anger.

And never, ever, had Mr. Skeeter Bill Robbins ever told her, Miss Dorothy Morrell, "Carlina, I'm done.   Do whatever the hell you want to do. I got no more to say."

Never.   The clipped words, the tightly controlled tone of voice, the finality of his argument, had slapped her in a way that still stung.   Slapped hard with words, but as always, never raising a hand to her.

Her own anger, and more so, the dread that continued to pull at her guts, had kept her from simply giving in right then and apologizing. Giving in and beginning the healing process between them.

She pressed her lips together and shook her head.   Her eyes burned from crying.   Her throat hurt from yelling.   Pain pounded in her head. Apologies would come, but not now, while the wounds of their arguments were still raw and angry.

Confused and bewildered, she though back over the last few days, picking apart every conversation.   Dissecting every argument.   At so many points of time, she could have changed her tone, her tack, her wheedling, her demands.   Yet each of those previous times, she and Bill had managed to remain civil, even if their impatience with each other had grown.

The events leading to their stand-off had begun not so long ago.   Two weeks, maybe a little more ago, Tiny Shuster and his Missus had been over to play pinochle.   It must have been a Wednesday night then.   Pinochle and home fermented hard cider, maybe a few bottles of that soda pop beer Budweiser and O'Doul's had been making for the last dozen years.   Long gone were the days of real beer - the kind that had actual alcohol content. It was more trouble than it was worth to try to smuggle what passed for beer in from Tijuana.   So, the fizzy apple cider or near beer.   And homemade pretzels.   Not as good as Mutti made.

How long had it been since Mutti had crossed her mind?   Mutti and dear Papa.   Dorothy thought back to her parents' arguments.   Papa would never have told off his wife.   Maybe he would have simply walked out of the kitchen into the dark of the night.   Off to some procrastinated chore, or to pull some weeds along the back fence of the garden, all the while puffing on his pipe – he never took to smoking cigarettes.   No, it would have been Mutti who had the last word in their arguments – not so much that her will had prevailed but that when Papa, as Bill, was done with the discord, he had simply walked away.

Oh, back to pretzels and beer.   How her mind wondered these days!

It was Wednesday, two, no three weeks ago.   In addition to the Shusters, Tiny and Missy, who came over weekly, Bill had invited Jack. And Jack had brought Myrtle. So instead of four-handed pinochle, they were playing six.   Pinochle with this bunch was never cut throat, always light-hearted, the competition friendly.   That didn't mean there was a lack of attention to rules or protocol.   No, house rules were always in force. No cheating.   Or at least none that could be caught.

They had cut the deck for partners.   Dorothy, Bill and Missy playing against Tiny, Jack and Myrtle.   Four or five hands had been played, the scores going back and forth.   With fizzy juice and pretzels being the order of the night, everyone's mood was mellow.

Dorothy had relaxed into thinking that Jack would make it through the entire evening without bringing up some harebrained scheme, one that Bill was sure to gladly fall into.   Bill had a way of pulling Jack's cock-eyed plans to success regardless of the unlikelihood – as long as there was no money involved.

She remembered well the moment that Jack finally had come up with his idea.   Bill had taken the bid and called spades as trump.   She was puzzling over which two cards she should send him.   She had a king and a queen in spades.   But she also had that jack of diamonds.   Jack of diamonds and queen of spades.   After all that was the name of the game.

She had glanced over at Bill wondering if she should try to slip a hand signal his way to ask if he'd rather have that jack of diamonds.   Just as she began to adjust her wedding ring with her thumb, when Jack made his announcement.

"Let's all go up to Paradise Trout Club for Thanksgiving.   All of us," he repeated for emphasis, grinning at the faces around the table.

Well, now, of all Jack's ideas, this one was actually intriguing.

Noah Beery's Paradise Resort was well known for fine dining, especially if one was partial to trout, and great fishing, though the end of November might not be the most inviting time of year to wet a worm.

Delightful bungalows for its guests the ads and newspaper articles boasted.   Then Dorothy stopped cold in her thoughts.   And what was whispered behind the backs of men's hands when their wives or girlfriends weren't around?

'Would-be-starlets available to entertain if the need or desire . . .' she snorted to herself '. . . desire should arise?'

She glanced around the table. She could tell that Tiny and Missy were all in – all in! And they weren't even playing poker. Myrtle was so dewy-eyed, or perhaps more aptly, cow-eyed, over Jack that there was no doubt where she would be come Thanksgiving Day. Bill looked across his cards at Dorothy and raised an eyebrow, asking her opinion. Surely there would be no need or desire for starlets among this crowd. Everything would be on the up and up.

"Sounds wonderful," Dorothy quickly replied, as she pulled the jack of diamonds and queen of spades from her hand. She slid them across the table. Bill picked them up and grinned across at her, winking with a short nod. Just what he had needed or wanted – or maybe he was nodding in agreement with Jack's invitation. She remembered she was still smiling as she picked up the cards Bill had sent back to her. King and queen of hearts. As she melded them, she gently tapped Bill's leg with her toe beneath the table assuring him he was, as always the King of her heart.

"Great!" Jack thundered as he slapped a double pinochle onto the table. "I'll drive."

Instantly Dorothy's mood dampened.

"Can't we take the train?" she asked, hopeful to miss out on being a passenger in Jack's sedan.

All five card players turned their eyes to Dorothy. Before Jack could jump in with his usual brusqueness, or actual rudeness, Bill answered for the group, "There ain't no railroad lines anywhere near them parts."

"None?" Dorothy wavered. "But I thought you could get to anywhere by rail."

"Those days are coming to an end," Jack trumped back into the conversation. "Besides, railroads take people from town to town, city to city. There ain't 'nuff people goin' to Paradise Springs to warrant the Southern Pacific to build a spur to some little old outpost."

Dorothy was determined not to be out talked by the likes of Jack Hulse.

"I don't think Noah Beery would take kindly to you referring to his resort as 'some little old outpost.' What I read in the papers, one would think it's God's own backyard."

"God don't run no railroad lines, girl, or we could take the train to just about anywhere," Jack guffawed, sounding as God-awful as any pack mule or trick burro for that matter.

Oh, God! Now what? She hardly dared to catch Bill's eye now.

"Come on," Jack offered, folding his hand of cards and laying them face down on the table, "let's go take a look at my car."

Jack's use of the word 'car' grated on Dorothy's nerves. A 'car', thank you, was built to ride the rails – dining cars, sleeping cars, boxcars, freight cars, all with heavy iron wheels perfectly built to roll down gleaming twin lines of steel rails.

As the other four players laid their cards on the table as well, Dorothy sighed and followed suit. Bill gently took her by the elbow to steady her on the walk through the darkness from the porch to Jack's car. She sighed. Her leg, the one she broke at the Exposition, seemed to hurt constantly any more.

Even in the moonlight, the Oldsmobile touring sedan was impressive, just as Jack liked everything in his life.

Including Myrtle, Dorothy mused. By the light of the porch light, she could see that the fenders on Jack's beauty were the same honey-golden color as Myrtle's starchy curls.

"Plenty of room for all six of us," Jack pointed out as he wound up to deliver yet another of his big spiels, pulling open the door to the backseat.

"Suicide doors, they call 'em," he explained as he ushered the women into the yawning cavern of the backseat. "Got lots of leg room. As comfortable as the couch in your front room."

Not even close, Dorothy silently refuted thinking of the overstuffed couch and chairs in her own living room, their welcoming cushions and cradling tufted pillows.

Jack's upbringing was showing through his veneer. Tenements had front rooms. Apartments had front rooms. Not that Dorothy had ever minded a front room, but then again, she didn't put on airs just to prove to others how important she was.

Once settled into the back seat, Myrtle pulled a slim cigarette case from within the folds of her bodice and offered them to Missy and Dorothy as she went on to retrieve a Banjo lighter as well.

"Oh, thank you, no," Missy gushed, sweetly turning down Myrtle's offer, settling further into the cushioned backseat.

Dorothy stared at the cigarettes, wanting one more now as much as any other time in her life. The anxiety – no, the dread caused by the prospect of traveling anywhere with Jack Hulse at the wheel surged through her. It felt as though electric sparks were dancing on the goose bumps up and down her arms and legs.

She closed her eyes and inhaled deeply of the cool of the night, savoring the crisp air of the autumn evening. She exhaled slowly and then smiled at Myrtle.

"I'm fine, thank you, dear," she said, making a point of calling out the difference in their ages. Myrtle shrugged, snapping the striker of her lighter to light up.

"Suit yourself," Myrtle answered as if she was well aware of Dorothy's cravings and didn't care one whit about age or its privileges.

"Dammit, Myrtle," Jack roared. "Not in the car! We've been over this and over this."

He brusquely helped first Missy and then Dorothy out of the backseat. He needn't have hurried. Myrtle had more than plenty of time to leisurely open the door on her own side of the car and calmly step out into the moonlight.

Dorothy shouldn't have been stunned. Nothing was past Jack, but to listen to him call Myrtle out in front of everyone was embarrassing and she went from being miffed with Myrtle's snippetiness to being mortified by Jack's callousness.

The magic of the evening evaporated for Dorothy. She felt drained and saddened as she followed their company back toward the house. She became aware of Bill's arm around her waist and leaned into him. He was more comforting than any the couch cushion or overstuffed chair.

He pulled a pack of ready-mades from his breast pocket and lit one up and handed the cigarette to her as they silently approached the porch steps, *Thank you, Bill, and thank you, God,* she silently prayed as she pulled in a deep drag. Lightheadedness hit her just as she knew it would, but it was fleeting. Besides, Bill's arm was still holding her close. Next, the cutting edges of the nervous energy bottled up inside her began to dull and then to dissipate, melting away like morning frost, fading like the smoke before her on the gentle breath of the evening breeze.

Jack be damned and he could take Myrtle with him, she thought as she leaned closer into Bill's embrace as they walked up the porch steps.

They never did finish playing that hand, Dorothy recalled. The cigarette butts had been snuffed out in the coffee cans filled with sand out there on the porch. Excited talk replaced Jack's tirades, pinochle forgotten in the whirl of making plans for the upcoming holiday.

"When'll we leave and when're we comin' back?" Bill asked, always the mind for details.

"Well, what you got goin' that week, Bill?" Jack came back.

"Not much. Startin' into the slow season for rodeos and shows like that."

For the past few seasons, Bill had partnered with Hoot, his cowboyin' friend from way back in the days before he'd met Dorothy. Not that Hoot did much cowboying anymore. Not real cowboying - not like the old days. Back in 1912, he won the all-around championship at Pendleton as well as the steer-roping world championship at Calgary - though not on the day that Carlina Eichhorn had sat in the grandstands. Same year, same place, though.

"Tiny? How 'bout you?" Bill turned to his right-hand man.

"You know better'n I do what I got goin' on that week," was all Tiny would say, grinning up at his boss.

"Settles it, then. Up to you, Jack. When we gotta have our bags packed by?" Bill asked.

Nightcaps from the *Medicinal Purposes* bottle had been poured, though Dorothy noticed Myrtle drank both hers and Jack's. For all his faults, for all his bluster, Jack wasn't much of a drinker, Dorothy had noticed.

"Let's leave here Tuesday, 'bout daybreak. It's only a few hours' drive up through Mint Canyon to Acton and then on to Paradise Springs. Give us plenty of time to mosey on over the mountains. Be to Paradise plenty early before dinnertime."

Jack was beaming. Being in the spot light always made Jack shine.

In the coming days, Dorothy approached the subject of how to get to Paradise Springs in any way other than driving with Jack by running first one and then another scenario past Bill.

"How about we take the train to the nearest city? We lease an automobile and then drive the rest of the way?"

"The nearest city? That would be either Mojave, San Bernardino, or by God, Dot, right here at our front door in Saugus! Right here," he repeated, "we are as close to the Paradise as any a them other places."

"But at least we'd be on the other side of the mountains if we went either to Mojave or San Bernardino."

"Listen to yerself, Dot! Yer proposin' we buy six train tickets, then rent a car fer what? We'll be no closer to Paradise Resort than as we are from here. If we drive from here, all we'll have to do is split the gas money. It's up to 18 cents a gallon this week but a hell of a lot cheaper than yer train idea."

He stopped to shake his head in disbelief. "What you got again' drivin' through the mountains, anyways?"

Dorothy could not even begin to explain her fears. She didn't understand them herself half the time but they were real. Debilitating.

A few days later, she tried a different tack. "How about we borrow an auto from Hoot? You know he'd let you in a heartbeat."

"Of course he would. That's not the point. We made plans to drive up with Jack. How would that look? Us ditchin' them to drive up ourselves?"

"At least you'd be driving."

She knew she was cajoling. Bill took pride in being a safe and reliable driver though they had no vehicles of their own. Never needed one. Bill just shook his head and refused to discuss it any further. At least, not then.

And now today. The eve of *The Journey*. It was raining. A light drizzle had started about noon. As the afternoon wore on, Dorothy worried as she watched the mountain peaks to the west beginning to turn white, and then as the snow cap crept down from the peaks, threatening to completely cover the slopes. Trying to ignore the changes in the mountains was like trying to ignore a toothache or a splinter. The snow wasn't going to go away. Not anytime soon.

Dorothy was passed cajoling, passed being patient in trying to convince Bill. Passed reasoning.

When he came in for supper, she laid right into him right away. Didn't even wait for him to finish washing his hands.

"Have you noticed it's snowing up in the mountains?" she demanded.

"Yup." Bill lathered his hands with soap and then leaned over the sink basin to suds up his face.

"That's all you're going to say? Yup?"

"Yup." He began to systematically lift water from the basin with his hands to rinse his face and scrub out his ears.

"Oh, good Lord! It's snowing!" she repeated, her voice growing shrill. "Dammit, Bill! The roads are going to be horrible."

"You don't know that for sure."

Bill reached for the small towel hanging next to the sink.

She gathered a deep breath. This was her last hope.

"Can't we just stay home?" It was more a demand than a question.

"Nope." Bill dried his face and hands using the small towel hanging next to the sink.

"Why not, for godsake?" Dorothy hadn't realized that in her desperation, she was now shouting, tears of frustration beginning to run down her face.

"We have been over this and over this," Bill began, his own voice raising to match hers. "These folks are our friends. Or I thought they were *our* friends. Maybe they're only *my* friends. *My* good friends. Me and my good friends, we've made plans. There ain't nothin' wrong with our plans and by our, I mean mine and Jack's and Tiny's. I don't know what yer goddam plans are, but me, I'm gonna go to Paradise with them boys and that's all there is to it."

"Dammit, Bill! Is this how it is? You? Your friends?" Dorothy yelled. "You are being so selfish. Thinking only of yourself. Doing whatever it is you and *your* damn good friends want to do. What about me? What about what I want? Do I ever come first?"

Bill's head snapped around to look her square in the eye and instantly Dorothy felt the hurt, the deep wounds the implication of her question had caused. Bill had always been her champion, had always been in her court, had always been the first to celebrate her successes. From Cheyenne to London and back again, no one had ever come before her. Not once.

"So, this is how you see it?" Bill suddenly sounded exhausted. Tired to the bone.

"This fightin' is over. Carlina, I'm done talkin' 'bout it. Do whatever the hell you want to do. I got no more to say."

XXVIII - NOVEMBER 1933 - MEDICINAL PURPOSES

The silence that followed was smothering her. The chill was beyond any scarves or gloves. Dorothy chewed her bottom lip as Bill turned quickly yet calmly on his heel and headed for their bedroom. Supper was forgotten. It would cool, might not ever be eaten for all she cared. On quiet feet of her own, she followed. He had already taken both of their suitcases from the top closet shelf, testament again of his constant concern for her. Or was it a challenge? Did he simply want to see if she were going to pack and join the party regardless of her constant complaining and whining the past three weeks? Dorothy bristled for a moment. Or was it simply arrogance? A firm conviction that she would follow him regardless of her unreasonable doubts and fears. She chided herself. Bill had never actually used the word *'unreasonable.'* Implied it, perhaps, but never said it.

Her first inclination was to take that damn suitcase and fling it as far into the rain drenched night as she could throw it. But that might seal the deal. Whatever *'The Deal'* was. The *'I'm Done Deal.'*

Just how far *'done'* could Bill be?

She studied his features as she slowly unbuckled her own suitcase and opened it. He seemed to have no thoughts more important than how to arrange a few articles of clothing in the best way. For Bill, there was always a *best way*. He continued to rearrange what little he had already stowed, adding a pair of dungarees to his socks and undershirts - blue jeans, they were sometimes called these days. A casual change up from the cream colored, 'ice cream pants' he usually wore if dressing up. He began the elaborate process of carefully folding and rolling several long-sleeved shirts to add his Spartan stash. She sighed, missing their traveling days. Missing their portmanteaus - those huge trunk-like packing wonders. Portmanteaus seemed to be standing on their sides, upended, opening to reveal drawers on one side and a hanging rod with those specially made wooden contraptions on the other side. They still had one somewhere. Overkill for a three or four day trip.

Bill finished stowing all his clothing into his suitcase. Carefully he closed it up and buckled the straps tightly to keep it closed. Without a word, he left the bedroom. Dorothy listened to his progress down the hall and into the kitchen. He must have set his suitcase at the backdoor, for the next sound she heard was the clinking of a ladle in the pot of stew she had set on the table just as Bill had come in for the evening. It was just beef and vegetables. Simple. She couldn't remember taking the biscuits out of the oven, but she must have. The kitchen would have been filled with smoke if she hadn't.

After stowing her underclothing, she rolled her own blouses and skirts - less carefully than Bill had - instead carefully wrapping that new electric iron in towel before placing it into the bottom of her suitcase. Her clothes always wrinkled no matter how carefully she rolled them. Several pairs of stockings. Another set of garters. An extra pair of shoes. Her calmness surprised herself as she fastened the buckles.

This, too, shall pass.

She only had to live one minute to the next. One hour to the next and soon the weekend would be over. God would still be in His heaven and all would be right with the world again.

She wasn't hungry so she simply exchanged her clothes for a nightgown and climbed into bed. Time would tell.

In her dreams the world was the pale green of early spring. Blossoms swayed on the branches of lemon and orange trees. Meadowlarks trilled here in California just as they had in Manitoba, in Oregon, in Wyoming. Sunshine sparkled on the dew. Dew that froze to frost. The flower petals that turned to snowflakes as first they danced lazily from the tree branches, then quickened and were swept up in moments of madness, rising to block the beams of sunlight until the world was nothing but swirling billows of snow and wind.

Dorothy woke with a start. She could hear Bill's gentle breathing next to her, close enough but still on the far side of the bed. She rolled over and curled herself into his back. Even in his sleep, he reached for her hand and pulled it to his chest. She relaxed and as she drifted off, she hoped her dream was nothing more than more reflections of her worries. Nothing more than closure for the uneasiness of the past 21 days.

Next she knew the decadent aroma of freshly ground coffee brewing gently nudged her to wakefulness. She threw back the covers that Bill had tucked around her. Swinging her legs over the side of the bed, she stretched and yawned, thinking of the dress hanging in her closet that she planned to wear today. She did not own a single pair of trousers. She thought them to be unladylike and unflattering, and yet on a day such as today which would likely be spent climbing in and out of that damn automobile, possibly walking through snow, she could see their advantage.

As she walked to the bathroom, she thought again of the ease of traveling by train. She really had to quit dwelling on it. It wouldn't make the day any better.

She squinted at her reflection in the mirror. Lately, she had been pulling gray hairs that were showing up in ever greater numbers. She sighed as she reached for her hairbrush. It was not where it belonged. Searching for it, she decided Bill must have packed a bathroom kit for the two of them. Probably already in his suitcase. She found a comb and smoothed her curls.

As she hurried back to the bedroom, she could hear Tiny and Missy laughing with Bill in the kitchen. Shoot! It was later than she realized. Even as she dressed, she heard Jack's Oldsmobile pulling up to the back of the house. A jaunty blowing of his horn further announced his arrival. She gathered her coat, scarf and gloves from the closet and as she hurried, she noticed her suitcase wasn't where she had left it last night.

"Good mornin', all!" Jack boomed as he burst into the kitchen, Myrtle at his heels. That man was like Father Time himself – he waited for no one or nothing.

"Hey, you!" Tiny replied to Jack before turning to Dorothy.

"Yer lookin' well," he said. He and Missy were sitting at the kitchen table sipping coffee.

God almighty, there'd better be some left for her.

"Grab yerself a cup," Bill offered Jack and Myrtle as he gathered both of their suitcase grips in one hand and a couple of traveling lap blankets in the other. It wasn't Bill's way ever to apologize, not with words, at least. Truth be told, she thought ruefully, he had nothing to apologize for, but as always, when he was ready to make up and get over the storm clouds their relationship had weathered, it was his way to do something for her, never to say much. She tried to catch his eye, but he was already out the door.

216

"Don't mind if we do." Jack pulled two mugs from the cupboard and poured for both Myrtle and himself. Would wonders never cease, Dorothy thought to herself.

"Ahhh, good mornin', Dot!"

Jack pulled down another mug and filled it to the brim. Dorothy shrugged off the urge to tell him she never drank her coffee black and thank you very much for not leaving enough room to add any cream. Sugar, yes, cream, no.

She smiled her best smile for Jack. He winked back, nodding as he lifted his coffee cup in a grand salute. Nodding back, she stirred sugar into her coffee. Better to start the day off on a positive note. Put her best foot forward. Let sleeping dogs lie. All of the above.

Dorothy took a deep breath as she assessed the others all sitting now at the table.

Missy and Tiny were still in their coats – they didn't intend to make Jack wait for them. She sipped her coffee and wondered if she would be able to surreptitiously top off her cup with a shot of whiskey – for *medicinal purposes*, of course – or better yet, top it off with a little of the hide out rum. The thought of Jack's possible reaction made her want to giggle. Was it really ever too early to start drinking?

"Is it still raining?" she finally decided to ask.

"Oh, yeah, but it's just comin' down real light. Nothin' to worry about," Jack promised.

She nodded, still eyeing the cupboard where the alcohol was kept safely behind the canisters of flour and sugar.

"Wind starting to pick up a little. Got new wiper blades on for the windshield."

Bill stepped back into the kitchen, rain dripping from his hat as he took it off. So much for coming down lightly.

"Well, folks, we 'bout ready to hit the trail?" Bill smiled across the kitchen at her, melting what little anger was left in her heart. She smiled back.

"Hey, Bill! You wanna ride shotgun or you gonna ride in the back with your missus?"

Dorothy held her breath waiting for Bill's reply. This would be the deal maker, him deciding where he was going to sit for next three or four hours.

"I don't much take to the front seat 'less I'm drivin'," Bill said. "Better off in back with my gal."

Bill made it sound as if sitting in the backseat was the only place he'd ever want to be, though Dorothy knew better. He hated backseats worse than he hated cold leftovers.

"Well, then, let's load 'em up and head on out!"

Jack rinsed his coffee mug and set it upside down on the sideboard. The others followed suit and soon the kitchen was empty except for her and Bill.

"Sorry I didn't have a cup ready for you this mornin'," Bill said as they made sure all the electric lights were all turned off. "I'da poured you two fingers of *medicinal purposes* to help you over the pass."

Dorothy gently lifted her hand to his freshly shaven cheek. "You are the best, Roy Raymond Robbins. God blest me the day you came into my life."

He lifted his own hand to cover hers as he bent to kiss her and she was more than happy to kiss him back. Jack chose that moment to lay on his horn. Still a cowboy's kiss was meant to be short and sweet. There would be more later.

She stood on the porch while he locked the door. Sure sign they'd be gone a while - locking the door. He perched his hat on her head as they walked together to the driver's side of the car.

"In you go," Bill said brightly, opening the door. What had Jack called it? A suicide door? Interesting expression for sure, though Dorothy could not imagine why anyone would want to end it all, let alone end it all by jumping from a moving car. She slid into the middle of the back seat. Missy was sitting on the other end of the long bench seat.

Bill folded himself into the seat beside her and then spread one of the traveling blankets across her lap and legs. Putting an arm around her shoulders, he pulled her close as Jack put the car into gear and started out onto the highway, windshield wipers keeping ahead of the rain.

"We won't be doin' any fishin', I suppose," Tiny said from the front seat.

"Nope." Short and sweet as usual was Bill's reply.

"Brought along some regular playin' cards as well as the pinochle decks," Tiny said. "I hear there is a good chance we can get ourselves something more than just fizzy juice and *medicinal purposes* up there."

Jack snorted while the others laughed. "Hear tell, some weekends it's been standin' room only up there. Good heavens, why do people think they gotta drink to have fun?"

No one answered his question. Discretion could be counted on to keep a conversation on positive notes. After all, more flies are caught with honey than vinegar.

Missy took up where Tiny had left off. "I can't wait to see the ball room. I wonder if there will be a band since it's the middle of the week."

"Remember, Toots, it's a holiday week. I wager there'll be a band," Jack said, unconcerned about what to do with his time.

"I heard there is a swimming pool. Heated water even," Myrtle put in.

Dorothy shook her head. She never understood the notion. All one needed was a bathtub. A bathtub in the privacy of a bathroom. No need to be half naked in front of all those people - all those other half naked people.

"Regardless, we'll find plenty to keep us busy, even it's just settin' on the veranda watchin' the world go by," Bill finally put in his two-cents worth.

The road began its climb out of the valley and into the foothills. Slushy droplets of snow began to mix in with the rain. Dorothy shuddered and sighed before deciding to concentrate on the pattern woven into Jack's woolen cap. Hounds' tooth, she believed they called it. It had become all the rage this last year. She studied it trying to figure out how the weavers had set up the warp and woof to create the design.

"Relax," Bill whispered to her as he straightened the traveling blanket that had fallen from her lap. She glanced out the side window. The snow was getting thicker. She could just barely see across the road to the hillside and the occasional trees that grew on the mountainsides.

Jack was driving more slowly now, carefully making his way through the storm and climbing higher and higher through the canyon. She turned her face into Bill's shoulder and slid one of her hands into his. His arm tightened around her shoulders, pulling her closer still.

"Sh-sh," he soothed as his fingers combed through her hair. His movements triggered a misty memory. How old had she been and where had she been? The memory clarified and she remembered now sitting on Mutti's lap, being held ever so close to her mother as Dorothy was crying. No, not Dorothy, but little Carlina was crying into her mother's shoulder. Mutti's fingers were tenderly trying to soothe her little daughter as they stroked her hair, combed through her curls just as Bill's were doing now. Mother and daughter were on a train. She couldn't quite remember why she had been crying so hard. She relaxed a little more into Bill's embrace, feeling safe and protected in his arms.

Then he began humming a nameless tune, a certain sign that he, too, was getting nervous.

"Dammit!" She was startled to hear Jack muttering. "I can hardly see the road ahead. I bet them headlights is completely covered with snow. Useless, that's what they are."

"Pull over. I'll get out and clear them off," Bill offered.

"Pull over? I can't even see where the shoulder of the road is," Jack growled back.

He slowed even further as they made their way through the swirling snow being driven by the wind, now howling around them. Dorothy became aware of the stillness inside the car. There was no more good-natured joshing, no planning for the afternoon, no more speculation on how much trout they would eat for supper.

In a tiny corner of her heart, Dorothy was glad. Let them all understand why she had been so nervous, then she remembered Bill was the only who knew of her fears. Maybe he was sorry now that they had come, but he would never say so. It didn't matter. There was only one way to go now and that was forward.

"Come on, man," Bill repeated. "If yer worried about the shoulder, just stop. There ain't no traffic on this road today."

Jack finally did as Bill had suggested and then added, "Boy, Bill, I think I'd feel better with you behind the wheel."

Jack turned to Myrtle.   "Babe, you better scoot on over the seat and set back there in the middle of them girls.   No sense in gettin' out in this storm."

Dorothy watched disinterestedly as Myrtle began her very undignified and unladylike clamber over the seat.

Bill squeezed her into a quick embrace and planted a kiss on her check as he reached for the door handle.   "Don't worry, kiddo," he said, trying to lighten the mood, "I'll be out and back in the car before you know it."

And he had been.   The first time.   The second time.   By the third stop, the process was almost routine.

After each stop, Bill had been able to drive several miles following the dim outlines of the sides of the road before the headlights were again covered with snow to the point he could no longer see to make his way up the road.

Dorothy marveled at the turn of events that had finally put Bill into the driver's seat.   She relaxed into her corner of the backseat and finally allowed herself to begin to mentally make plans for the afternoon.   Too cold for much more than sitting before a roaring fireplace, curled into Bill's embrace.   Maybe some *medicinal purposes* to celebrate the beginnings of their Thanksgiving's celebration.

They were finally nearing the summit and it wouldn't be many more miles and the snow and wind should lighten up.   Then the road would just be wet with rain as they made their way down into the valley past Acton. One last time, Bill stopped the car and as he started to open the car door, he turned to Dorothy and the others in the car.

"It'll be okay," he reassured her in particular. "We're gonna make it safe and sound after all."

XXIX - AUGUST 1941 - FOGHORN CLANCY - SYRACUSE, NEW YORK

Dorothy snubbed out her cigarette, the first one of the morning, wondering how many more would be needed to make it through this day. She poured herself another cup of coffee from the percolator setting on its trivet. It was going to be an at least two cup morning, and perhaps a two finger afternoon. Time would tell.

Years. Years and years, it was since she'd been to a rodeo. Even more since she'd been to a rodeo in the state of New York. 1916, perhaps? The Stampede at Sheepshead. Shoot! She and Bill had been there. She'd watched while he battled bronks and spun his fancy rope. In turn, he had cheered her on as she rode to third place in the cowgirls' bucking horse competition.

Bill Picket, Hoot Gibson, Guy Weadick, and all the rest of the crew who had been there had thought that the Easterners were a hard crowd to please. Even harder to draw into the stadium – not even the enthusiastic endorsement from Colonel Theodore Roosevelt himself, could fill the seating in the grand stands. If they had only known. At least no one had ended up being summoned to court on counts of cruelty to animals.

Sheepshead Stampede. What a fiasco! After the Stampede was over, there was no cash to pay out the prize monies. Worry turned to panic as competitors scrambled to find ways to raise enough money to get home. Wherever it was they called home.

A vigorous knock at the front door told her that her company had arrived. A long forgotten tingle of anticipation began in the pit of her stomach as she carefully got to her feet, reaching as always for her cane. The cane she would deposit in the coat rack before opening the front door. The walk would loosen up tight muscles, warm up aching joints and as always, give her time to put on her brightest smile. Her show smile. Her Gawd Almighty Queen of the Goldarn World smile. What she would give to hear Bill's pleasing drawl right about now!

"How do you do, Mr. Clancy?" Dorothy beamed at her guest standing on the front stoop, hat in his hands. "It's been a very long time."

"Indeed, indeed it has!" he boomed.

"Come in. Come in and have a seat."

Foghorn Clancy followed her into her living room. Framed photographs of Bill and her lined the bookshelves and Sue's scrapbook was showcased on the coffee table.

"It's a pleasure to meet with you again, Miz Robbins," Clancy thundered, pleasantly, kindly. "It's been too long. Too long!"

"As always, my pleasure as well," Dorothy laughed, basking in Clancy's jovial mood.

God, it was good to laugh now and again.

"Could I get you a cup of coffee or a glass of iced tea?" Dorothy asked, suddenly remembering her role as hostess to her guest, glad she had not yet taken her seat. Getting to her feet without her cane was sometimes hard first part of the day.

"I have lemonade in the ice box as well," she added.

"Well, now, lemonade will suit me fine. That'll be great."

"Make yourself at home and I'll be right back," Dorothy said making her way through her tiny dining area and on to the kitchen.

"Mind if I take a look around? Blazes! This is as good as a cowboy hall of fame!"

"Not at all. Be my guest," Dorothy called back, thinking how much better it would be once all the pleasantries were over and they could get down to the business of the day.

When Dorothy returned from the kitchen with the pitcher of lemonade and her best two pressed glass tumblers – free inside the Quaker Oats she usually had for breakfast, if she did have breakfast – she saw that Clancy had taken a seat on the sofa and had opened her scrapbook. He held it in his lap and carefully turned the pages as though he was respecting their age as he admired postcards and photographs and scanned through newspaper clippings. He stopped short of pulling letters from their envelopes, figuring he would be crossing the line of privacy if he did.

"I see you've found my book of treasures," Dorothy said proudly as she set her tray onto the coffee table.

"I hope you don't mind," Clancy replied.

"Not at all. My life is an open book," Dorothy said.

And I wrote every damn chapter myself!

"As you know, I want to write about you for a feature we call 'Memory Trail.' It's a regular in the *Horns and Hooves* magazine. And I hope you're still up for my invitation to accompany me to the rodeo this afternoon."

"By all means," Dorothy replied, pouring the cold lemonade into the tall green tumblers. "It's been years since I've been to a rodeo. I'm looking forward to it," she added, hoping to convince herself.

But how many years? No need to go into unimportant details. To count the years would be to count back to a time of tragedy. Of heartbreak. Disaster.

"I've been a guest of the JE Ranch Rodeo a time or two before," Clancy said. "And you may have heard that Hoot Gibson is the featured guest for the performances here at the state fair."

"I hadn't heard," Dorothy began hesitantly. "It's been forever since I've seen him."

About the same number of years since she'd been to a rodeo, actually.

"As I recall, your husband, Skeeter Bill, was the manager at Hoot's ranch in Saugus out in California."

Dorothy nodded, pensively thinking back to the days she had played the part of hostess for the guests at the Hoot Gibson Ranch Rodeo. It had been an undemanding part, seldom needing to be played. Smile and wave. Smile and wave. Hoot made sure he kept himself in the spotlight.

"Those rodeos kept Bill plenty busy," she replied, skirting her own role for the time being.

"What do old cowboys do when they're too stove up to climb aboard the steers or bronks?" Clancy asked, though actually introducing his next thought.

"Why, they go to dreamin' about bein' the head of their own rodeos!" he answered his own question.

Dorothy bristled slightly, but kept her show face intact. Bill had never been an "old cowboy," bent and twisted with the rheumatism, much less "stove up."

"You know better than most," Dorothy replied. Clancy had been chasing rodeos, not as rider, but an announcer for decades. Hobnobbed and rubbed shoulders from the least to the greatest.

"From the time I first was acquainted with Bill," Dorothy explained, "he had one or more irons in the fire. Performing, competing or supplying rough stock," Dorothy said, defending a man who no longer needed defense.

Clancy hooted in agreement. "Bill sure loved the show."

"You remember when Austin took the rodeo to London?" Dorothy knew it was a rhetorical question. Of course, Clancy and the entire rest of the rodeo world remembered the Imperial Rodeo.

Clancy nodded.

"Sure, Bill went as a contestant," she continued. "Competed in fancy roping and bronk riding, but more importantly, Tex Austin had hired him on as one of his arena directors. The challenge of keeping the show moving, making sure the rough stock was brought to the holding pens at the right times, sometimes playing nursemaid to the cowboys, sometimes shaking hands with esteemed guests . . . it was a thrill greater than the roping or riding. It fired him up."

Dorothy paused to think back to the summer of 1924, to collect long ignored memories. To again feel the rush of hope.

"After the rodeo closed at Wembley, he stayed on a few weeks to help Austin finish wrapping up all the loose ends. Bill was so sure that the rest of Europe was a field ready to harvest, so to speak. Fresh, new ground, teeming with anxious spectators ready to jump at the chance to see a glimpse into the Wild West. He thought maybe he could start in Monte Carlo, chase the money, go from there."

Here Dorothy paused again. How far should she explain? She decided to leave Big Talking Walker out of today's memories. No need to dwell on foolishness.

"Before he returned to the States, he helped me convince Tommy Kirnan to let me join his company for the post Rodeo tour into Ireland and France."

"Oh?" Dorothy had Clancy's undivided attention, as he carefully closed the scrapbook and set it back onto the coffee table.

"He was a sweet talker," she mused. No one knew better than she did.

"But he never found any sponsors? No one to back his European rodeo plans?" Clancy asked.

"No, but he didn't let it slow him down. As soon as we got back in '25, he was back to chasing shows and rodeos." Dorothy nodded, more to herself and her memories.

"Of course, where Bill went, I went, but I was done with competition. Every ride in London took me forever to recover from," she laughed brightly, signaling Clancy that she might have been joking. No need for his sympathy over sore muscles long forgotten.

"Those days, he got so he was more into looking for livestock to buy. He used to tell me about his horse-trading father, buying up herds – sometimes gathering wild horse herds – and selling them to the US Army. Might be he was just carrying on an old family tradition."

"Mind if I smoke?" Clancy asked, startling Dorothy out of her reverie. Her stories and memories must be lagging, if Clancy had nothing better to think about than a cigarette.

"Of course not," Dorothy brightly replied, deciding to skip straight ahead to Mr. Hoot Gibson, star of the silver screen and All-Round Cowboy of the Pendleton Round Up of 1912. Talk about old cowboys!

"Need a refill on that lemonade?" Dorothy asked, returning Clancy's focus to the here and now.

After she had topped off both of their glasses, she continued.

"It's interesting that Hoot is here at the State Fair," she hedged. "Bill and Hoot's rodeo trails overlapped, ran together and sometimes bounced off each other from way back before I ever knew Bill, long before I left Winnipeg to come to the United States."

"So who knows how they became acquainted?" Clancy asked.

"No. Could have been behind the chutes, maybe out in the arena throwing saddles on outlaws, or . . ." Dorothy laughed quietly ". . . over drinks after – or before – the show. Long before Prohibition."

"Hard times. Hard times," Clancy chuckled, thinking that just a little vodka would make a great glass of lemonade even better. Something to keep in mind for later this evening.

"It was just a little over ten years ago, Hoot and Bill fell in together and life was never the same after that.

"All the challenges that Bill had fallen in love with at Wembley were now right at his fingertips. Hunting all over the west for steers and then bulls, buying up the 'buckin'est bronks' as Bill would have said. Shipping by rail instead of driving them on the hoof as his father had. Advertising Hoot Gibson's Golden State Rodeo. Word of mouth. Newspapers. You name it. He was in his element.

"Nothing he liked better though, than taking the show on the road! 1932, I think it was, he put the kit and kaboodle into train cars and headed for Dallas for the State Fair. No train trip for Hoot, though. Flew in by way of his beloved Blackhawk biplane. Put it on display the whole week." She shook her head, still in awe of man's ability to fly. She wouldn't mind one last flight high above the earth.

"And you?" Clancy asked.

"Oh, you could say I was the official hostess."

Not that Hoot Gibson with his bevy of starlets and cronies ever needed a hostess. He was top hand at playing host. Nothing too fine, nothing too outrageous, Hoot spared no expenses. Not that any of the in-crowd ever stayed around long enough to need a hostess, Los Angeles a short train trip away – the Southern Pacific ran special trains up from Los Angeles and back from Saugus just for the show – and a shorter still by car.   But if a title was needed, this was a perfect one.

Clancy checked his pocket watch and cleared his throat.

"Miz Robbins, we'll need to be leavin' soon.   Maybe the next five or ten minutes.   That gonna be all right with you?"

"I'll just get my hat and we'll be on our way," Dorothy answered.   Her hat.   Her triple X Stetson.   Today, it would be her crowning glory even if she were only wearing a light summer dress and jacket and not a fine tanned leather split skirt and vest over a billowing cowgirl's blouse.

XXX - AUGUST 1941 - DAYS GONE BY

Dorothy straightened her skirts and took a deep breath. It was going to be just fine, she kept telling herself. All they had to do was make it the six miles from her front door to the State Fair Grounds. There was hardly a cloud in sight let alone a hint of snow! Clancy closed her car door and whistled a nameless tune as he made his way to the driver's seat.

"Do you keep in touch with any of the old crowd anymore?" he asked as he climbed into the driver's seat and slipped his key into the ignition.

"No, ahhh, no," Dorothy said as she shook her head. Too many years had passed since she and Bill had traveled the circuits with names like Reine Hafley, Fox Hastings, Rose Smith, Ruth Roach, Mabel Strickland, and

Prairie Rose Henderson. One of her favorite photographs included herself with all of them taken in Texas. She thought back, struggling to remember. Was it at the Triangle Ranch Rodeo in King County? Must have been somewhere around 1927. The end of her glory days. Fourteen years and a life time ago.

"Who do you wanna know about?" Clancy offered as he slowly pulled his big touring car out into the street.

"Oh, Ruth Roach, or Bea Kirnan, maybe Vera McGinnis? We all went to London the summer of '24," Dorothy added, knowing full well that just like herself, Vera McGinnis had been trampled badly in 1934 and was quietly retired now, just where, though, Dorothy wasn't sure.

"Ruth, she married a Texas rancher name of Salmon a few years back. Probably sipping ice tea and settin' on the front porch 'bout now hopin' to catch a breeze," Clancy chuckled.

Dorothy nodded, thinking of the 'soft-spoken, rough-riding golden girl of the West,' who like many of the cowgirls back in the day, wore huge bows in her hair framing her face under her Stetson. Ruth Roach, once the wife of the world renowned steer-wresting champion Bryan Roach. By 1924, though, she and Bryan had split the sheets and she was then Mrs. Nowata Slim Richardson - both of whom were winners of some pretty good day money at Wembley. Strange, she thought, as she remembered that Bryan and his newly wedded wife, Lois, had been in London that summer as well. Politicians weren't the only ones who made strange bedfellows.

"Bea Kirnan," Clancy mused. "You mighta heard that Tommy passed away back in '37. Don't remember now the particulars. Heard tell that right after Tommy passed, she tried her hand at running an eatery in Wichita Falls, but that didn't go over so well. She mighta been one of the world's best trick riders and fancy ropers, but must not'a been much of a cook. Where she is now, I'm not for certain, though I think I recall someone saying she'd headed to California to try her luck there."

"No, I hadn't heard," Dorothy answered quietly. All too well, she knew the loneliness that would be overshadowing Bea's life. As far as finding one's luck in California, Dorothy hoped it would work for Bea as well as it had for her.

"What about Tad Barnes? I mean Tad Lucas?" Dorothy asked, smiling a little at the memories of the no nonsense, yet free-spirited woman who made her own luck by working hard to excel at everything she did.

"She's still chasing the rainbow," Clancy replied. "She went to Australia just last year to ride daily in the rodeo shows at the Aussie's Royal Agricultural Show," Clancy added. "I bet that sounds familiar to you! Contracted to ridin' two shows a day."

Dorothy smiled indulgently and nodded.

"Just like the Brits, the Aussies call her a 'buck-jumper.' But even better than ridin' bronks, or racin' in cowgirl relays, she's one hell of a gal in the trick saddle."

Dorothy nodded in agreement.

"Watching her sometimes made me think she was flying, or close to it."

Clancy slowed for traffic as he turned onto Burnet Avenue. He seemed quiet as he merged with traffic and headed west.

"What about Fox Hastings? I haven't heard much about her for years," Dorothy asked.

"Fox, you say?" Clancy's gravelly voiced mellowed. "I shoulda let her go to London with you folks. She had lots more goin' for her than just bulldoggin'."

'The hell you say, Dorothy thought.

"I always wondered why she didn't come. Her husband Mike went."

"I know, I know," Clancy replied. "But I wanted her billed as the World's Only Woman Bulldogger . . ."

"Even though she wasn't," Dorothy interrupted, remembering to smile sweetly across the car at her companion.

You can say anythin' you want, long as you say it nicely and smile big enough, Bill had told her over and again.

"Well, now, close enough," Clancy insisted. "As her manager, when I heard all the scuttlebutt about those Cruelty to Animals folks screamin' at Cochran and Austin, I figgered they'd never let a woman compete."

"They? Exactly who did you think was going to try to stop her?" Dorothy asked.

"Didn't matter. 'They' could've been Cochran and Austin or them Brits. Either way, I figgered she wasn't goin' to be allowed to be wrestlin' any steers in London."

"In the end, that competition was shut down after just a few rounds," Dorothy replied, miffed at now knowing why Fox wasn't with them in London. She inhaled deeply, counted to ten, and exhaled. It was water under the bridge.

"Damnedest part was that she broke her leg that June bull doggin' in Oklahoma. It was just before the Fourth of July Round Up in Belle Fourche, South Dakota," Clancy growled.

Dorothy nodded once more to herself. *Water under the bridge, water under the bridge,* she repeated again.

"But do you know where she is these days?" Dorothy reiterated.

"After she split up with Mike, she married another bull dogger, Chuck Wilson," Clancy began. "Kinda dandy story about them gettin' hitched. They were in New York for the Madison Square Round Up in 1929. Tied the knot just before the round up opened. Believe her and Chuck bought up a ranch in Arizona. Last I heard, anyway."

A companionable stillness filled the car as Clancy made his way through traffic and Dorothy thought back on the changes the past decade had brought.

Bonnie McCarroll, gone. Thrown and trampled at the Pendleton Round Up in 1929. She hadn't been killed outright, but had clung to life for a week and a half, before her heavenly pickup men, or women for that matter, Dorothy thought stubbornly, had reached down to take her home. Damn it.

Marie Gibson. Dear Ma Gibson. Canadian born just as she was – *officially, that is.* Naturalized citizen by marriage, just as she had been. Her husband, Tom, hadn't wanted to leave their ranch in Montana in 1924, so she'd gotten her own passport and gone to London by herself. By herself and over 300 cowboys and cowgirls from the US and Canada.

Killed at a county fair rodeo, for heaven's sake! A county fair! A stopover engagement in a little southeast Idaho town between the huge rodeo contests at the Chicago World's Fair and Madison Square Garden. On a goddamn horse named *Kiss*.

As they approached the fairgrounds, the parking lots filled to overflowing brought back memories of the problems Bill had had with finding enough room for parking year after year at Hoot's rodeos in Saugus. Success brought its own trials, she supposed. Clancy slowed to a near crawl but continued to make his way through the rows and rows of parked cars. How he was ever going to find a parking spot was beyond Dorothy.

"Press pass, please," ordered a parking lot attendant as they neared the stadium. Clancy produced a press card, at which the attendant waved him passed and pointed out some reserved parking behind a roped off area.

"Well, this is certainly first class," Dorothy laughed, as they pulled to a stop. Clancy made his way around the car to open her door and help her out. Gratefully, Dorothy took his hand as she swung her feet around so when she stood, she'd have both feet beneath her at once. Smiling behind the pain in her lower back, she took Clancy's elbow and followed him into the stadium and up the stairs to where they would be sitting.

"Here we go," Clancy said, as they reached their seats. He handed her a rodeo program, front cover emblazoned with a picture of a bronk rider. It had been drawn it to appear that the horse and rider were bursting through the shiny paper of the front cover.

"Thank you," Dorothy replied, the feel of the slick paper cover taking her back again to London. The program cover of the First International Rodeo sported a steer wrestler in midair as he left his horse, one hand already grasping one of the steer's horns. How ironic, that the iconic and enduring image for the rodeo featured the event which would become forbidden.

A band concert was in full swing, playing popular selections as the spectators continued to pour into the stadium. The band members were dressed in Indian attire of various styles sporting a rainbow of colors. Full feathered headdresses and ornately beaded vests and beech clothes were in distinct contrast to gleaming brass instruments.

Dorothy opened the program to the list of events.

"United States Indian Band," Dorothy read aloud. "My goodness. Who knew?"

But Clancy was busy talking to an old acquaintance that had recognized him and had missed what Dorothy had said. The two were laughing and joking in the way old friends do that haven't seen each other in a long while. No matter. Dorothy took the opportunity of having a few minutes to herself to read the history of the band, officially the Oneida Indian Band, and was surprised to learn it had been around for more than a half century.

As she turned the pages she suddenly found herself looking at a full page picture of "Our Guest Star – Hoot Gibson." Dressed in an embroidered Western cut shirt, the brim of his snow white Stetson angled across his forehead, his steely eyes fixed and looking off into the distance.

Still a handsome man.

She glanced quickly though his biography on the next page. ". . . he became a star almost overnight and the rest is history." Indeed, and getting closer to "being history" every year.

"I'm glad to see there are still cowgirls riding bronks on today's program," Dorothy pointed out to Clancy now that his friends had moved on.

"Fewer and fewer rodeos still let 'em compete." Clancy nodded. "I got on good authority that even the rodeo at Madison Square Garden is more'n likely gonna shut 'em down after this season."

Dorothy frowned her disapproval but kept her peace. Just as many men were injured or killed as women, but no one was putting a stop to their competitions.

The cheerful band music quieted signaling the beginning of the afternoon's rodeo events.

The Grand Entry featured staid cowboys – on equally serious looking horses complete with breast collars and cruppers – riding solemnly and sedately into the arena, Old Glory whipping smartly in the afternoon breezes next to the New York state flag.

Each to their own, Dorothy thought as she and the crowd rose to their feet to the band's rendition of "The Star Spangled Banner."

"Ladies and Gentlemen," the announcer's voice boomed over the loud speaker, "please put your hands together to welcome our Dancers of the Rangeland as they take us though an old time Quadrille on horseback."

To Dorothy's surprise the band started up again, this time playing a medley of cowboy and western tunes familiar in every way. She hummed along to the Bob Wills tune, "Rose of San Antone." Bill had loved to include cowboy dances at Gibson's rodeos at or in conjunction with many of the rodeos he helped to produce.

She was further amazed when four cowboys in brightly colored shirts on prancing black horses seemed to spring onto the exhibition grounds from one end of the arena and four cowgirls in matching blouses but on white horses made their showy entrance from the other end. Horses with their riders circled the ring in countering directions and finally formed a square in the middle of the arena.

Dorothy was speechless and awestruck as the dancing horses and riders went through familiar dance moves, dosado, grand right and left, promenade, bending the line and weaving the ring. The equestrian dancers had finished their moves with their horses alternating in color in a perfectly straight line. In unison, the horses all bowed on one knee as their riders doffed and waved their hats to the cheering crowds.

"I've never seen anything like this!" Dorothy exclaimed as at last the music came to an end. "Simply amazing!"

"This is the most beautiful square dancing I've ever seen!"

Clancy laughed a deep belly laugh. "High praise comin' from you!"

The announcer's voice boomed and echoed as the more usual rodeo events began to take place. Steer riders, trick and ropers, and then the cowgirls' bronk riding.

"Brings back memories, I bet," Clancy remarked as the first of the cowgirls was climbing into the chute, watching Dorothy closely for her reaction, trying to judge what she was thinking.

"Oh, yes! I can almost feel that horse's muscles twitching and jumping as that cowgirl climbs down into the saddle," Dorothy replied.

Oh, God, how would it be, she thought. The sweet odor of horse sweat, acrid man sweat, her own sweat. The dust being raised by hooves pawing nervously, and the quiet that came as she blocked out the entire world and all her senses became focused on the horse beneath her.

She found herself holding her breath as the gate burst open and the bronk charged into the arena, head down, heels flying.

"Come on, come on, hang in there," Dorothy chanted breathlessly. "You can do it. You can do it! Come on! Come on, girl!"

The whistle sounded and the pickup man quickly crowded into the still bucking bronk, easily swinging the rider from her saddle and onto the ground. Cheers and applause drowned out the shouts of the cowboys and the snorting of the bronk down in the arena.

"They don't ride them like we used to anymore," Dorothy said wistfully. "I mean, to a standstill. Goodness, but that girl was good."

"Hummm, yer right, a course."

Clancy's reply seemed noncommittal though and she turned to see what he was paying attention to.

"What?" Dorothy asked in surprise as she realized that Clancy's attention had been on her during the entire ride rather than the cowgirl from Nebraska.

"You!" Clancy laughed. "I hardly ever seen anyone so taken in by watchin' a buckin' horse rider. Eyes a-sparklin'. Clappin' and a hollerin'."

"Really?" Dorothy could feel a flush of self-consciousness coming on. "Hollering? I didn't realize."

"Ain't seen nothin' like it since last time I took my boy to the circus. You are a sight to behold," Clancy answered.

Dorothy laughed, soothing away her embarrassment.

"As long as I don't try to jump down into the arena, we'll be okay!" She returned her attention to the arena below them.

"And now, ladies and gentlemen, without further ado," the announcer boomed, "please welcome the one, the only Western Motion Picture Star, winner of the World's All-Around Cowboy's Championship at the great Pendleton, Oregon Round-Up on his beautiful Palomino stallion, Mister-r-r-r Ho-o-o-o-ot GIBSON!"

A roar of approval filled the air as the stallion, Pal, galloped full tilt through the arena in a figure eight, Hoot's familiar figure on his back, silver mountings on his saddle and bridle flashing in the sun.

Dorothy sadly shook her head as she watched Hoot's familiar figure so comfortably riding his horse around the ring. It was 1941, for Pete's sake, nearly three decades since he had won the all-around title at Pendleton in 1912 and four years since the last time he'd played in any new films to grace the silver screen.

She tried to distract herself by flipping through the rest of the printed program Clancy had given her. Past the pictures of a daredevil cowboy riding Roman style, straddling two horses, jumping them over an automobile, past the page of the poetry of a cowboy challenging a "spooky-eye demon" to a bucking duel, past the pictures of the rodeo clowns – unsung heroes among the rough riders, to the list of Rodeo Officials, and there to her surprise was Hoot Gibson of Nebraska, of all places, listed as Assistant Arena Director.

"Oh, my God!" Dorothy exclaimed even as she noticed that a line or two below, Fog Horn Clancy was listed as a "General Representative" of the rodeo, whatever in the hell that meant.

"What? What's wrong?" Clancy turned and tried to assess Dorothy's look.

She raised an eyebrow and searched Clancy's face.

"Did you know that Hoot was working for Colonel Eskew?" she asked.

"Humm," Clancy shrugged. "Didn't think it was an important detail to mention."

"Maybe not," Dorothy replied, "but I hadn't realized that his life had come to this."

"Come to this?" Clancy repeated, dumbfounded. He hesitated as if carefully thinking over what he was to say next. "Good Lord, Dorothy. He's still out there front and center, center of attention, still pullin' in the spectators, pleasin' the crowds. Looks to me like he's still doing what he loves best."

Dorothy realized she may have just overstepped her bounds with Mr. Fog Horn Clancy.

Pull it together, girl! Get that all-American smile back on your face and make it to the end of the show. You've been tougher straits than this.

"I suppose we'll be visiting with Hoot before we leave," she said brightly, smiling up at Clancy, as if discovering that Hoot was in her own backyard was the better than sliced store bought bread, instant coffee, or hot boloney sandwiches – though none of which particularly pleased her at all.

XXXI - AUGUST 1941 - AFTER THE SHOW

Hey, there, Clancy!" Hoot hollered to Mr. Foghorn Clancy from across the arena. The crowds of spectators had thinned after being bidden adieux by Gibson himself as his parting words had been the closing event of the afternoon's rodeo. He and Pal had taken their bows before he doffed and waved his hat to the appreciative rodeo fans and had galloped from the arena at least a half hour ago.

Dorothy and Clancy now sat waiting in front row seats and Dorothy was sure that the coming rendezvous with Hoot had been part of Clancy's carefully orchestrated plans for the day.

Knowing her voice wouldn't carry, she smiled and waved as Hoot continued on his way toward them. She could feel the pent up frustration, maybe even some old anger, from the past few years melting away in the sunshine of Hoot's joie d'vivre. Eternally optimistic, it was no wonder he and Bill had been able to work together seamlessly, always sure that today would be better than yesterday and tomorrow better yet.

Hoot made his way over the front of the arena and easily hoisted himself over the fence.

"Goodness, Miss Dorothy!" Hoot greeted her. "Just how the hell have you been?"

Dorothy searched his face, so familiar even after all these years, and was surprised to see shadows of sorrow in his eyes as he took her hand and helped her to her feet.

"Shakin' hands surely isn't the way to say hello after all these years," he said gruffly as his arms swallowed her in a friendly bearlike hug. "Gosh, Dorothy, you look great."

"As do you, Hoot!"

Dorothy was surprised to find tears gathering, threatening to spill down her cheeks as she tried to swallow the lump in her throat. She put her hands to his shoulders and decided it was now high time for a kiss on each of his cheeks.

Her warmth in returning his brotherly embrace seemed to release both of their flood gates as tears began to course down their cheeks.

"Oh, my God, girl! I am so sorry! I am so damn sorry!" Hoot's voice choked through his tears and he pulled her into a closer embrace. She buried her face into his shoulder, clinging to her husband's boss, his partner, his co-star, and sobbed as a stunned Clancy stood looking on. In his wildest dreams, he would have never imagined such a reunion between the two.

He stood helplessly watching the grief and sorrow that had seemed so far gone, so healed over become explosively raw, wondering if arranging this meeting had been a good thing.

Taking a deep breath, Clancy turned away and shoved his hands into the pockets of his pants and watched as a breath of breeze blew dust across the exposition grounds. Was it his imagination, or were the chute gates creaking as the light wind blew through them? Horses nickered and steers muttered from the holding pens behind the chutes. The seats in the stadium were now empty and pigeons flew low, looking for forgotten popcorn, lost hotdogs or cotton candy. In almost every way, it was an ordinary afternoon.

Ordinary except for the display of renewed heartbreak unfolding before his eyes. He studied the two from the corner of his eye as Hoot finally loosened himself from the embrace, trying to regain his composure, and Dorothy pulled a handkerchief from her pocket to dry her eyes as the two stepped apart.

"Well, now that is a hell of a way to say hello," Hoot said and then he grinned, back at the top of his game, once again all bravado and show.

"I'll say," Dorothy agreed, letting a little laughter lighten the moment.

She suddenly felt self-conscious of her graying hair, her crooked spine, the lines of age showing at the corners of her smile and her eyes. But if Hoot were still anything like Bill, he'd be eying her tall gray Stetson that had managed to stay on her head through it all.

"I miss him," Hoot began cautiously. "I know you do, too."

Dorothy only nodded, not ready to return to her tears. She turned to Clancy.

"As you can see, I haven't seen Hoot since before the accident," she explained. "My back was broken and so Hoot was left to take care of Bill's final arrangements."

She refused to say the word *funeral*.

"You were in a body cast, as I recall," Hoot added and then apologized, "I should've come to see you."

"Those were hard times," Dorothy replied. "No need to replay any 'should have beens.' We'll let bygones be bygones."

"Thank you, Dottie. Thank you."

Hoot's use of Bill's pet name for her used to irritate the hell right out of her, annoying her at his uninvited familiarity, but now it seemed to further help to soothe away raw emotions of the last eight years.

"What have you been doing to keep yourself busy?" Hoot asked, bringing the conversation back to the present.

"Oh, I have a little apartment house here in Syracuse," Dorothy began. "I do my thing, my tenants and neighbors do theirs."

"What? You don't regale them with stories from your rodeo days? How your rides thrilled hundreds, why, more likely thousands?" Hoot stopped quickly, deciding mid-sentence not to say "in your glory days." No need to pour salt into old wounds.

Dorothy smiled ruefully. "They only know me as Mrs. Robbins, the landlady who takes their rent. That's my only claim to fame these days."

"These days? Sounds kind of lonesome."

Immediately Hoot could have kicked himself.

"Oh, I still have plenty to do. Keeping house for one isn't as easy as you'd think especially when I get into a book or the newspapers, and all the little household chores get put off until I come to my senses and decide I'd better get on the stick and spruce things up."

Hoot highly doubted that anyone raised by a German *hausfrau*, even one who had raised her children in the middle of Manitoba, would ever really allow herself to be surrounded by dust or disorder.

He thought back to the cozy bungalow she and Bill had lived in during his years as the manager of his Golden Gate Rodeo, there had never been a doily or dish towel out of place. Floors shining. Handmade rugs regularly and thoroughly beaten, hanging on the clothes line out back.

Remembering them, Hoot asked Dorothy, "Do you still make those rag rugs?"

Dorothy chuckled and nodded.

"Of course! I'm always working on a couple of them all the time. I keep my ears to the ground and my eyes open to find the kind of woolen scraps I need to use."

Dorothy was surprised that the conversation had turned so dramatically away from Bill and rodeos to something as mundane as using worn out woolen clothing to create rugs.

"How did you put 'em together? I remember some long hook thing."

"Bill made me the wire hooks I use."

236

She left it at that.   No need to confuse these two men with the description of the long hours of cutting on the bias, folding, loading her rug hook with woolen strips before using stout cotton thread to crochet the network that supported and held the fabric strips together.

Clancy cleared his throat.   "Dorothy, yuh mentioned earlier to me some of the movies yuh'd been in back in the day," he cut in, feeling the need to redirect the conversation back to the purpose of this day; writing the biographical article for the *Hooves and Horns* magazine.

Dorothy flushed, standing next to an actual headliner like Hoot Gibson who knew her history as well she did.   It may have been a few years since his last moving picture, but he'd always had his name in the credits.

"Well, now, first I suppose we ought to mention *A Man's Land.*   You know, one of Hoot's movies?" she said as Hoot grinned and nodded.

"I did a bit of stunt riding for *the beautiful* Marion Shilling during the runaway horse scenes but stunt doubles never get their names in the credits."

Dorothy laughed and then she sighed.

"Poor Bill.   Even though his name was in the credits, it seems he never got to be more than the bumbling side kick."

Take that, Hoot, as the dig I meant it to be!

"We both knew better than that," Hoot defended himself.   "He had talent and tenacity.   Not many men would have taken on the role of sidekick as well as he did."

"On a different note, though," Dorothy brightened and continued, turning back to Clancy, "I worked with each of the Farnum brothers.   *A Tale of Two Cities* with William, and *The Squaw Man* with Dustin."

Would anyone even remember the Farnums these days?   Where had the years gone?

"Oh, and I loved working with Mabel Normand and Wallace Beery."

Name dropper, she thought to herself, though she was sure that was what Clancy was after.

"Of course, that was long before the days of talkies."

Oh, so, so long ago!

Uncredited, bit parts, stand-ins, a face in the crowd but, she reminded herself, a pretty face in the crowd.   Sometimes doubling for the Hollywood starlets who didn't know the business end of a horse or their way into a saddle – or how to take a fall without coming up covered with bruises.

Suddenly she remembered something more substantial.

"While we were in London," Dorothy said, warming up to her memory, "Bill and I were in a short film directed by a Brit – name of John Betts.   An interview, of sorts.   A type of documentary, I suppose.   We never saw the finished product.   In it, Bill and I were filmed trying to explain the origins of rodeo.   How every event had its beginnings on working ranches.   The Truth, as we knew and understood it."

She sighed.   "I don't think it would have been a very popular piece of work considering the audience."

"Don't ever remember Bill mentioning it," Hoot put in, frowning a little.

"It wasn't anything theatrical like the two of you in *The Dude Bandit* or *The Fighting Parson*. It was just sitting and talking in front of a moving picture camera," Dorothy explained, laughing, eyes sparkling. "I can't think of a reason why it would have ever come up between you and Bill during one of your moving picture shoots. Heaven knows, you two would have been too busy during rodeo season working out details during planning or producing to talk about days long gone."

She grew somber and sighed. "That film is probably in some dark vault gathering dust."

Clancy made mental note to avoid mentioning lost footage when he wrote up his article on Dorothy. He turned to Hoot.

"Why don't you join us? Maybe grab a bite to eat somewhere?" Clancy asked.

"Be happy to," Hoot replied as he offered his elbow to Dorothy and the three of them began making their way out of the stadium to the press parking lot.

"What was it I heard about you riding your first bronk on a dare?" Clancy asked as they walked along.

"Oh, it was back when I first met Bill. I was opening Wild West Shows for Frank Griffin. Boy, the Boss hit the roof when he heard what I'd done. Good heavens! He was completely unimpressed that I had outridden Nettie Hawn. Nettie Hawn, Cowgirl Champion of the World of 1913! Rode a wicked bronk named Snake at Pendleton. *Snake.* Now that's a great name for an outlaw horse." *Better than Blondie!*

"Griffin blustered and stormed about, thundering about my safety and how I could have been hurt – and not been able to meet my obligation for 'daily appearances,' I'm sure.

" 'You could have been killed!' Griffin yelled. 'Or worse!' he added. At the time I could not believe that there was anything worse than being killed."

As Clancy opened her car door for her and she stepped into the front passenger seat, Dorothy decided she would add one more opinion before explaining further. She waited until he and Hoot were both seated in the car with her.

"Cars are great for being able to pick and go any time and most anywhere you want, but I myself would not ever have one."

"Oh?" Clancy asked. "Not even if someone gave you one?"

"No. Not even then," Dorothy replied firmly.

"And why not?"

Clancy figured she'd say something to the effect that cars were too big or too fast or that she doubted she could ever learn to drive one.

"I never had much use for them ever," she started, "but it was just a short drive in a car with good friends – much like today – that took Bill from me. Only difference between today and back then is the weather. You may remember hearing about it or maybe reading about the accident in the papers.

"Bad, bad snowstorm. Visibility was next to nothing. Bill got out of the car to clear snow from the headlights and another car plowed right into us, only to be rammed by another coming up behind it.   Instantly, in less than a blink of an eye, *our lives* became just *my life.*"

Dorothy continued in a more somber tone, repeating herself.   "Yes, once I wondered what could be worse than being killed, but now I know."

A strained silence fell over the trio as the two men sat, still as statues, afraid to encourage her to continue, but hanging on to hear whatever it was she was planning to say.

"Worse than being killed can be living," she said firmly.   "Living for months in a body cast, not able to do a damn thing for myself.   Having neither hearth nor home to come to after finally being released from the hospital.   Learning a whole new way of thinking and coping.   Living my life so far from all that I love or have ever loved.   Losing those connections.   The distance that wasn't measured in miles, but time. Living alone with just memories for company."

Stunned silence fell, and Dorothy felt she needed to switch it up and return to the jovial sunshine shining brightly just a few moments ago– no need to prolong the gloom.   Better that she break and dissipate the uncomfortable and overwhelming sadness she had somehow allowed to slip into their conversation. No more room for despair on a day like today.

Dorothy turned to look both men in the eye and put on her very best Opening the Show smile.

"Now, Hoot, don't you or Clancy think for one minute that I am looking forward to going over to the Other Side anytime soon!"

She chuckled and shook her head, just once, to punctuate the positive, as the men relaxed and returned her smile.

Now to regain the *joie de vive* of earlier in the day with Hoot and Clancy. *Always leave them smiling Boss insisted.*

"The truth is, boys, I still have a lot of living yet to do!" she assured them.   "Besides, this little gray haired lady is too old for an early grave!"

Clancy and Hoot immediately fell over themselves in assuring her she was still very much a spring chicken.   Men.   Sometimes so predictable.

Still chuckling, Clancy put the car into gear and backed out of his parking spot as Hoot lit up a cigarette.   The afternoon was back on track.

Dorothy's smile faded as she studied her hands folded in her lap.   The Truth.   It had gotten her this far.   It would continue to get her through until from the Other Side, the pickup men – and women she reminded herself – maybe even Bill or Marie Gibson – were at her side to tell her "good ride" and take her on home.

AFTERWORD

After Skeeter Bill Robbins was killed in 1933, Dorothy Morrell seems to have disappeared. Unlike her glory years between 1913 and 1924, when her name regularly appeared in newspaper stories from California to New York, and even Europe, after 1933 there are few clues to follow and very little is known of her remaining years.

- 1936 – Dorothy Carolina born Eichhorn applied for social security benefits in California.
- 1941 – Foghorn Clancy interviewed her in Syracuse, New York, and wrote a one page article chronicling her life story as she told it for the *Hooves and Horns* magazine.
- 1944 – *Rodeo Romances*, another magazine affiliated with Clancy, published a story, *Tenderfoot Champ* written by 'Dorothy Morrell Robbins – Famous Bronc Rider' in its fall issue. The details of the multi-page article closely followed the story line of the *Hooves and Horns* article, though fleshing out with more details in a friendly, chatty voice.
- 1949 – She was pictured with Tillie Bowman in front of the chutes at a rodeo in Union, Oregon.
- 1953 – A "life claim," was made on her social security number. While usually a claim for disability benefits, it may have been the year she passed away. On that record is the *notice '03 Sep 1976: Name listed as DOROTHY C ROBBINS'* leading to an assumption that she may have passed away in either late August or early September 1976. However, on the social security "life claim" for Addison Perry Day, one of the judges at Wembley, a similar note was added *(29 Nov 1978: Name listed as ADDISON PERRY DAY)* when in fact, Mr. Day passed away in 1955.

SOURCES AND STUFF

*Poems written by "Skeeter Bill" Robbins
**Poems written in the style of "Skeeter Bill" Robbins by the author
***Poem written in the styles of "Skeeter Bill" Robbins and Rudyard Kipling by the author

The author chose to use the spelling of certain words such as bronk, and aeroplane contemporary to the time period.

Caroline's German speaking family would have pronounced her name "Car-oh-leen-a." To help the English reader more correctly and closely pronounce her name, the spelling "Carlina" was chosen.

Images relating to Dorothy and her story can be found at:
https://www.pinterest.com/grammabobbi/dorothy-morrell-bucking-horse-rider/

I   **Spring 1913   From Calgary to California**
- Wikipedia. "Calgary Stampede." Retrieved 1 Oct 2017 https://en.wikipedia.org/wiki/Calgary_Stampede
- Dolly Mullins was at the Calgary Stampede in 1912, but there is no evidence that Caroline Eichhorn was, likely did not meet each other.   Mark this part of the story "creative."
- Clancy, F. (Oct 1941) Memory Trail. *Horns and Hooves*, p 5 – Dorothy explained how she decided to use the surname Morrell.

II   **February 1891   Hamburg**
- Staatsarchiv Hamburg; Hamburg, Deutschland; *Hamburger Passagierlisten*; Microfilm No.: *K_1743*
- Year: *1891*; Arrival: *New York, New York*; Microfilm Serial: *M237, 1820-1897*; Microfilm Roll: *Roll 562*; Line: *49*; List Number: *251*
- http://www.bruzelius.info/Nautica/Ships/Merchant/Sail/C/Caitloch(1874).html *History of the sailing ship Caitloch which capsized in the port of Hamburg in 1891*
- Procedures for processing Immigrants onboard Steamships - Ocean Passenger Travel http://www.gjenvick.com/SteamshipArticles/TransatlanticShipsAndVoyages/OceanPassengerTravel/1891/07-ProcessingImmigrantsOnboardSteamships.html#ixzz4DStBM3uA
- Information about the Rhaetia: http://www.nims-leistiko.info/nims-leistiko/Rhaetia.htm

III   **June 1901   Winnipeg, Manitoba**
- Year: *1901*; Census Place: *Winnipeg (City/Cité) Ward/Quartier No 5, Winnipeg (city/cité), Manitoba*; Page: *1*; Family No: *2*

- *Elections Canada. "Saint Boniface – Historical data" retrieved 1 Oct 2017 from* http://www.elections.ca/res/cir/maps/mapprov.asp?map=46009&lang=e
- *RochelleS. "German/Russian Borscht" Retrieved 13 Jul 2016 from* http://www.food.com/280970

IV October 1913 Rosie
- (Fri, Oct 3, 1913) Daring Riders of Rodeo Parade With Girls of Portola. The San Francisco Call, p 2 - First mention found of "Miss Dorothy Morrell, the famous Canadian rider"
- (Mon, Oct 6, 1913) Rodeo on for a Week. San Francisco Chronicle, pg 2 – "Owing to a sprained wrist, Dorothy Morrell, a Canadian cowgirl and motion picture horsewoman did not appear in the saddle."
- (Fri, Oct 10, 1913) Will Continue "Bulldoing" Rodeo Sport Not Stopped. Oakland Tribune, p 6. "Miss Dorothy Morrell attempted to ride "Rosie" the bucking burro, and was thrown heavily."
- (Sat, Oct 11, 1913) Burro Throws Fair Rider - Romantic Courtship Ensues. Oakland Tribune, p 3.
- The poem in this chapter was written by the author in the style of "Skeeter Bill" Robbins

V April 1914 On a Dare!
- Furlong, Charles Wellington. (1914) The World's Work ...: A History of Our Time, Volume 27, p 457. Garden City & New York: Doubleday& Company, – "whereas any old cowboy is welcome to risk his neck . . ."
- Larkin, Mark. (Thu, Apr 29, 1915) "I Rode My First Broncho On a Bet," Said Dorothy Morrell, the World's Champion Rider. Santa Cruz Evening News, p 7.
- See also (Wed, Aug 30, 1916) Women Are To Take Prominent Part In Rodeo. The Bakersfield Californian, pg 3. "During the Bakersfield Rodeo of April, 1914, Dorothy Morrell took her first lessons in horseback riding from a local cowman."

VI May 1914 Captain of the Cowboy Company
- (Sun, Apr 26, 1914) Klamath Buccaroos Would Like to Fight The Oregon Daily Journal, p 9. "Skeeter Bill" Robbins, a local cowpuncher . . . has been elected captain of a cowboy company, which telegraphed to President Wilson its willingness to serve.

VII 18 June 1914 Begin with Breakfast
- No evidence has been found to show that Dorothy and Bill visited San Francisco or the fair grounds of the Panama-Pacific International Exposition, though Bill had reported to his mother that he would be riding there during the Exposition.
- Ewald, D and Clute, P. (1991) San Francisco Invites the World. San Francisco: Chronicle Books. p 23, "Each Sunday, starting about a year before the opening, people assembled on the fairgrounds for a charge of 25 [cents] to watch the progress of the fair. . . Often there were as many as 50,000 people in attendance."
- (Fri, May 11, 1914) Help Wanted – Female Oakland Tribune, p 21. Used to extrapolate a possible wage for Dorothy.
- (Tue, Jul 21, 1914) Great Sport at Big Week. Santa Cruz Evening News, (Santa Cruz, CA), p 6
- Dowd, K. (Thu, Oct 24, 2016) "The Short History of the Coolest Commute: the Air Ferry." San Francisco Gate. Retrieved Jul 2017, from

http://www.sfgate.com/bayarea/article/history-seaplane-air-ferry-San-Francisco-Oakland-10331533.php

VIII **July 1914**   **San Francisco Across the Bay**
* No evidence has been found to show that Dorothy and Bill visited San Francisco or the fair grounds of the Panama-Pacific International Exposition, though Bill had reported to his mother that he would be riding there during the Exposition.
* Wilder, L. (1974) *West From Home: Letters of Laura Ingalls Wilder, San Francisco, 1915*. New York City: Harper and Collins.   Some of the things Rose and her mother enjoyed doing during Laura's visit to San Francisco were inspiration for Bill and Dorothy's activities.
* Dowd, K. (Thu, Oct 24, 2016) "The Short History of the Coolest Commute: the Air Ferry." *San Francisco Gate*. Retrieved Jul 2017, from http://www.sfgate.com/bayarea/article/history-seaplane-air-ferry-San-Francisco-Oakland-10331533.php
* (Fri, May 15, 1914) Aeroplane Service at San Francisco. *The Daily Advertiser*, (Lafayette, Louisiana), p 1
* (Sun, Oct 3, 1915) Fair Aeronautist Surprises Friends. *Oakland Tribune*, p 11
* (Tue, Jun 9, 1914) World's Greatest Exposition Nearing Completion. *The Gastonia Gazette*, (Gastonia, North Carolina), p 12

IX **June & July 1914**   **The List**
* (Fri, Dec 18, 1914) Southern Pacific Route. *Santa Ana Register* (Santa Ana, California), p 12. Description of types of cars included in cross country trains.
* "George Washington (Inventor)" *Wikipedia*. Retrieved Oct 3, 2017 from https://en.wikipedia.org/wiki/George_Washington_(inventor)
* (Tue, Jul 21, 1914) Great Sport at Big Week. *Santa Cruz Evening News*, (Santa Cruz, CA), p 6
* (Aug 17, 1914) Thousands Coming to See Greatest of Frontier Days. *Wyoming Tribune* (Cheyenne, Wyoming) p 2

X **August 6, 1914**   **Train to Cheyenne**
* (Jun 6, 1914) Wyoming Boy Making Good. *Douglas Enterprise* (Douglas, Wyoming), pg 1
* (Mon, Jun 15, 1914) Southern Pacific Rail Schedule *San Francisco Chronicle*, p 12. Train for Ogden, Cheyenne, etc to leave from Oakland Pier.
* "Pullman Sleeping Cars add Comfort to Overnight Travel." *Railswest*. Retrieved Jul 26, 2016 from http://www.railswest.com/technology/pullman.html
* (Aug 7, 1914) Seven Footer is on Way to Join Frontier Stunts. *Cheyenne State Leader*, p 3
* (Aug 14, 1914) A Converse County Boy. *Douglas Enterprise*, p 1
* Lund, C. "Always Keep an Edge on Your Knife." *MetroLyrics*. Retrieved Oct 3, 2017 from http://www.metrolyrics.com/always-keep-an-edge-on-your-knife-lyrics-corb-lund.html. "be sure it's upside down . . . it keeps the luck from runnin' out."
* Price, J. (1990) *Wild Horse Robbins*. Huron, South Dakota: East Eagle Press.
  – Biography of Frank B. Robbins, Roy's younger brother.   p 2 "Bill Kimball was a stepfather who didn't treat the Robbins boys very well."
* Robbins, D. (1944) Tenderfoot Champ. *Rodeo Romances*, vol 4, no 2. p 74

XI **August 7, 1914**   **Almost Mrs. Robbins**

- Only evidence found to date that Dorothy/Caroline had been previously married is her "divorced" status on the marriage license for her and Bill/Roy. "California, County Marriages, 1850–1952," database with images, FamilySearch (https://familysearch.org/ark:/61903/1:1:KZ3T-CH8 : 24 September 2017), Roy Robbins and Caroline Eickhorn [sic], 15 Oct 1915; citing Yuba, California, United States, county courthouses, California; FHL microfilm 1,651,351.Robertson, C. (2010).

XII October 4, 1914 A Little to the Right of the Middle of Nowhere
- Grant, R. (1986) from *Pages from Converse County's Past*, Heritage Book Committee, Douglas, Wyoming, 1986, p 327. Details of BF and Sue May Robbins lives

XIII October 4, 1914 Supper
- (Aug 22, 1914) Champion Buster Not Decided: Four Will Fight Finals Tonight. *Cheyenne State Leader*, p 1 "After a hard and interesting series of pretty rides by the contestants for the world's championship in the Ladies' Bucking contest, Miss Dorothy Morrell of Winnipeg, Canada, was proclaimed to be the best in the field."
- (Aug 23, 1914) Floyd Carroll Keeps Championship Title in State: Great Rides. *Cheyenne State Leader*, p 1 "Miss Dorothy Morrell, Winnipeg, Canada, first: title of world's champion; $150 in gold and $250 gold mounted saddle.

XIV October 4, 1914 Evening
- Though Bill and Dorothy were billed as attendees of the Pendleton Round-Up and Bill competed, there is no evidence that Dorothy participated as a competitor in any of the events.
- (Sep 17, 1914) Reno Day at Fallon Today. *Nevada State Journal* (Reno, Nevada), p 7
- (Sep 21, 1914) Personal Mention. *East Oregonian*, p 5
- (Sep 21, 1914) Crowds Begin to Arrive Here for Round-Up. *East Oregonian*, p 1
- (Sep 25, 1914) Wild Horse Race Exciting. *The Oregon Daily Journal* (Portland, Oregon), p 7.   Skeeter Bill finished second.
- (Sep 24, 1914) Hotfoot Wins First Contest. *The Oregon Daily Journal*, p 7. Skeeter Bill pulls leather.
- (Sep 26, 1914) "Skeeter Bill" Robbins Tells in Verse of Ride on a Bucker, *East Oregonian* (Pendleton, Oregon), p 6.   This poem was written by Robbins.

XV October 5, 1914 An Hour Shy of Burnt
- (Aug 14, 1914) Dorothy Morrell, Movie Star, Here for Frontier Days Show. *Wyoming Tribune*, p 5
- (Aug 18, 1914) Frontier Day Now on at Cheyenne. *Aspen Democrat-Times* (Aspen, Colorado), p 1 Predicts 25,000 tourists.
- (Aug 18, 1914) The Puncher in the Scrambled Shirt is Skeeter Bill Robbins. *Wyoming Tribune*, p 5
- (Oct 8, 1914) Moving Picture Artists. *Bill Barlow's Budget* (Douglas, Wyoming), p 5
- (Oct 23, 1914) (Untitled). *Bill Barlow's Budget*, p 8. Discussed Dorothy and Bill marrying in not "very many months."

XVI April 14, 1915 Hell Bent for Leather
- (Apr 15, 1915) 101 Ranch Cowgirl Is Painfully Injured. *San Francisco Chronicle*, p 4

- Ewald, D and Clute, P. (1991) *San Francisco Invites the World.* San Francisco: Chronicle Books. p 55, Photograph of: "One of the two Cadillac ambulances belonging to an emergency hospital located in the Service Building."

XVII **April 15, 1915**   **Tune of Your Old Love Song**
- Creativity disclaimer: as for the names of the reporters from the Oakland and San Francisco newspapers, neither paper credited the name of its reporter.   The San Francisco article was short and to the point, while the article in the Oakland paper was longer and written in a familiar voice. None of the names attending medics or doctors are known either.
- (Feb 19, 1915) Along the Joy Zone. *San Francisco Chronicle*, p 5. Advertisement for Miller Brothers' 101 Ranch Real Wild West
- (Apr 16, 1915) Plucky Cowgirl Has Broken Last Bronco. *San Francisco Chronicle*, p 4
- (Apr 18, 1915) Career Ended – Must Not Ride. *Oakland Tribune*, p 28 – Contains verse referring to "That Tune of Your Old Love Song."
- (May 16, 1915) Candidate for Zone Queen Was Injured at 101 Ranch. *Oakland Tribune*, p 21
- (May 29, 1915) Dorothy Morrell "Queen" of 101 Ranch Employees. *San Francisco Chronicle*, p 4
- "California, County Marriages, 1850-1952," database with images, *FamilySearch* (https://familysearch.org/ark:/61903/1:1:KZ3T-CH8 : 24 September 2017), Roy Robbins and Caroline Eickhorn [sic], 15 Oct 1915; citing Yuba, California, United States, county courthouses, California; FHL microfilm 1,651,351. – Caroline's status "divorced"

XVIII **June 2, 1915**   **At the Convention**
- (Apr 29, 1915) "I Rode My First Broncho on a Bet," Said Dorothy Morrell, the World's Champion Rider. *Santa Cruz Evening News*, p 7 – Also, front page headlines referred to the sinking of the Lusitania
- (May 8, 1915) Because She Loved Horses and Hated Nursing Miss Morrell Became Champion Broncho Rider. *The Wichita Beacon*, p 15.   Article also printed (Jun 15, 1915) *Chicago Day Book.*
- (Jun 2, 1915) Experience of Suffragist at Capital. *San Francisco Chronicle*, p 11
- (Jun 3, 1915) Women Gaining from Iceland to China – They Vote Even in the Isle of Man. *San Francisco Chronicle*, p 4 – Includes photograph of Morrell with Suffragette Sash with 101 Ranch watch-brooch pinned to it
- (Jun 3, 1915) Congressional Union Hold Second Conference. *San Francisco Chronicle*, p 4
- (Jun 7, 1915) Dorothy Morrell Unable to Ride at Frontier Days. *Wyoming Tribune*, p 5
- (Jun 11, 1915) Famous Cowgirl Will Never Ride Again. *Kemmerer Republican*, (Kemmererer, Wyoming), p 5

XIX **May 1924**   **The Voyage**
- "California, County Marriages, 1850-1952," database with images, *FamilySearch* (https://familysearch.org/ark:/61903/1:1:KZ3T-CH8 : 24 September 2017), Roy Robbins and Caroline Eickhorn [sic], 15 Oct 1915; citing Yuba, California, United States, county courthouses, California; FHL microfilm 1,651,351. Caroline's status: "divorced"
- Robertson, C. (2010). *The Passport in America – The History of a Document.* Oxford, United Kingdom: Oxford University Press.
- Creativity disclaimer: The author is unsure how contestants were invited or chosen.

- National Archives and Records Administration (NARA); Washington D.C.; NARA Series: *Passport Applications, January 2, 1906 - March 31, 1925*; Roll #: 2530; Volume #: *Roll 2530 - Certificates: 422350-422849, 21 May 1924-21 May 1924. Dorothy's birthdate had originally been typed as the same date as Bill/Roy's. It was erased and typed over.*
- (Mar 9, 1924) British to Stage All-Nation Rodeo Early in Summer. *The Houston Post,* p 22
- (Mar 14, 1924) British Syndicate Will Spend $500,000 On Wembley Rodeo. *The Akron Beacon* (Akron, Ohio), p 14
- (Mar 25, 1924) AD Day to Judge at Rodeo in London, Eng. *The Winnipeg Tribune,* p 7
- (Apr 7, 1924) Famous Rodeo Riders Visit Bakersfield. *The Bakersfield Californian,* p 6 – "Skeeter" has received the appointment of assistant arena director.
- (Apr 15, 1924) Brenham Man in World Rodeo. *The Houston Post,* p 1 "A Ship has been chartered and free transportation from New York to London and return has been provided for contestants and their stock."
- (May 4, 1924) Real Stars for the Riding Prince. *The Times* (Shreveport, Louisiana), p 64
- (May 4, 1924) Famous Cowgirl Will Go Abroad. *Detroit Free Press,* p 14 Includes details of bon voyage party given by "Lady Bob" Montgomery
- (May 9, 1924) Western Cowboys on Way to Imperial Rodeo. *The Winnipeg Tribune,* p 6 Includes names of Albertan cowboys including "Andy and Arthur Lund from Raymond."
- (May 12, 1924) All About the Rodeo. Explanation by the Promoters. Manager Smiles at "Cruelty Stunt." Advises Critics to "Quit Eating Beef." *The Guardian* (London, England) p 9
- (May 24, 1924) Prince of Wales Gets Opportunity – Skeeter Bill Robbins and Jack Hoxie to Teach Him to Ride. *The Bakersfield Californian,* p 6

XX   14 June 1924   Opening the Show
- (Jun 8, 1924) "Outlaw" horses with wicked records. *The Observer* (London, Greater London, England) p 5 Advertisement for "First International Rodeo or Cowboy Championships"
- Simpson, C. (1925) *El Rodeo - One Hundred Sketches Made in the Arena During the Great International Contest (1924).* London: John Lane the Bodley Head Limited.
- (Jun 15, 1924) Cowboys Thrill 90,000 In Stadium At Wembly [sic] – American and Canadian Rodeo Declared Most Exciting Show England Has Ever Seen. *The Baltimore Sun,* p 11
- Nevinson, H. (Jun 16, 1924) The Crowd and The Spectacle. *The Guardian,* p 7 – This article along with Simpson's chapter on the Opening Ceremonies give great detail to weather, general description of the arena, the use of electric amplifiers, and the Irish bagpipers. Also is highly critical of the rodeo in general calling it "cruel and unworthy of our race." Reports that the crowds applaud the steers that avoided the ropes and bulldoggers. Steer Roping Events will no longer be open to the public.

XXI   17 June 1924   After the Ride
- (May 2, 1924) Did Kipling Pull Ludicrous Boner? *The Bakersfield Californian,* p 8 – Kipling named "roads, gates, etc., at the British Empire exhibition at Wembley Park."
- Bronner, M. (Jul 7, 1924) Britons Weep As Cowboys Bulldog Steers, But Calmly Watch Foxes Pulled Apart. *The Ogden Standard* (Ogden, Utah), p 6

- (Jul 6, 1924) Cowboy "Real Poet." Rudyard Kipling Says, After Chat With Skeeter Bill. *The Cincinnati Enquirer*, p 65
- Simpson, C. (1925) *El Rodeo – One Hundred Sketches Made in the Arena During the Great International Contest (1924).* London: John Lane the Bodley Head Limited.   Skeeter's poem quoted on p 166
- (Jul 21, 1924) U. S. Cowboys Return to N. Y. With Monocles – 117 Members of Rodeo Company Pleased at Treatment in England. *Detroit Free Press*, p 13
- (Jul 31, 1924) "Don't Forget." *The Bakersfield Californian*, p 7 – Reported on Kipling handing Robbins a self-addressed envelope and the words of a "bystander." "Keep that, Skeeter; it'll be worth $500 someday."
- (Jul 29, 1924) Spanish Princess Greets Western Cowgirl. *The Evening News* (Harrisburg, Pennsylvania), p 16 Photograph of "Eldest daughter of the King and Queen of Spain, in animated conversation with Dorothy Morrell, American Cowgirl, and "Skeeter Bill" Robbins, cowboy poet, exhibiting in rodeo in London.   This meeting was not written into this story.
- (Jul 31, 1924) Skeeter Bill Meets Rudyard Kipling - Dorothy Morrell Interviews Royalty. *The Bakersfield Californian*, p 7
- (Jul 31, 1924) Poet of the Empire and Poet of Range Read Each Other's Poems. *The Bakersfield Californian*, p 7 - Includes Robbins untitled poem, opening line "The cowboys are in London."
- *"hand us dope"* –share the inside scoop
- McGinnis, V. (1974) Rodeo Road, My Life as a Pioneer Cowgirl. New York: Hastings House Publishers.   P 186 "The first afternoon we showed to ninety-three thousand people, who loved every "blimey, blinking, bloody" second of the performance.

XXII June 1924   Brush With Royalty
- Porter, W. (Sep 1985) When they took the West to London. *True West, vol 32, no. 5, p 10-17*   Includes photographs of rodeo program cover, Tex Austin fancy roping, and the dinner party hosted by the Prince of Wales, later the Duke of Windsor, who reportedly "went to visiting among the tables."
- McGinnis, V. (1974) *Rodeo Road, My Life as a Pioneer Cowgirl.* New York: Hastings House Publishers.   P 186. "The only request our hosts or hostesses made was that we wear our western clothes – boots, hats, spurs and all."

XXIII June 1924   Dinner
- Porter, W. (Sep 1985) When they took the West to London. *True West, vol 32, no. 5, p 16.*   A *Billings Gazette* article is quoted in which Aubrey and Mabry McDowell recount their evening at the dinner party hosted by the Prince of Wales.
- "Food Aboard RMS Titanic." *RMS Titanic - Ship of Dreams.* Retrieved Oct 4, 2017 from http://www.titanicandco.com/menu.html   Used a guide for menu at dinner party.

XXIV 9 September 1924 "Tour of Wembley Champions"
- (Jul 27, 1924) London Is No Place for Cowboy Opines Arizonan Back From English Rodeo. *Arizona Daily Star* (Tucson, Arizona), p 6 - Comments on belief that the English are "fine people" but that their "parties end up in a drunk." Also mentions "Twenty of the 185 performers who went over remained in England to appear in theatrical performances."   Reports that ironically, that while the Prince of Wales is a fan and supporter of the Imperial Rodeo, he stayed away due to his place "as secretary to the humane society."

- Lait, G. (Week ending Jul 5, 1924). Challenges Thrown at American Riders in London's Great Rodeo. *Clipper - Oldest Amusement Paper in America*, p 23 Reports "day money" and championship winnings for all Wembley contests who ended up "in the money." Dorothy Morrell came in 4th in the "Cowgirls' Bronc Riding." Bill split 4th in "Fancy Roping" with Frank Walker, Strawberry Red Wall and Carlos Miers.
- McGinnis, V. (1974) *Rodeo Road, My Life as a Pioneer Cowgirl.* New York: Hastings House Publishers. P 188. "Eight of us took things into our own hands; we were not going to be cheated out of seeing Paris. Early on Sunday morning ... we chartered a plane, took our own guide, and flew across the English Channel, landing in Paris around nine a.m." Went on to further say, they barely made it back Monday in time for the afternoon rodeo.
- *Ibid,* Recounted her joining with Tommy Kirnan for the post rodeo tour. Their show was at the Coliseum Theatre for 30 "days and nights."
- (Apr 25, 1924) Ardwich Empire Advertisement. *The Guardian,* p 1. "Texas Walker, The Famous Novelty Roper."
- (Aug 15, 1924) More Rodeo - Importing Many more Horses and Steers - Tour of the Great Citiies. *The Guardian,* p 7 "Texas Walker, who was born in Leeds, has chosen his native town as the depot and headquarters." Further boasts of "novel features" the rodeo will present.
- (Jul 6, 1924) Mr. Cochran and the Coliseum Show. *The Observer,* p 7 Cochran is highly critical of Kirnan's post–Wembley tour. "Two or three cowboys exhibition of rope spinning and other suitable performances for music hall display." "No bucking horses to remain in England." "To advertise show as a "rodeo" is misleading" and "belittles a magnificent sport." Further reported that the programme will begin the week of July 14 with eight Rodeo Champions.
- (Sep 27, 1924) Dorothy Morrell Writes to Local Friends; In Paris. *The Bakersfield Californian,* p 9 Includes full text of a postcard to a "friend."

XXV 23 December 1924   Reunion
- (Oct 18, 1915) "Skeeter Bill" Robbins Will Spend Winter Here. *The Evening Herald* (Klamath Falls, Oregon), p 3 Refers to winter Bill and Dorothy spent in Klamath County
- (Jun 9, 1924) Wild West Riders. Lassoing in London Streets. London, 7th June. *The Age* (Melbourne, Victoria, Australia) p 10 refers to charabancs - stretch, open topped vehicles
- (Jun 7, 1924) "Ro-Day-O." *The Guardian,* p 8
- (Aug 19, 1924) Rodeo in Dublin: Two Accidents, *The Guardian,* p 7 "During the rodeo performances in Croke Park, Dublin, last night, before 20,000 spectators, Charles Alderidge, one of the cowboy, was knocked unconscious . . . Miss Vera McGinnis also met with an accident."

XXVI 24 December 1924   Christmas Eve
- (Aug 22, 1924) Devonshire Steers for Rodeo - "More Dangerous Than Americans." *The Guardian,* p 7
- (Sep 1, 1924) Rodeo At Sea - Exhibition on a Cunard Liner. *The Guardian,* p 11 - "Five hundred passengers watched the performance, which included the rope tricks of Bill Robbins, the cowboy poet.. . Texas Walker . . . said he would return to England to arrange a rodeo on a bigger scale than at Wembley, and would seek the co-operation of the R.S.P.C.A."
- (Sep 15, 1924) Elko is in Holiday Attire for celebration this Week. *Reno Gazette-Journal* (Reno, Nevada), p 4 - Catlin Shale Oil Celebration. Walker and Robbins were in attendance.

- (Oct 23, 1924) Cowboy to Face Charge at Elko. *Reno Gazette-Journal*, p 6 – Texas Walker arrested and charged with writing alleged fraudulent checks totaling over $2000 during the Catlin Shale Oil Celebration
- (Nov 1, 1924) Wales is Welcomed Home. *The Los Angeles Times*, p 1. "Texas" Walker, a rodeo director, walked a few paces behind the royal party in his broadest brimmed hat, chaps, spurs, boots, and the rest of the a cowboy's garb, including a lariat.
- (Nov 18, 1924) Leeds Rodeo – Promoter Determined To Go On. *The Guardian* p 8

XXVII   November 1933   Jack of Diamonds, Queen of Spades
- (Nov 29, 1933) Skeeter Bill Robbins Killed in Car Crash. *The Bakersfield Californian*, p1 – Lists survivors of the crash, including "Mrs. Robbins was the only one critically injured."   The relationship between Mr. and Mrs. "Tiny" Shuster, Jack Hulse, Myrtle Gallagher and the Robbins is unknown

XXVIII   November 1933   Medicinal Purposes
- (Nov 29, 1933) Skeeter Bill Robbins Killed in Car Crash. The Bakersfield Californian, p1 – Lists survivors of the crash, including "Mrs. Robbins was the only one critically injured."

XXIX   August 1941   Foghorn Clancy
- Clancy, F. (Oct 1941) Memory Trail. *Horns and Hooves*, p 5

XXX   August 1941   Days Gone By
- Clancy, F. (Oct 1941) Memory Trail. *Horns and Hooves*, p 5
- (1941) *Grotto Rodeo - Edgerton Park - Jul 14-19, 1941 - Rochester, N.Y.* Rochester, N. Y.: Drexler Print Shop, Inc.   Used as a reference for the rodeo Dorothy attended with Foghorn Clancy just a few weeks later. Retrieved Jul 17, 2017 from *mcnygenealogy.com/book/grotto-rodeo-1941.pdf*

XXXI   August 1941   After the Show
- Clancy, F. (Oct 1941) Memory Trail. Horns and Hooves, p 5
- Brooks, G. (2005) Good Ride Cowboy [Garth Brooks] on *The Lost Sessions (CD)*, Nashville: Pearl Records

Made in the USA
San Bernardino, CA
17 October 2018